THE LONGING FOR HOME

BOSTON UNIVERSITY STUDIES IN PHILOSOPHY AND RELIGION

General Editor: Leroy S. Rouner

Volume Seventeen

Volume Sixteen
In Pursuit of Happiness

Volume Fifteen
The Changing Face of Friendship

Volume Fourteen
Can Virtue Be Taught?

Volume Thirteen
Selves, People, and Persons

Volume Twelve
On Community

Volume Eleven
Celebrating Peace

Volume Ten
On Freedom

Volume Nine
Human Rights and the World's Religions

Volume Eight
Civil Religion and Political Theology

Volume Seven
Knowing Religiously

Volume Six
On Nature

Volume Five
Religious Pluralism

Volume Four
Foundations of Ethics

Volume Three
Meaning, Truth, and God

Volume Two
Transcendence and the Sacred

Volume One
Myth, Symbol, and Reality

The Longing for Home

Edited By

Leroy S. Rouner

UNIVERSITY OF NOTRE DAME PRESS
Notre Dame, Indiana

Library of Congress Cataloging-in-Publication Data

The longing for home / edited by Leroy S. Rouner.
     p.   cm. — (Boston University studies in philosophy
and religion; v. 17)
   Includes biliographical references.
   ISBN 0-268-01324-1 (paper : alk. paper)
   1. Home—Philosophy.   2. Home—Religious aspects.
I. Rouner, Leory S.   II. Series.
B105.P53L66   1996
128—dc20   96-30449
                                               CIP

Manufactured in the United States of America

FOR ELIOT DEUTSCH

Interpreter of Indian philosophy, guiding guru of the East-West Philosophers' Conferences, noble spirit with a genius for friendship. He has integrated philosophies of East and West in his own creative work, and his Institute lectures have beckoned us to the intellectual and spiritual life of the coming world civilization.

Contents

Preface   ix

Acknowledgments   xi

Contributors   xiii

Introduction • *Leroy S. Rouner*   1

PART I: TALES OF HOME

Longing for Home • *Elie Wiesel*   17

Of Dwelling and Wayfaring: A Quest for Metaphors
• *Erazim Kohák*   30

The Only Henniker on Earth • *Werner Gundersheimer*   47

The Longing for Home • *Frederick Buechner*   63

PART II: THE MEANING OF HOME

Home Is Where We've Never Been: Experience
and Transcendence • *Leroy S. Rouner*   81

Are We at Home in the World? • *Rémi Brague*   95

Places of Experience and the Experience of Place
• *Katherine Platt*   112

The Man Who Committed Adultery with His Own Wife
• *Wendy Doniger*   128

Home and Zakhor—Remember! • *Alfred I. Tauber*   148

Shekinah: The Home of the Homeless God
  • *Jürgen Moltmann*   170

PART III: NOSTALGIA AND HOPE IN A HOMELESS AGE

Dwellers, Migrants, Nomads: Home in the Age
  of the Refugee • *Edith Wyschogrod*   187

Hospitality: Home as the Integration of Privacy and
  Community • *Rosemary L. Haughton*   204

Ecofeminism and the Longing for Home
  • *Karen J. Warren*   217

The Indian Diaspora and Its Conception of Home
  • *Bhikhu Parekh*   230

The Terror of Land Loss, the Dream of Finding Home
  • *Martin E. Marty*   243

Author Index   265

Subject Index   267

Preface

Boston University Studies in Philosophy and Religion is a joint project of the Boston University Institute for Philosophy and Religion and the University of Notre Dame Press. The essays in each annual volume are edited from the previous year's lecture program and invited papers of the Boston University Institute. The Director of the Institute, who is also the General Editor of these Studies, chooses a theme and invites participants to lecture at Boston University in the course of the academic year. The Editor then selects and edits the essays to be included in the volume. In preparation is Volume 18, *Human Nature*.

The Boston University Institute for Philosophy and Religion was begun informally in 1970 under the leadership of Professor Peter Bertocci of the Department of Philosophy, with the cooperation of Dean Walter Muelder of the School of Theology, Professor James Purvis, Chair of the Department of Religion, and Professor Marx Wartofskky, Chair of the Department of Philosophy. Professor Peter Bertocci was concerned to institutionalize one of the most creative features of Boston personalism, its interdisciplinary approach to fundamental issues of human life. When Professor Leroy S. Rouner became Director in 1975, and the Institute became a formal center of the Boston University Graduate School, every effort was made to continue that vision of an ecumenical and interdisciplinary forum.

Within the University the Institute is committed to open interchange on fundamental issues in philosophy and religious study which transcend the narrow specializations of academic curricula. We seek to counter those trends in higher education which emphasize technical expertise in a "multi-versity," and gradually transform undergraduate liberal arts education into preprofessional training.

Our programs are open to the general public and are regularly broadcast on WBUR-FM, Boston University's National Public Radio affiliate. Outside the University we seek to recover the public tradition of philosophical discourse which was a lively part of American intellectual life in the early years of this century before the professionalization of both philosophy and religious reflection made these two disciplines topics virtually unavailable even to an educated public. We note, for example, that much of William James's work was presented originally as public lectures, and we are grateful to James's present-day successors for the significant public papers which we have been honored to publish. This commitment to a public tradition in American intellectual life has important stylistic implications. At a time when too much academic writing is incomprehensible, or irrelevant, or both, our goal is to present readable essays by acknowledged authorities on critical human issues.

Acknowledgments

The monumental task of transforming a manuscript into a book falls annually to Dr. Barbara Darling-Smith, Assistant Director of the Institute. She divides her time between the Institute and Wheaton College, where she is Assistant Professor of Religion, and this year was voted "Teacher of the Year" by Wheaton seniors. At the Institute she has become a legend in her own time. It is rumored that she can recite from memory the entire *Chicago Manual of Style,* and I have no reason to doubt that. Her expertise in proofreading and manuscript preparation is matched only by her many graces as a colleague and friend. Chief among these are her ebullient spirit, her indefatigable optimism, and her breezy good humor. This year she has been ably assisted by Charity Rouse's hard work.

The Institute is honored by the participation of each of our various authors, and grateful to each of them.

Ann Rice at the University of Notre Dame Press guides the manuscript through the publication process, and this year has been extraordinarily patient with our numerous delays. And, as always, Jim Langford, Director of the Press, has been an invaluable resource as our publisher, intellectual colleague, and fast friend.

Funding for this year's program has come from the Lilly Endowment, the Stratford Foundation, and several generous friends.

"Wild Geese," from *Dream Work* by Mary Oliver, copyright © 1986 by Mary Oliver, is used by permission of Grove/Atlantic, Inc.

Contributors

RÉMI BRAGUE is Professor of Philosophy at the University of Paris I (Panthéon-Sorbonne). He has also taught at Pennsylvania State University, the University of Burgundy (Dijon), the University of Lausanne (Switzerland), and Boston University. He has written a number of books, including *Le restant*, *Du temps chez Platon et Aristote*, and *Aristote et la question du monde*; his *Europe, la voie romaine* has been translated into eight languages. His Ph.D. is from the University of Paris IV, and his awards include the Reinach Prize from the Association des Études Grecques.

FREDERICK BUECHNER, an ordained Presbyterian minister, has served as chair of the Religion Department at Phillips Exeter Academy and School Minister there. He is the author of numerous novels and books of essays, including *Lion Country* (a National Book Award nominee), *Godric* (a Pulitzer Prize nominee), *The Return of Ansel Gibbs* (winner of the Richard and Hinda Rosenthal award), *A Long Day's Dying*, *The Magnificent Defeat*, *The Hungering Dark*, *The Alphabet of Grace*, *The Book of Bebb*, *The Wizard's Tide*, and *The Clown in the Belfry*.

WENDY DONIGER completed two doctorates in Sanskrit and Indian Studies (from Harvard and Oxford) and is Mircea Eliade Professor of History of Religions at the University of Chicago. Her books include *The Ganges* (for children); *Siva: The Erotic Ascetic* (which has been translated into French and Italian); *Women, Androgynes, and Other Mythical Beasts*; *Dreams, Illusion, and Other Realities*; and many others. She is a Fellow of the American Acad-

emy of Arts and Sciences and past president of the American
Academy of Religion.

WERNER GUNDERSHEIMER is Director of the Folger Shakespeare Library, and he has taught at a number of universities,
including the University of Pennsylvania, where he chaired the
Department of History and was Director of the Center for Italian Studies. Among his many books are *Life and Works of Louis
Le Roy*; *The Italian Renaissance* (an anthology of source readings,
with commentary); and *Les simulachres et historiees faces de la
mort* (a facsimile edition of Holbein's *Dance of Death* woodcuts,
with historical introduction). He has received a Fletcher Jones
Fellowship and a John Simon Guggenheim Memorial Fellowship.

ROSEMARY L. HAUGHTON has written thirty-five books, including
The Catholic Thing, The Passionate God, The Re-Creation of Eve,
and *Song in a Strange Land*. *Transforming Spaces: The Vision of
Hospitality* is due out next year. A fable for children entitled *The
Tower That Fell*, with her own illustrations, will be out soon. Since
1981 she has been a member of Wellspring House in Massachusetts, a community nonprofit corporation that provides shelter
for homeless families and has developed innovative projects for
low-income housing, community education, and local economic
development.

ERAZIM KOHÁK is Professor of Philosophy Emeritus at Boston University and Professor Ordinarius at the Institute for Philosophy at
Charles University in Prague, Czech Republic. His Ph.D. is from
Yale University, where he was a Danforth Fellow, a University
Fellow, and the recipient of the Cooper Prize in Classics. He has
written *Idea and Experience: Husserl's Project of Phenomenology
in* Ideas I; *The Embers and the Stars: A Philosophical Inquiry into
the Moral Sense of Nature*; and *Jan Patočka: His Thought and
Writing*, as well as other books.

MARTIN E. MARTY is the Fairfax M. Cone Distinguished Service
Professor at the University of Chicago, where he received his

Ph.D. He is senior editor of the weekly *Christian Century*, editor of the fortnightly newsletter *Context*, and coeditor of the quarterly *Church History*. The author of forty-five books, his most recent is *Under God—Indivisible*, Volume 3 of his *Modern American Religion*. He is past president of the American Academy of Religion and a Fellow of the American Academy of Arts and Sciences, for which he directed the Fundamentalism Project, soon to be published in six volumes.

JÜRGEN MOLTMANN received his doctorate and his habilitation degree from the University of Göttingen. He is Professor of Systematic Theology Emeritus at the University of Tübingen and the author of numerous books, including *Theology of Hope*; *Religion, Revolution, and the Future*; *The Crucified God*; *The Church in the Power of the Spirit*; *The Future of Creation*; *The Trinity and the Kingdom*; *On Human Dignity: Political Theology and Ethics*; and *God in Creation*. Among his many honors are the Elba Literary Prize and the Gifford Lectureship.

BHIKHU PAREKH obtained his Ph.D. from the London School of Economics and is Professor of Political Theory at the University of Hull. He has taught at a number of universities, including, most recently, serving as Visiting Professor of Government at Harvard University. His books include *Marx's Theory of Ideology*; *Gandhi's Political Philosophy*; and *Colonialism, Tradition, and Reform*; along with several others. He was Deputy Chairman and for a year Acting Chairman of the Commission for Racial Equality in Great Britain, and was elected the British Asian of the year in 1992.

KATHERINE PLATT's Ph.D. in Social Anthropology is from the London School of Economics and Political Science. She is Assistant Professor of Cultural Anthropology at Babson College and is Faculty Associate at the Center for Middle Eastern Studies at Harvard University. She has taught at Boston University, Harvard University, Wellesley College, the University of Southampton (England), the London School of Economics, and the University of Minnesota. She is the author of a number of scholarly papers

and was the recipient of a Junior Faculty Research Assistantship
Grant from Harvard University.

LEROY S. ROUNER is Professor of Philosophy, Religion, and Philosophical Theology and Director of the Institute for Philosophy
and Religion at Boston University, where he has most recently
been Acting Chairman of the Philosophy Department. His Ph.D.
in Philosophy is from Columbia University. Author of *Within
Human Experience: The Philosophy of William Ernest Hocking*; *The Long Way Home* (a memoir); and *To Be at Home: Christianity, Civil Religion, and World Community*; he is also general
editor of Boston University Studies in Philosophy and Religion.
He has edited fourteen of those volumes, in addition to a number
of other books.

ALFRED I. TAUBER is Professor of Philosophy at the Boston University College of Arts and Sciences and Professor of Medicine
and of Pathology at the Boston University School of Medicine. He
is also Director of the Boston University Center for the Philosophy and History of Science. His M.D. is from the Tufts University
School of Medicine. He wrote (with Leon Chernyak) *Metchnikoff
and the Origins of Immunology: From Metaphor to Theory*, and
his latest book, *The Immune Self: Theory or Metaphor?* is in press.
He has also edited a number of books, including *Organism and
the Origins of Self*.

KAREN J. WARREN is Associate Professor of Philosophy at Macal-
ester College and she has taught philosophy in grades K-12,
colleges and universities, and a prison. She has edited four an-
thologies: *Ecological Feminism*; *Ecofeminism: Multidisciplinary
Perspectives*; *Ecological Feminist Philosophies*; and *Feminism and
Peace* (with Duane Cady). In addition to writing numerous arti-
cles, she has produced an environmental ethics critical thinking
game and two videos, one of which won first place at the Chicago
International Film Festival, Education Division. Her Ph.D. is
from the University of Massachusetts.

ELIE WIESEL is the Andrew W. Mellon Professor in the Humanities at Boston University. His numerous books—which include novels, essays, stories, portraits, legends, a cantata, plays, and memoirs— have won various awards, including the Prix Medicis for *A Beggar in Jerusalem*, the Prix Livre Inter for *The Testament*, and the Grand Prize for Literature from the City of Paris for *The Fifth Son*. Among his other books are *Night*, *The Town Beyond the Wall*, *The Gates of the Forest*, *Souls on Fire*, and *Four Hasidic Masters*. He has also been awarded the Congressional Gold Medal of Achievement, the Medal of Liberty Award, and the 1986 Nobel Prize for Peace.

EDITH WYSCHOGROD received her Ph.D. from Columbia University. Her books include *Emmanuel Levinas: The Problem of Ethical Metaphysics*; *Spirit in Ashes: Hegel, Heidegger, and Man-Made Mass Death*; and *Saints and Postmodernism: Revisioning Moral Philosophy*. She is J. Newton Rayzor Professor of Philosophy and Religious Thought at Rice University and has also taught at Queens College of the City University of New York and at the State University of New York, Stony Brook. A past president of the American Academy of Religion, she was also a Fellow at the Woodrow Wilson International Center for Scholars.

Introduction

LEROY S. ROUNER

The Longing for Home continues the Institute's exploration of fundamental human issues which have not received much recent scholarly attention. Philosophers and theologians have not regularly addressed this topic in their formal work, but it is an issue which underlies much contemporary life and thought. The politics of the Middle East is heavily influenced by the desire of Diaspora Jews to return home to Jerusalem. The American debate over "family values" bemoans the loss of common ground in morality and things spiritual which, until recently, helped define what the American adventure was all about. We are nostalgic for the settled, secure life of small towns in the American heartland, where people once knew what they ought to do, and most of them did it. This is the soft, dreamy nostalgia of modern folk who have chosen mobility over stability in order to get ahead in life, and are saddened by the price they have had to pay. But the great spiritual event of the contemporary world may well be the hard, desperate nostalgia resulting from genocide and the radical displacement of peoples the world around, so prevalent in our time that one of our authors refers to this as the Age of the Refugee. Home is the longed-for refuge of displaced millions.

Much of our nostalgia is geographic and cultural. We want to go back to a place where we were happy, where the ways were familiar and reliable, where we knew who we were, and where we were; a place where we were recognized and understood. Like Hannah Arendt's yearning for the Athenian *polis*, and Gandhi's yearning for the Indian village, we want a place where we know people, and where we are known; a place where we can be somebody. But we modern folk have lost our roots, and our fight against anonymity is made poignant by the realization that we can't go home again. The world that we remember

1

does not, alas, await us; yet that sad fact only intensifies our longing for home.

So the more important dimension of this nostalgia is in the "rag and boneshop of the heart," where we are restless because of the inescapable ambivalence of our moral and spiritual lives, and our faint, persistent awareness that we are somehow not quite who we had always hoped and intended to be. This nostalgia is not geographic or modern; it is the universal nostalgia of the human condition. In the essays which follow, home is usually a place, and always certain people, but this universal human yearning-for-we-know-not-what is regularly in the background.

Our first group of essays are "Tales of Home" because, while philosophically and religiously reflective, they are also autobiographical stories. We begin with Elie Wiesel, who turns the question of home around by noting that its opposite is exile, and that ours is the era of displaced persons, "orphans of hope and serenity, burdened with wounded memories. . . ." Remembering the story of Adam and Eve, he sees exile as the human condition, and sets his own story within the story of the Jewish people. Physical exile was not the only exile the Jewish people had to endure. "Still at home, in the Promised Land, the children of Israel lived under pressure of foreign powers to exile their souls." From Hadrian's cruel edict that all practicing Jews were to be put to death, to the Spanish and Portuguese Inquisitions, the world seemed intent on robbing the Jewish people of their soul.

Wiesel makes the Holocaust immediate for us as he tells the story of his return to his childhood home in the town of Sighet, Hungary, "where I had discovered the face of poverty and the magic of friendship." But he could not stay. He did not recognize his home, not because it had changed, but because it had not changed. He felt at home only in the cemetery, and stayed just a day. When he left, he took the town with him, and the question: what is the home one is longing for? He has two answers, one biographical and the other theological. Home is Sighet, and home is Jerusalem; but not simultaneously. "When I am in one, I long for the other."

Erazim Kohák is a Czech philosopher who came to America as a young man and today, toward the close of his academic career, has returned home to teach in Prague. His essay is a search for metaphors which might help us understand the universal human longing for home. Shall we be dwellers, rooted in the good earth, with lives grounded in stability; or shall we be wayfarers, delighting in the discovery of what lies just beyond the next curve in the road, or over the hills and far away? He confesses that his primal instinct as a child was to be "a dweller on the land and tiller of the good earth, deeply rooted in the land of [my] ancestors. . . ." But, in fact, his life has been one of constant change. "God knows how many . . . homesteads I have tried to conjure up on anonymous plots of land on which life cast me only to uproot me yet once more." Even when he knew he would stay only for a few months he would try to put down roots. "It had nothing to do with reason or reality. The need to belong, the need for a place of homecoming, is far more basic than either of those."

So the dweller became a wayfarer, but Kohák's final metaphor for the human condition is that of the pilgrim. He has a bond with Wiesel as he notes that pilgrims are much like exiles in that both have a home which sustains them, but that home is not a place. Rather, it is a posture, a willingness to be at home in a world which we know is not final and forever. As human we are both free and incarnate in our world, and Kohák concludes, "As both free and incarnate, do we not need to learn precisely the pilgrim's fusion, the attitude of dwelling, of love and labor, in a life of wayfaring?"

Werner Gundersheimer tells the story of his very early years. He was a German Jewish child, born in the late 1930s in Germany, at a time when few German Jews were having children. Escaping the Holocaust with his parents, he came to America, only to have his parents leave him for a year with a Christian minister's family in Henniker, New Hampshire, when he was just three years old. I knew him as a bright and happy little kid, part of our summer neighbor's family at Ossipee Lake, but lost track of him after 1941. Fifty years later we rediscovered one another, and my wife and I took him and his wife back to Ossipee.

His recollection of those early boyhood summers and of his life with the Tucker family are full of precise detail. He also describes the allure of the Christian culture which surrounded him, even as the Tuckers helped him maintain his Jewish identity. He does not agonize over deprivation. He celebrates what was present. Initially desolate and alone he nevertheless immediately made a new home for himself. Who knows why some of us grieve endlessly over our childhood deprivations, and others celebrate whatever gifts they are given? His adaptation to American life was enthusiastic and complete. His story is not about mere survival; it is about flourishing—a case study in how a very small boy learned what Kohák calls the way of the pilgrim.

Frederick Buechner was so intrigued by our theme that he has subsequently written a book of his own by the same title. His story begins with a celebration of home as both a specific place and a personal presence. The place is not his own home, but that of his grandparents, and the presence which enlivened it for him was his grandmother, Naya. While his own family moved often during the Depression for economic reasons, the grandparents' house was an elegant house with servants and an aura of stability and permanence. It was also beautiful with a "beauty that I took in through my pores almost before I so much as knew the word *beauty*—the paintings and books and green lawns. . . ." But mostly that house became home because of the serenity and well-being generated by Naya's presence. He goes on to tell the story of the home which he and his wife made for their children, and then asks what a *true home* might be.

Buechner recalls a character from one of his earlier novels whose homecoming is the occasion for recognizing "most poignantly that he is at a deep level of his being homeless and that whatever it is that is missing, he will spend the rest of his days longing for it and seeking to find it." Then Buechner recalls how he himself found what he was seeking as a result of a sermon of George Buttrick's at Madison Avenue Presbyterian Church in New York City in December of 1953, which asked, "Are you going home for Christmas?" Buechner, who is now an ordained Presbyterian minister, comments, "Home is where Christ is was what Buttrick said that winter morning, and when the next autumn I found myself to my great surprise putting aside whatever career I thought I might have as a writer and going to Union Seminary instead, at least partly because of the tears that kept coming to my eyes [during Buttrick's sermon], I don't believe that I consciously thought that home was what I was going there in search of, but I believe that was the truth of it."

Our second group of essays focus on the meaning of home, or what Buechner calls *true home*. My essay is on a theme which recurs in this book, the idea that *true home* is transcendent, and therefore a place where we have not yet been. Developing an argument which William Ernest Hocking first proposed in *The Meaning of God in Human Experience*, I suggest that this yearned-for metaphysical home is part of our experience of ourselves and our world, and theoretically should be discernible in any of the three primary objects of our experience—ourselves, other selves, and physical nature. For purposes of this essay I have chosen to focus on physical nature.

My argument is that our experience of nature, while it may take place in isolation, is always a social experience, and that we are aware of the natural world as also being known by someone other than ourselves. While this view may seem odd, I argue that it is not counterintuitive. It seems odd only because so much in post-Cartesian philosophies of nature is abstract, and has robbed us of our immediate intuitions regarding our experience. I stress the understanding of philosophy as the examination of belief, and argue that the people who are expert in an understanding of nature are those who have extensive experience of wilderness—especially mountaineers, whose view of nature is notably unsentimental. I conclude with reference to the mountaineer Robert Leonard Reid's *Mountains of the Great Blue Dream*, where he speaks of his belief that nature is a presence, and of our experience of ourselves in relation to nature as a discovery of a transcendental reality which is our true home.

Rémi Brague's question is "Are We at Home in the World?" and he begins his answer by a careful examination of what it means to be in the world before asking if we can be at home. He argues that the history of Western philosophy has been a conversation between two different answers to the question he poses. One answer is initially Platonic, with Stoic elements added in classical antiquity, and Jewish and Christian elements added in the medieval period. This view won out over Epicurean and Gnostic views which tended to be what we would call "unworldly." With the collapse of the medieval world view, however, the Epicurean lack of interest in this external world, and the Gnostic view that we can be at home only in a world totally beyond this world, have both now become influential.

Brague points out that a paradoxical alliance between Epicurean and Gnostic views has been taken up by technology. "Like Epicureanism, [technology] rejects teleology and looks for efficient causes only. Unlike Epicureanism, it does not content itself with adjusting to a world that is radically indifferent to our pursuits, but endeavors to correct it. Like Gnosticism, it considers that the world as it now stands is not good and wants mending. Unlike Gnosticism, it does not dream of flying off. The catchword of technology could be: since the world is not our home, let us build us a home in it." Brague rejects this modern synthesis and proposes that we find a way of being at home in this present world as it is. He examines the views of Plotinus, Kant, and Heidegger as a way of shaping a point of view which might make that possible. He concludes with an examination of a phrase from Kant's third *Critique*, "beauty as a symbol of morality," and suggests that "the very fact that we can identify natural beauty as a symbol of what is most human in us—that is, ethics—shows that we are, in this world, neither parts and parcels, nor strangers, but guests."

Katherine Platt is a cultural anthropologist exploring "the culturally and experientially lively boundary between the inside and the outside which transforms space into place." The inside of a meaningful place is a container of experience, and her essay argues that home is the penultimate place of experience, second only to the body. She goes on to focus on the connections of identity to the experience of a home place, and the liveliness of the inside/outside boundary. With these tools in hand, she turns to an examination of three rather different cases. One is the Eastern European Jewish shtetl or ghetto of the early twentieth century; another is the childhood home place of women in rural Iran; and the third is the Arab peasant village of pre-1948 Palestine.

Interested in what Victor Walters calls "the energies of places," she also uses ideas taken from the research of Edward and Mildred Hall, who pointed out that some places, like outdoor cafes, gather people together, while other places, like railway stations, scatter them. Gathering places make us pay attention to one another, whereas scattering places turn our attention away from each other. Platt's conclusion about her case studies is heartening. She notes the grim facts of homelessness in our Age of the Refugee, but adds that "these are not the only facts about displacement. Less grim is the human ability to hold onto home meanings when home has vaporized. Less grim is the human ability to mobilize the energy housed in these home meanings for the purpose of structuring new experiences, for creating new order out of chaos. Less grim is the human symbolizing skill of turning ourselves inside out to create new places of experience."

Wendy Doniger's essay is wide ranging as she explores world mythology for an answer to the question why we prefer the real world that we know to the seductive world of fantasy. In this she follows Brague's insistence that the "unworldly" amalgam of Epicureanism,

Gnosticism, and technology will not give us our much needed sense of being at home. The home she explores is the relationship of husband and wife. "There is," she tells us, "a widespread, cross-cultural (if not universal) mythological theme of a woman who, faced with a choice between her mortal lover or husband and an immortal god who resembles him in every way but his mortality, chooses the mortal." The reason for this, she suggests, is that much of what the woman loves are the mortal imperfections of her human lover. The prototypical woman wants her man "sweaty, blinking, earth-bound, dusty."

The adultery theme illustrates the same preference for human companionship. Doniger cites a Telugu myth from South India where a human man impersonates a god in order to sleep with the god's wife, while his own wife has impersonated the goddess in order to sleep with the god. The two masqueraders meet, fail to recognize each other, and make love, only to realize that they had gone to all that trouble to end up in bed with each other. Doniger notes, "The round trip to the marital bed via the attempted adultery is a voyage to the longed-for home via a fantastic odyssey. It is the longing for the self that can only be found via the detour of the Other." In all these masquerades, Doniger argues, "the mask frees the true self, lures it out of its repression, creates a safe-house for it to live in. Even outside the stage and the page, people masquerade as themselves. The sexual selves nest within one another like so many Russian dolls; one by one we peel them off, only to discover that the innermost doll is the same as the doll on the outside. Our masquerades are driven by the longing for the self who existed 'before the world was made.'"

Alfred Tauber's essay is a reflection on a fundamental Memory which is, at the same time, personal to him, definitive for the Jewish people, and universal for humankind. He therefore stands with Elie Wiesel, whose essay begins: "What follows is a meditation by a Jewish man on a subject common to all members of the human family: the meaning of our natural longing for home." Tauber opens with a vivid account of a Yom Kippur service which he attended with his father when he was no more than five years old. The participants were seeking God's forgiveness, and they were afraid, but they were a community and the boy was filled with awe. Forty years of wandering later, Tauber tells us he has "often recalled that closeness, the sense of community enveloping me. More, I reflect on an innocence and intensity of feeling, which seems long lost but nevertheless remains with me." This loss of innocence, and our sense that we are essentially innocent in spite of this loss, is a theme I touched on in my essay.

Beginning with the celebrated text from Deuteronomy, "A wandering Aramean was my father," Tauber turns to the Jewish admonition *Zakhor*—"Remember!"—and remember especially, Tauber tells us, the spiritual wasteland of the wanderer. Diaspora is the Jewish condition, and the Shekinah, or Divine Presence of God, has been lost to the wanderers, as has the home in Jerusalem, until the day when the Messiah comes. Memory, for Tauber, is thus mythic, "a mystical time" where the past is made present in remembrance. He concludes as he began, with the recollection of a Sabbath service when he suddenly had a vision of his grandmother. He turned to the rebbe sitting next to him and said "'Rebbe, I see my grandmother.' Without looking up, between mouthfuls of the fish he was eating, he matter-of-factly responded, 'Of course, she is happy you are home.'"

This section concludes with Jürgen Moltmann's reflections on a theme which Tauber introduced, the Shekinah, "the home of the homeless God." Moltmann is particularly interested in contemporary Jewish reinterpreters of this theology of the Divine Presence, especially Ernst Bloch and Franz Rosenzweig. He points out that there is a Christian Shekinah theology as well—"The Word became flesh and dwelt among us (John 1:14)"—and he asks what this can mean for Christians and Jews. Moltmann's own influential book on the *Theology of Hope* has much in common with Bloch's understanding of the "principle of hope." He quotes Bloch's poignant desire to find with God "what gleams forth to everyone in childhood and where no one as yet ever was: home." Here once again is the theme of transcendental yearning for the home where we have never been.

Moltmann concludes with three remarks about our own human homecoming. One is that "the initial result of Jewish and Christian experiences of the divine Shekinah is an inward unrest, and the perception of this world as a history open to the future." The second is the contrary experience of "the Shekinah [as a] deep inward rest, and the perception of this world as God's home." And finally, Moltmann concludes, "To be on the move and to come to rest; to arrive home and to go out: we have to fulfill the claims of both these dimensions of our lives. Repose and movement aren't opposites. We have to preserve repose in movement, and remain capable of movement in repose. In the rhythm of the two our life is alive and in harmony with God who journeys with us, and who dwells among us." Like Kohák and Gundersheimer, Tauber and Wiesel, Moltmann is a pilgrim.

Our final section begins with Edith Wyschogrod's close examination of the Age of the Refugee. She begins: "What is home in a time of enforced exile, the age of the refugee? What can the expression *to dwell* mean in the era of homelessness? How is home to be construed when the circumambient world of life-giving elements—elements in the ancient pre-Socratic sense: earth, air, fire, water—have become sources of pollution or death, in this age of environmental collapse and apocalyptic weaponry?" She argues that "the images of home as a settled existence and as deterritorialized wandering . . . can offset each other to useful effect." Here she is in company with the "pilgrim" theme made specific by Kohák. She examines the idea of settled existence and its undoing, by evoking what Platt had called the "inside" and the "outside" of our experienced world. The "inside" is home as measurable space, implement, dear and beloved, community, covering; and the outside is "a sense of home that is linear, wandering, errant." She asks: "How does life in the elemental reshape itself in new contexts: the desert, the ocean, outer space, the American West? How do individuals and communities become nomadic?"

Nomads, she argues, are distinguished from settlers by their zones of freedom. Migrants, on the other hand, move in response to political persecution, poverty, or the threat of genocide. In the end she finds that home as groundedness, shelter, covering, is indispensable. "Without housing bodily existence breaks down, a dissolution that is occurring in vast areas of the world." Like Platt, she has a concluding moral response to the situation she has been examining, reflecting on the homelessness of the Thai prostitute, or the Yanamamo expelled from the Brazilian jungle. "Yet even if the real and the imaginary are fast becoming indistinguishable in this age of images, the very images of their displacement and unshieldedness shatter my sheltered existence and my nomadic pleasure."

Rosemary L. Haughton has a different perspective on the world of home and homelessness. She proposes the notion of hospitality "as a way to break open the dualism of thought, policy, and practice that is . . . responsible for the terrible dead end into which we have wedged ourselves as a society." Hers is an attack on Enlightenment ideas and values, especially the resulting notion that prosperity is the level of profit, "regardless of the quality of life either of the people who produce goods . . . or of those who buy them." She sees encouraging signs, however, in scientists who recognize that detached observation is not possible; and especially in those educators who recognize Paulo Freire's critique of "banking education"—putting in and recovering information "as if it were chunks of some valuable commodity." Noting that she is neither a philosopher nor a scientist, but a gardener, homemaker, and writer, she proposes an investigation of home as a paradigm, and hospitality as the way home functions.

Hospitality, she notes, is much more than a social function or a gesture of temporary generosity. In times of war, or under oppressive regimes, hospitality is at the risk of one's own life, and is a life or death matter to those to whom it is extended. And in the interplay between host and guest the notion of hospitality becomes "a solvent of social and moral dualisms" as it is based on an inclusion of the other. To be a source of hospitality, a home must brave the weakening of specific identity in order to be inclusive to a wider community than its own inner circle. Haughton writes as one whose life work is now living in a home whose mission is to provide hospitality for homeless families. Her experience is that hospitality creates a realm which is neither private nor public, but rather communal. This is not socialism, "since that is about the abolition or centralization of ownership and so, in a sense, the abolition of the possibility of home as a defining experience for groups of people. Without ownership there cannot be hospitality; but ownership becomes something different—legally, emotionally, morally—when it is governed by a question: ownership for what? And the answer is itself hospitality, of space, of ideas, of creativity."

Karen Warren is concerned with ecofeminism and its understanding of home. She thinks of home in three distinct senses. The first is "the house sense." Home is a dwelling place. The second is "an intentional community," by which she means a deliberately chosen abiding place of one's affections. The third sense is "bioregional," a natural place laced with local natural history and human lore. In this context the longing for home is essentially a longing for relationships that sustain and nurture one, and are life-affirming. This leads to her fourth ecofeminist sense of home as just such a place where these needs for sustenance are met.

Her criticism of many homes is that they are unhealthy or dysfunctional, especially when controlled by the values and ideas of patriarchy. "They are characterized by rigid roles, inflexible rules, a primary value on exaggerated rationality and control, where basic individual needs tend not to get met." These are homes of domestic abuse, emotional neglect, sexual assault, disrespectful gender-role expectations, and the like. In response to the question why one should call life-affirming homes "ecofeminist," she lists six important insights into the nature of women and homes that make up this definition. These criticize the privatization of the notion of home, and here she shares much common ground with Haughton. She also looks toward a notion of home that will include a new valuation of the nonhuman, noncultural, natural environment. She concludes with the vision of earth as seen from outer space, suggesting that the earth is home to us all. "Earth is a home which must be clean and well kept, nurtured and respected, protected from unwarranted exploitation and destruction."

Bhikhu Parekh's essay is concerned with the Indian diaspora and its conception of home. Parekh is a political philosopher, and he begins by noting that the term *diaspora* originally referred to people who had no homeland of their own and thus was long confined to the Jews. But as homelessness of large numbers of people became a characteristic of the modern world the term has been enlarged to cover a variety of folk. Parekh cautions, however, against obscuring the "deep differences between the self-consciousness and self-confidence of those diasporic communities who have no home of their own (for example, the Jews, until recently), those who do not think in terms of a home (for example, the Gypsies), those who do have a home (for example, the Indians, the Irish, and the Chinese), and those who have a continental but not an identifiable national home (for example, the Africans).

His conclusion takes us back to Kohák's definition of the pilgrim. He notes that diaspora Indians have no home where "one has struck deep roots and which commands one's total affection and loyalty." Clearly, diaspora Indians have learned how to take their home with them. But he adds, "This does not mean that diasporic Indians are homeless or rootless; rather that like the banyan tree, the traditional symbol of the Indian way of life, they spread roots in several soils, drawing different kinds of nourishment from them and relying on one when the rest dry up. This is why overseas Indians are among the greatest travelers. Traveling, which to them is not going *away* from home but rather going from one home to another, is the only way they can stay in touch with their multiple homes." He ends with the comment that they "perhaps symbolize the predicament of postmodern humanity in the increasingly globalized and multicultural world."

Finally, Martin Marty explores "The Terror of Land Loss, the Dream of Finding Home." He begins with biblical references to Jeremiah and Israel, and then, quoting Walter Brueggemann, notes that "the sense of being lost, displaced, and homeless is pervasive in contemporary culture." Marty's work has been largely in American religious history. He argues that "the literature and the actions of Americans through the centuries suggest that most of the people successfully conflated home with land as natural environment and land as national experience: homeland." The American land was therefore somehow both revelatory and redemptive. It was who God was for us, and it was how God was blessing us. And here again the pilgrim theme recurs, as in Marty's quote from Jacques Maritain, the French Catholic philosopher: "Americans seem to be in their own land as pilgrims, prodded by a dream. They are always on the move—available for new tasks, prepared for the possible loss of what they have. They are not settled, installed. . . ."

But settlement, Marty argues, is the sacralization of land and place. "The American place became a holy land to so many, not because it was a scene of hierophanies, some sightings of God or divine agents, and thus a place for shrines that marked where heaven met earth . . ." but rather because it was a place where one could take one's shrines with one. Catholic Americans, for example, are famous for their Saint Christopher medals, Christopher being the patron saint of travelers. And once again the celebrated persona of the longing for home is neither the settler nor the wanderer, but the pilgrim whose sense of home is equipment for life's unexpected journey.

So where is home? Who is home? What does it mean that in our heart of hearts we yearn for what is not yet, and we sense that home is where we are headed, and perhaps where we have been, but not where we are now, no matter how much we feel at home in our world? As Rémi Brague noted, we are not strangers, but we are not owners either. We are guests in the world.

All this is strange. I live in a much cherished and magical place, only twenty miles from where I was born. It has been a lodestar of my world and life ever since we came here some forty years ago. My devotion to it is fierce, but when I am home alone it does not even look the same as it does when children and friends and grandchildren are here, and I have no congenial feeling, only thorough familiarity, as I walk from room to room, or wander my meadows and forest. Like Frederick Buechner's house on Woodland Road, it is a beautiful place; but much as I love it, I know it is not mine. We have it only for a while. As Erazim Kohák would say, it is a way station on a pilgrim journey. So where is our *true home*? Somehow, somewhere, there is a transcendent realm of reality. Our present experience of the world contains only hints and guesses of this transcendence, but many of our various authors have given voice to a conviction which I share with them—that it is this transcendence which gives ultimate meaning to our longing for home.

PART I

Tales of Home

Longing for Home

ELIE WIESEL

WHAT FOLLOWS IS A MEDITATION by a Jewish man on a subject common to all members of the human family: the meaning of our natural longing for home.

The Bible begins with the letter *bet*. It begins with a *bet*, not with an *aleph*, because we are meant to discover that the beginning belongs to God, not to us. But—why a *bet*, not a *gimmel* or a *yod*? *Bet* is a house. Thus we are told that the Book of Books is a shelter, a dwelling place. A place in which men and women laugh and weep, read and write, work and sleep. A place in which people love one another before they start quarreling—or the other way around. In other words, it is a home.

In the Bible, as in life, the home precedes everything else. It precedes even life itself. First God created the world. Adam and Eve came later.

The home is unique, as is the human being who is called upon to live in it. It is possible that man or woman come from dust to return to dust, come from nowhere to go nowhere, but we are born somewhere, at a precise time and a particular place not of our choosing. But wherever that place is, it becomes home. Therein lies one of the mysteries of human existence: *to be* means to admit our limits in space as well as in time.

When does a house turn into a home? When we move in? When we furnish it, sleep in it, eat in it? What is it that makes a bunch of stones and wood into an enchanted place from which one may escape to return, be it in dreams, a disabused adult if not a wise old man? What is a home?

In Talmudic literature, the question is quite simple. *Bayit ze isha*—"home is a woman." It is the woman who transforms man into husband, and house into home. It is she who creates the ambiance and conditions of family life. She is the homemaker. Usually—at least in the Talmud—it is to meet his wife that a man comes home. But what if the man is not married? Then he meets his mother. And we may guess the way she welcomes him: "*Nou?* When will you get married?" (There is another interpretation of the Talmudic saying: *Bayit ze isha*—home is a woman—refers not to the wife but to the mother: her womb is the house for her children.)

If we are to believe King Solomon—whose expertise in the field is beyond dispute—for a married man, home is a center of happiness or of malediction. When, under what circumstances, does paradise become hell? When does the refuge of home become a prison? Furthermore, what is worse: to be a prisoner in prison or a prisoner at home? Where is one's yearning for freedom endowed with more grace? Above all, how is one to explain the profound nostalgia that, at times, one feels for home? Such a desire is inevitably fulfilled, for, as Thomas Wolfe said, "You can't go home again." Once we leave home, it is for good.

And yet, though the longing we refer to lies beyond the concrete world, it is real and lasting. It can remain submerged for periods of time but it never fails to surface. Is it because one wishes to plunge into a universe still intact and friendly or perhaps rediscover an innocence that has been lost, even shamed?

Longing implies distance. But then, one can stay at home and still feel distanced from an object, a place, an image, a memory, a human being. Longing also implies estrangement. When does longing occur? It can occur anytime. Like Kafka's characters, one awakens in a strange place, discovers oneself estranged from something or someone. Thus it is only natural to think of home with a genuine sense of longing.

Still, what is home? Let us turn it around: what is the opposite of home? Being a stranger? Let us think about exile. Being a stranger in exile is the opposite of living at home. And similarly, longing means to be in exile and yearn for redemption which, in the Jewish tradition, is interpreted as returning home.

In exile, distances constantly grow and estrangement deepens. The unfortunate lot of the exiled is that he or she is always kept at a distance and considered a stranger by all others. Albert Camus's stranger goes further: he is present at his mother's funeral, but not really; he sees and observes everything as through a curtain. At the end, he no longer belongs to the person he is; he has exiled himself from himself.

Exile is a theme that has preoccupied philosophers since the dawn of critical thought. Today it is more timely than ever. Isn't the twentieth century the age of the expatriate, the refugee, the stateless—and the wanderer?

After the liberation of Europe, fifty years ago, a new species of human appeared in special camps for so-called Displaced Persons. Shifting between a past of fire and ashes, and a future of sealed gates, yesterday's prisoners and survivors of unprecedented tragedies, rejected by all civilized nations, with the sole exception of the State of Israel, dwelled in a state of utter humiliation. Displaced persons: their official name suited them well. Orphans of hope and serenity, burdened with wounded memories, these homeless men and women were indeed displaced. Their spiritual beings were in exile. Their language itself, filled with pain and anguish, was displaced: it fell on deaf ears and indifferent hearts.

As for the present, it is enough to read newspapers and watch television news to realize that the reports and images we have just seen seem to have emerged from biblical narratives. In truth, our century is marked by displacements on the scale of continents. Armenians, Kurds, Muslims, Hindus, Bosnians, Rwandans: political and economic refugees, victims of religious persecutions, ethnic cleansing, and racial oppression. Never before have so many human beings fled from so many homes.

Home? Where is home? To children, the question may sound silly. They know that home is not simply a geographical location, a number on a house. Children know things that adults have already forgotten. They know where home begins—inside certain gates—and where it ends: outside familiar doors. Children know that beyond home lies the frontier. For adults, who love to complicate things, the problem is somewhat more complex. To some, home means an infinite capacity to dream; to others, it is a peculiar attraction to nightmares. Why do some nurture a desire to flee home and others to return to it? Is their path the same? Is the road of departure identical to that of return? Why is home a safe refuge to some and a prison to others? Let us insist on what we stated earlier: the opposite of home is not the prison—which may, eventually, become home—but exile. More than prison, exile suggests uncertainty, anguish, solitude, suspicion, hunger, thirst, and a constant feeling of guilt.

Exile remains part of the human condition. That we know since the origins of creation. After Adam and Eve, all their descendants were exiled from a woman's womb into a cold and indifferent world.

Were Adam and Eve luckier than most? Granted, Adam was taken from God's vision and Eve from Adam's rib. So what? Did that make them happier? I feel sorry for them. Born adults, they were deprived of their childhood. For their children, things have been and will be different. To be born to life, they—we—needed fathers and mothers who, in due course, were there to guide us, protect us, spoil and reprimand us. Parents and offspring, all have the same beginning and the same end. And, at one point or another, all are compelled to experience some form of exile.

At birth, the infant's first breath is an outcry. A protest against being expelled from the warmest of surroundings into a world that could surely go on without the little intruder. The infant is no longer protected. It is still loved, but not as before. Neither boy nor girl will ever again be loved as they were one minute earlier. In the outside world, they will be strangers condemned to an endless series of uprootings.

What does the child feel when he or she is for the first time taken to school? Who will ever resolve their fear of separation? What do they think about, as they bite their lips so as not to burst into tears? Don't they tell themselves that they are being sent into exile by their own parents?

Barely have they made friends, than they must separate again for a new school that has been found for them. New friendships are forged? They don't last long. A further exile is awaiting them at high school and college, where, irony of ironies, some professor is giving a course on . . . exile. The children's room at home has been occupied by others or perhaps made into a study. Have we left out military service? And marriage? The first of many job changes? Isn't unemployment a sad and degrading form of exile, as is homelessness? At the end, all mortals find a last exile or a last home—what do they call it, a resting place?—in the grave.

Is history, then, nothing but a journey from exile to exile? Social exile, criminal exile, political exile, religious exile. The first exiled persons? Adam and Eve were expelled from paradise for having been too curious. Their eldest son—Cain—was next in line. Having slain his brother Abel, of whom he was jealous, he was sentenced to eternal wandering. The first man to be exiled for redemptive reasons was Abraham: God did him a favor by ordering him to leave home and go to Canaan. His journey will last to the end of time. The first exiled youngster who made good in a foreign land? Joseph—who was also the first biblical man to suffer from an amorous woman's spite. The first political refugee? Moses. He could have stayed in Egypt but chose to flee into the desert and then go back home. Both Joseph and Moses have something in common. While they were away, they seem not to have missed home too much. Neither seems to have thought of their families who, in Egypt, faced troubles of various sorts. Eventually both were reunited with their families, in Egypt. In Egypt, Jewish exile was of a collective nature. It was to last beyond Egypt. As a form of punishment? Tradition also ascribes some positive traits to exile. Talmudic sages maintain that, in exile, Jews had opportunities to teach others the lessons of life and its values.

Is this why the people of Israel had to endure so many exiles? The Babylonian exile took place even before the destruction of the first Temple in Jerusalem. The king and his children followed several decades later. Jeremiah narrates the end of the last king, Zidkiyahu. His tormentors killed his sons before his eyes, then blinded him so that he would never stop seeing their death in his burning memory.

The second fall of Jerusalem created a mass deportation of a larger magnitude. Titus brought the heroic Judean warriors into captivity to Rome where jubilant crowds mocked and insulted them in the streets. Chased from Jerusalem, from the Galilee, Jewish refugees, poor and martyred, dispersed to the four corners of Europe. They settled here and there, trying to start normal lives. It was not easy. So? Who claimed that to be Jewish is easy? Here today, elsewhere tomorrow. The chronicles of Jewish martyrology are books of tribulations. There is hardly a place in Europe where Jews have not been—for a while. In other words, there is hardly a home in Europe from which Jews have not been chased.

At times, not only communities but entire cities are condemned to wandering. Take the Hasidic experience and geography. Guer and Wizsnitz, Lubavitch and Bratzlav, Czanz and Bobov, Satmar and

Sadigour are no longer in Poland, Romania, Hungary, and the Ukraine but in Jerusalem, Bnei Brak, and Brooklyn.

Is home a concept linked to space or is it also anchored in time? Is home related only to the question "Where?" not "When?" If time is the only factor, then we are all, so to speak, homeless—for time is perpetually in motion. But then, couldn't it be said that, as we move in life, we take our home with us?

However, physical exile is not the only one my people had to endure. Still at home, in the Promised Land, the children of Israel lived under pressure from foreign powers to exile their souls. The Jewish soul exerts a strange attraction over many political and spiritual rulers. Assyrians, Greeks, Persians, Romans: all sought to appropriate it, as if they could not live without dominating it. Thus they tried all methods. They used force and seduction, threats and promises, riches and deprivation. More often than not, in vain. The Jewish soul was—and is—determined to remain Jewish rather than allow itself to be exiled into other souls.

Must we recall Hadrian's cruel edict? Whoever practiced the Jewish religion was sentenced to death. To observe the laws of Shabbat, to circumcise one's son, to teach or study Torah meant to risk torture and capital punishment. The tears of Rabbi Ishmael, the melancholy laughter of Rabbi Akiba, the last words of Rabbi Hananya ben Tradyon: in the promised land of Judea, the foreign occupants were at the service of Death, whereas the Jewish soul remained faithful to God, the home of all souls.

Things did not change with the passing of years. In exile, Jews were constantly exposed to pressures aimed at uprooting their souls. During the Crusades or the *jihads* fidelity meant death. Conversion or assimilation was rewarded with life—and successful careers in subsequent centuries in Italy or Austro-Hungary where, said Heine, conversion was an entry ticket into society. But very few accepted such spiritual exile.

Before the Spanish and Portuguese Inquisitions and expulsions, Jews felt "at home" in these countries. They held influential positions in government and were admired for their philosophical insight as well as for their creativity. It lasted throughout the Golden Age until, under Torquemada's pressure, the very pious King Ferdinand and Queen Isabella ordered the Jews to choose between physical or spiritual exile.

And rich and poor, learned and unlearned, abandoned their terrestrial belongings, determined to safeguard their identity and the home of their Jewish soul.

But the Jewish soul is open to only one influence and knows only one home: Jerusalem. There is a mysterious longing between Jews in exile and Jerusalem.

Is exile necessarily and unavoidably evil? Socrates thought so. At his infamous trial, he was given a choice: exile or death. He chose death. But perhaps exile *is* death. To experience a disappointment in love, a betrayal of friendship, a bankruptcy can lead to a decision that life is not worth living. A father realizing that he is unable to feed his family, or a writer to discover the proper words to express his or her despair, or an adolescent to find a goal for her efforts—what they all have in common is the belief that salvation may come by exiling life—or exiling themselves from life. Madness is a consequence not of uncertainty but of certainties, said Nietzsche, who knew quite a lot about exile, madness, and suicide.

Exile means breaking with family, friends, acquaintances, surroundings, culture, language, and work. Exile means beginning again—elsewhere—an existence filled with ambition, anxiety, and occasional reward, in the midst of new friends or adversaries.

Except for romantic expatriates who worship literature, mainly their own, the effect of exile on its protagonists is basically negative. Jewish prophets were deprived of their powers outside the Holy Land. "Ein ha-shekhina shora ele be-Israel," says the Talmud—"The Shekinah dwells in Israel alone." Ezekiel? An exception that proves the rule. Generally, in ancient times, exile was considered a malediction, a punishment—and still is. One left home for a city of refuge only when one committed involuntary manslaughter. To escape the avenger's wrath, the culprit was ordered to stay away from home, in exile, until the death of the High Priest. Hence, we are told, the mother of the High Priest would be a frequent visitor in the cities of refuge offering their residents food and clothes, to keep them happy, so they would not pray for the death of her son which would bring them freedom.

As for voluntary exile, for the sole purpose of travel, it was not viewed favorably by the Masters and teachers in Palestine. One could leave the Galilee or Jerusalem for Babylon only to study or teach there. Today one might add poetry, music, and painting to the list of special authorizations. Had Homer, allegedly blind, chosen to stay home, would we have had the opportunity to savor the intellectual and poetic riches of *The Iliad*? Had Alexander the Great not taken with him on his campaigns a young philosopher named Aristotle, would Greek philosophy have been exposed to Oriental and Jewish thought? Can we imagine Spinoza in Spain rather than Amsterdam, Heinrich Heine locked in Germany, Mozart bound to Austria, James Joyce and Samuel Beckett permanently attached to Ireland?

For poets, novelists, and social observers who often travel so as to reflect on what they see and hear, to reflect is to travel. They travel in time as well as in space. Their thought or their fantasy carries them, exiles them to imaginary shores while staying anchored in their familiar scenery which they love or hate. Only mystics draw their strength from exile. Yet even they experience nostalgia. Even they hope one day to return home. But what is home for them? God. Always God, God everywhere. For mystics, nothing is worse than to be exiled from God. As for God, he too is exiled by himself from himself. Kabbalistic texts stand by this affirmation. God's statement *"Imo anokhi be-tzara"* ("I share its distress") is interpreted as follows: When the people of Israel entered exile in Egypt, God accompanied them there, as he is with them wherever they are. The concept of *Galut ha-Shekhina* ("the exile of God" or of God's presence) is part of Jewish mysticism. But how can God who is infinite and everywhere be "away"? Away from whom? From where? We do not know where he is when he is away, but we do know that when this happens, he is nostalgic. The Shekinah too aspires to go home, and be united with God.

In simpler terms, exile above all means separation. Separation not only from a place but from a human being is to go into exile. When nostalgia intervenes, it is in order to return to that place, to that being. There is no nostalgia without separation.

Yet, according to Hasidism, distance implies danger, for it leads to estrangement. Do not go too far away from your origins. Lost in the forest, the traveler must shout, louder and louder, so as to be heard far away. A prince who has lived in exile too long, says Rabbi Nahman of Bratzlav, runs the risk of forgetting his princely condition.

Therein lies the danger of exile: forgetfulness. To leave in order to return is both useful and creative; to leave and forget to come back is neither. Forgetfulness by definition is never creative; nor is it instructive. The one who forgets to come back has forgotten the home he or she came from and where he or she is going. Ultimately, one might say that the opposite of home is not distance but forgetfulness.

One who forgets forgets everything, including the roads leading homeward. Forgetting marks the end of human experience, and of longing too. As long as memory is awake and functioning, it is active; as long as it is active, it penetrates the depths of our consciousness. It reveals hidden experiences, vanished faces one wishes to see and touch again, suppressed events one would like to relive with the passion of our youth.

Like everybody else, I carry within me a nostalgia, a longing that grows deeper and more pervasive with each passing day. Like everybody else, I am searching for the paths I must follow if I want to return to the place I had left eternities ago. That place is still home to me. It is the town of my childhood; it is my childhood.

Since I left it—more precisely: since I was forced to leave it—I have not stopped dreaming of returning. But the house which was mine no longer is. It remains far, far away, on the other side of oceans and mountains; perhaps on the other side of life. That's how it is: nostalgia can create heartwarming links in time but in space they are heartbreaking. It is because I wish to go back in the past that the present keeps me imprisoned. Is it fear that opposes nostalgia? Fear of being disappointed? Fear of discovering that my village or your home do not live up to the image we have kept of them in our memory? Fear that the mountains in our childhood are actually hills, and that the huge river is not so huge after all? That the forest, which in our childhood seemed so big, so dense, so frightening, and so mysterious, is nothing but a few pine trees you can buy very cheap? I have dealt with the theme of longing, its ironies and torments, in many of my works. Twenty years after the last Jew was driven out of Sighet, my childhood home, I decided to return there—just to see once more the small Carpathian city where I had discovered the face of poverty and the magic of friendship, where I had lived years of anguish and happiness. I failed to recognize it. Because it had changed? No, because it had *not* changed. Petrified, resigned, condemned to evolve outside time, it lived only in the memory of those it had expelled from its territory.

I found once again its gray houses, rendered sad by the approaching twilight. The park. The churches. The movie house. It is because it remained so faithful to its image that the town seemed strange to me. Because of its resemblance to itself, it betrayed itself. Here, life continued as before, except that most of its inhabitants, the Jews, had been deported to places in Silesia where they were robbed of their lives.

I remember: in 1944, in the ghetto, people tried to hang onto a fragment of hope in spite of logic. They said to one another: "It is inconceivable, after all, that the Hungarians would send us all away! How could the town go on functioning without its physicians and businessmen, without its watchmakers and tailors? The town needs us; society needs us! It is in its own interest to keep us here!" Well— a few short weeks later, proof was offered that the town could go on perfectly well without its Jews. Their disappearance wasn't even noticed. The formerly Jewish houses were lived in; in the streets people seemed busy. It was as if Jews had never dwelled within these walls. Passersby didn't stare at the stranger in their midst. In their eyes, I wasn't even a stranger. I was nothing. The longing I then felt? To reenter life and become a child again, the child I was before childhood was lost. So I looked and looked for that child, for that adolescent, in places that used to be familiar to me.

Of the thirty-odd synagogues and houses of study that, once upon a time, were the pride of our community, only one was still open. The largest one, the main synagogue where my father attended services on Shabbat and the holidays, had been burned down by the Germans. Eyewitnesses reported that the flames could not be extinguished for days. Apparently, most principal synagogues in occupied cities had undergone a similar fate. The enemy saw in the ransacking of holy places a desirable goal.

The only open synagogue—we called it the Sefardi Shul—was somewhat luckier. It was not destroyed. But what is a synagogue without Jews? Impoverished and humbled, this last surviving shul seemed to be waiting for ghosts. Its wretched state filled me with sadness. I felt in peace, and at home, so to speak, in one place only: in the Jewish cemetery. Outside, I was in hostile surroundings. Here, I felt safe, welcome, and protected by a great family. Strange; it was the first time I ever visited this cemetery. I was too young before. And yet the place fascinated me. Even as a boy, I imagined the dead chatting with God and his angels, or with one another. At times, I felt like sneaking in when no one was around. There was always someone to order me to go home or to the Heder. Now, there was no one to order me to do anything. I walked among tombstones, listening to echoes from my youth stifled by the silence of the dead.

I stayed twenty-four hours in the town of my childhood and left. I thought: "It's the last time; it's my last visit." It was not meant to be. There were others, each lasting several hours, never more than a day or a night. Hardly had I arrived than I wanted to leave. For the last time. It was always like that. Each time it was meant to be the last time. And each time I took the town with me.

Occasionally, I discuss the subject of longing with friends. Some share my views, and my longing for the past; others refuse to go back. Why revisit the hateful, distorted faces of neighbors? Why walk again in streets where their childhood had been humiliated? What's the use of measuring now the immensity of yesterday's loss?

And yet. With the passage of time, more and more survivors do go back to their hometowns. Not alone. With their children. For the sake of their children. As if to tell them: look, look well; these are fragments of our common past; now you will perhaps understand why, at times, our eyes grew suddenly dark as they looked at you with love as you slept in the crib or played in the garden.

Usually, the children return from those pilgrimages more shaken than their parents and grandparents. That is because they have witnessed a tragic and irrevocable fact: their parents' homes will forever remain violated, in ruins, never to be replaced. Still, that does not mean that survivors' children are not able to offer their parents some joy and a certain measure of serenity. Quite the contrary; they alone can do that. Is there any greater happiness in the world, resonant with more hope, than that of the survivor when he or she embraces a child, a future which often bears the name of the survivor's father or mother?

Where then, what then, is the home one is longing for? Is it to be found only in the past, never in the future? Mine belongs to both. In other words, constantly shifting from biography to theology, it is both in Sighet and in Jerusalem. But not simultaneously. When I am in one, I long for the other.

Wherever I go, said Rabbi Nahman, my steps lead me to Jerusalem. It was the dream of my dreams. No city, no landscape nourished my dreams with as much passion and fire. In Sighet, I knew Jerusalem better than Sighet. I knew how to go to the Temple, at what time, with whom. I could easily describe the color of its dawn, the density of its dusk. I heard the prayers of the priests and the songs of the Levites. I was there in spirit.

If all my writings represent a celebration of memory, their sub-text is a song of songs of longing for Jerusalem, the only city in the world that has its fiery replica in heaven.

On occasion, while visiting Israel, I stumble upon journalists wanting to embarrass me by asking why I do not reside in Jerusalem, since I love it so deeply. It is a painful but valid question. Usually I answer without answering. I say, though I do not live in Jerusalem, Jerusalem lives in me. Is there a better answer? Having longed for Jerusalem since the beginning of our life in exile, why aren't all Diaspora Jews going there? Is it that, for my part, I prefer the longing over reality? Years ago, I was asked by a reporter where I felt most at home. I answered: "In Jerusalem . . . when I am not in Jerusalem."

I come now to the end of my pilgrimage to the sources of nostalgia. What can one say in conclusion? That Adam was lucky to have been expelled from paradise? That God's punishment contains its own reward, namely, the ability to long for a paradise lost? Would the paradise be a paradise if it were not lost? But what about the longing for the future? Moses did not long for his Egyptian past but for his Jewish future. Messianic redemption implies the distant kingdom of David transformed in hope for a better future, a future when every human being everywhere will feel at home—at last—at home in his or her faith, country, and socio-ethnic environment.

Is that true longing? Longing for the humanity in human beings that moves them away from the need to conquer, to dominate, and above all to humiliate others?

I am fond of this kind of nostalgia.

But there is another one.

There is a legend which tells us that one day a man spoke to God in this manner: "Almighty God, let's change about. You be man and I will be God for only one second." God smiled gently and asked him, "Aren't you afraid?" "No," said the man, "and you?" "Yes, I am," said God. Nevertheless, God, being kind and compassionate, granted the man's desire. God became man and the man took his place and immediately availed himself of his omnipotence. He refused to revert to his previous state. So neither God, nor man, was ever again what he seemed to be. Years passed, centuries, perhaps eternities. And suddenly, the drama quickened. The past for one, and the present for the other, were too heavy to be borne. As the liberation of the one was bound to the liberation of the other, they renewed the ancient dialogue, whose echoes come to us in the night, charged with hatred, with remorse, with love, with despair, with hope, with all these mixed into one, but most of all, with infinite longing. And all the rest is commentary.

Of Dwelling and Wayfaring:
A Quest for Metaphors

ERAZIM KOHÁK

" . . . And the place thereof shall know it no more."

That line has haunted me down the years. I know the scene well, having visited it many times in troubled dreams. The weed-grown barnyard where none have dwelled since the ploughman departed, sunlit in the uncanny silence of dreams. The sunshine of waking hours is alive with the buzzing of insects, the song of birds and the sound of the brook. In a dream, there is silence. My tread makes no noise, I cannot hear my heart beating. The stone barn faces me, its whitewash long since faded to an indistinct tan. The weathered door hangs ajar, crooked on a single hinge. None have passed through it in all these years. It is overgrown with wild roses glowing red in the sunlight against the darkness within. That is the curtain of forgetting from the ageless tales my mother once heard from her mother and told me in her turn, in another life, before the war, when the world was young and we so innocent. It is all so familiar, yet nothing welcomes me. I have returned, and I am a stranger here, as in all the places where I have sought to dwell. Deep in my bones I sense the reverberations of the psalm, " . . . and the place thereof shall know it no more."

(Erazim Kohák, "Transition: Ploughman, Pilgrim, Conqueror," in *The Psychoanalytic Review* 81, no. 1 [Spring 1994]: 101; altered)

I should like to undertake an inquiry into the metaphors that drift like faded etchings through the margins of our awareness. That, admittedly, is not a strictly philosophical endeavor. I shall not try to adjudicate between Lukács's and Kojeve's reading of the master/slave dialectic or to construct ingenious arguments proving some thesis or other. This really will be just a quest for metaphors. Still, I do not think it an idle undertaking because I do not consider metaphors idle, mere poetic descriptions of a prosaic reality. Metaphors, I believe, shape the context of our experience as a meaningful whole, deciding in the process not only what is primary and what derivative, but also who we ought to be and how we ought to act.

Consider, for example, the unfortunate pseudo-Darwinian metaphor of the *Übermensch*. In France, he took on the guise of an artistic genius of bohemian habits, exempt from the constraints of mere mortals. In Prussia, he became a military officer; in Russia a revolting Titan hurling stones at the Olympus—and in America, a reporter in a blue union suit who leaps tall buildings at a single bound. In all those permutations, he remained unabashedly masculine, even when repackaged as "Superwoman." It was silly, not at all for real. Yet generations of adolescents grew up feeling like failures—actually, like 98-pound weaklings—if they failed to live up to the image. I am not at all sure that we should count it a joy that today the various images of the Superman have given way to the superconsuming CEO who owns a Lear Jet and Julia Roberts. It is all fanciful pretense, yet life has taught me to take care what I pretend since that is what I am likely to become. A metaphor is a mask that molds the wearer's face.

My concern is with a deeper layer of metaphors, those of being human. I rather suspect that Western thought in the century just ending made an unfortunate mistake when it took Hegel's aside about the master and the slave as its root metaphor for the relations of humans to each other and to the world—not that there would be any lack of masters and slaves in our history. The Avar horsemen swooping out of Asia upon my Slav ancestors in the Pannonian basin acted it out colorfully and cruelly. So have many others. The power of Hegel's metaphor is precisely its ability to subsume under itself a whole range of situations which have as yet no definite meaning structure. Even the emerging relation between a hard-currency tourist and a Prague waiter can be readily subsumed under the metaphor of the master and the slave, with all the overtones of domination and smoldering rebellion. It is a handy excuse for overcharging the tourist, but it has some unfortunate side effects. If we so constitute our relations with each other and the world, we cannot but consider ourselves in a state of permanent warfare which, at least according to Hobbes, renders life nasty, short, and brutish. It is a destructive situation since there can be neither accommodation nor cooperation between domination and rebellion.

I suspect that human transactions lend themselves readily to the Hegelian model because there genuinely is an inherent tension built into our being. We are freedom incarnate, actual only as we commit ourselves to the particularity of time and place, yet never identical with nor reducible to that particularity. Certainly, we can articulate that tension, permeating all aspects of our being as humans, in terms of the metaphor of Man [sic] the Master dominating the Earth as well as his (lesser) fellow humans. Is that, though, how we wish to constitute our being and our world?

I would suggest that there are other metaphors, equally adequate but significantly less destructive. My own metaphor of choice is that of the ploughman, a dweller on the land and tiller of the good earth, deeply rooted in the land of his ancestors, tending it with calloused hands and passing it on to his descendants. That is what I wanted to be. The books from which I drew my childhood metaphors were heavy with nostalgia, the aching love that cried, the beloved country! When in distress with fortune and men's eyes, I have ever sought refuge in Karel Rais's village romance, *Zapadlí vlastenci,* and on the latest of my make-believe ancestral homesteads. God knows how many such homesteads I have tried to conjure up on anonymous plots of land on which life cast me only to uproot me yet once more. Yet again and again I would stoop down and once more build up, with worn-out tools, the vision of a home, a place of belonging. All my life I have planted figurative tomatoes along *la strada.* I even managed to become attached to Erdberg, a rather homely corner of Vienna where I sublet a flat by total chance for what I knew would be a six months' stay. I would wander through local museums that even the old-timers did not know, finding old prints and maps, noting the details of each street. It had nothing to do with reason or reality. The need to belong, the need for a place of homecoming, is far more basic than either of those.

In the history of my native land, there is Johannes von Tepl's *Der Ackermann aus Böhmen* ("the ploughman from Bohemia"), interestingly translated into English as *Death and the Ploughman.* At about the same time, in the latter half of the fourteenth century, William Langland was writing his *Piers Ploughman.* For both, it is the dweller of the land, the tiller of the soil, who stands as the image of passionate integrity against the uprooted folly and knavery of the time, the corruption political and ecclesiastical, vanity of vanities. The Psalmist may rue that "the place thereof shall know it no more," but Robert Frost replies, "When to the heart of man was it ever less than a treason . . . to bow and accept the end of a love or a season?" The tiller of the land defies the transience of time.

What is the ploughman's strategy? It is easy to trot out cheap pseudo-Freudian images and claim that the ploughman weds the earth as he puts the blade to the furrow. Latter-day dwellers, even if they have not read Heidegger, speak of returning to the land, to nature, to the simplicity of Walden or of my own once and future clearing in New Hampshire. Common to all such images is a vision of a world outside time, a world that has a rhyme and a reason, a rhythm of its own.

The effective life-world of our time notoriously has none of that. Our time, in addition to being money and being always short, is linear, an infinite sequence of identical moments distinguished from each other only by an arbitrary numbering. It is now precisely 1994.11.02.20:32. There is a time for everything, says the Preacher. Our time seems more like a time for nothing. We have effectively abolished the diurnal cycle of light and darkness with a flick of the light switch. Nominally, there still is summer and winter, but, in the centrally heated, air-conditioned environment our computers require, that is something we watch through a double-glazed window. We have become like gods, arbiters even of night and day. And it is an immense burden.

Those who choose to dwell close to the land return to a world that can sustain itself because it has a rhythm and an agenda of its own. The effective world of our life consists entirely of human products, fashioned solely to serve human needs. In a world of artifacts and constructs, it is easy to convince ourselves that we are the source of all value and that the world exists only to serve us. It is a burden no lighter for being self-inflicted. The dwellers, tired of being masters of all they survey and unwilling to be its slaves, choose to return to a world that has a life of its own.

They return, finally, to a world from which they do not simply take, a world to which they need to give of themselves, and receive themselves back at its hands. Life close to nature is not a program in virtual reality. It requires a heavy investment of love and labor. Here moments do not dissolve. They take on the tangible form of barns and meadows and stone fences. In the process of incarnation, life receives a stability it could never have in fiction or in electronic simulation. Whatever turn my personal fortunes may take, life still goes on in its ageless cycle and sustains me, bearing me with it when my strength fails.

A neighbor, long since dead, once recounted to me the death of his daughter sometime before the First World War. "Died in the afternoon, she did. I laid her out in the parlor, where Sarah kept her best china, with the little pink flowers. Then I milked the cows, hitched up and drove to town for the preacher. It was getting dark by the time I got back and I still had to feed the chickens and bring them in. That night I sat up with her some, so she would not be lonesome. But I milked early in those days. Guess I didn't really have time to mourn her proper, the way you do." I felt humbled—and envious. He was a dweller on the land.

The rural metaphors of dwelling belong to another age, and yet they are perennial. Dwelling is not a function of the modes and means of production or of social organization. It is a function of being human, the structure—or, to borrow Patočka's favorite term, *the movement—* of incarnation. A life is not a body. Anyone who has ever stood in wordless grief over the body of a loved one knows the difference. Though the body is still there, the narrative that was the person has taken a turn we cannot follow. The American personalists, Borden Parker Bowne foremost among them, were wont to say that a person is invisible. Edmund Husserl would have it that a person is a presence we apperceive in perceiving a living body. Life is just more. Yet that life can be actual only as it becomes incarnate. That is the ontological root of the movement of dwelling. The strategy of the ploughman is the strategy of incarnation, life becoming flesh. Life seeks reality by entering into space and time in ways as tangible as the stone fences, the red-boarded barns, and the cows, the beautiful cows who know their people. To become actual, life has to commit itself to the tangible, vulnerable particularity of the moment. "He who would seek to save his life shall lose it"—in the very literal sense of missing out on it, of never living it. Only in risking incarnation do we become actual.

It is that recognition which in our time has given rise not only to profound insight but also to rather trite prescriptions for curing the ills of civilization. The trouble with our age, we have been told, is that it has become "alienated." We have lost the art of dwelling, of giving ourselves to the soil and finding ourselves in it. We have lost the patience to dwell. In seeking to prevent our lives from leaking into the world, we have become estranged from the world of living nature and from the living depth of our own being. As a diagnosis, that may actually be quite accurate, though as a prescription it is somewhat problematic. Ever since Jean-Jacques Rousseau—and Virgil before him—we have been told to return to living nature or what remains of it, to reconnect with our unconscious depth or the Ground of our Being, to think like a mountain. All of those are surely noble and eminently worthwhile activities. I am no stranger to them myself. Are they, though, really a cure for our malaise? Should we become ploughmen and dwellers on the land, merging into the life of Gaia? And, for that matter, can we?

I am not now thinking of the practical difficulties of resettling the twenty-eight million residents of Mexico City or of greater New York on Walden Ponds. I am thinking philosophically: is estrangement the original sin and is a return to the ground, both in the literal and in the figurative sense, the cure? I am troubled right at the start about just when and how we are supposed to have become estranged. In ecological circles, it was fashionable to blame Descartes—and God knows he richly deserves all the blame we can possibly heap upon him. But did humankind really live in a blissful harmony with nature and with its own unconscious until Descartes came along? It would take a rather strained reading of history to claim that. Technology is another villain of choice, and again truly worthy of blame. Yet already the sharpened stick with which our earliest ancestors killed their prey is technology. Where does the break come? Or is reason the villain? That, too, is a fashionable claim. Yet the great plagues of our times—Nazism, nationalism, fundamentalism—speak in the tones of authentic, unconstrained emotion, a voice of the deep calling to the deep, undistorted by critical reason. Or is the problem simply reflective consciousness? Would we dwell poetically, as Heidegger would have us do, if we could only return to the prereflective spontaneity of our ancestors, of Native Americans, or of the traditional culture of your choice?

I doubt it. That is the paradox of incarnation: the more intensely humans seek to return, to sink roots, to be at home, the less are they able to do it. Call up your own images. Mine is one of standing at Prague's weed-grown airport, shabby and forlorn after forty-two years of isolation. This was the return I had longed for since I was fourteen years old, and I was like unto them that dream. I was coming home, to a cherished language, to a people who would not ask me what my accent was and how to spell my name, to places I walked so many times in my daydreams, dreams, and nightmares—and I was an exile once more. So much of my life remained on Bay State Road in Boston, on the sun-struck beaches of Cape Cod, in the blue-green world of New Hampshire. Longing to dwell, to have a home, I had loved it all so intensely that so much of me remained behind, fused forever with that time and that place.

That is the paradox, and not mine alone. The more humans would be at home, the more they give of themselves to the land, the less they are and the less they can be at home. Certainly, there are people who live out their lives in the space of a day's journey by horse and wagon, and I have often envied them. During my New Hampshire years, I loved dismissing the whole world as "th' other side of Brattleboro." Yet even though humans may not move in place, though they live out their lives amid familiar places and familiar people, they cannot help moving in time. The familiar places are transformed with each passing year. The fence has crumbled, the old pear tree died; old Bowker is gone and so is her pup; the companions of long ago have died or changed. Within my neighbor's lifetime, Sharon had gone from a prosperous farming community of four hundred to a spread of abandoned farms and secondary forests with twenty inhabitants and then to an affluent bedroom community for ex-urbanites and their toys. By the time my neighbor died, he felt as much an exile as I. "And the place thereof shall know it no more."

The Prayer Book has it that "in returning and rest we shall be saved," yet there is no returning; there is no resting. It is not a matter of some original sin, separating us from some authentic being to which we could return. There is a tension built into the very dynamic of being human upon this earth, ever in the world, yet never of it. The problem is not just that we are alienated dwellers, but that we are irreducibly both dwellers and wayfarers.

The image of the wayfarer is the second great metaphor of human presence. To our dweller imagination, the condition of the wayfarer is hard to conceive except as a temporary state or as a curse. Abraham, the wandering Aramean, our father, was on his way to a promised land. So was Odysseus, for twenty years longing, albeit somewhat unconvincingly, for the hearth smoke of Ithaca and the embraces of the girl he left behind him. So was Moses, for forty years leading his people through the wilderness. Never mind that he did not get to enter the promised land, seeing it only from afar. At least it saved him a disappointment. He, too, was on the way home, not knowing he could not arrive. Like Abraham and Odysseus, he thought of wandering as a temporary condition, a prelude which would end when they had safely arrived at their destinations and could live happily ever after, much like the protagonist of a Hollywood film. A happy ending means homecoming and living happily ever after.

In my childhood imagination, the wanderer was personified by Gustave Doré's 1856 print, illustrating Eugene Sue's interminable travesty of a novel, *Le Juif errant,* the Wandering Jew. It shows a figure of a man with a flowing beard and a cloak to match, a slouch hat and a staff, trudging through a mountain pass in what appears to be the Jura Alps, doomed never to arrive, ever to wander on. I would stare at the picture in awe and fear, dreading his stumbling upon a German Army road block.

Actually, the story itself is of a much older date. Its putative scriptural basis is in John 18:22, which recounts Jesus' defense before the high priest. An officer of the temple "struck Jesus with the palm of his hand." None of the canonical Gospels record the story enshrined in medieval legend—that Jesus turned to his assailant, now on the way to Golgotha, and said, "I go but thou shalt bide till I come again." The legend first appears in Roger of Wendover's *Flores historiarum,* which recounts that the Archbishop of Armenia, then visiting England, reported meeting an aged man, named Cartaphilos, who had struck Jesus a millennium earlier and has ever since wandered over the face of the earth, doomed to find no rest until the Second Coming. In a later version, dating from 1602, the name has changed to Ahasuerus, the king of the Medes and the Persians in the Book of Esther, and the tale acquired a distinctive anti-Semitic tinge. It has served that purpose ever since. To the dwellers, wayfaring is a curse.

Is that, though, how we should imagine the eternal wanderer? Albert Camus's interpretation of the myth of Sisyphus suggests a different reading. Camus's Sisyphus accepts his lot. Rolling the boulder up the steep slope ceases to be for him a means to an end, ever frustrated as the boulder slips from his hands at the top of the slope. Rolling stones may be drudgery, but hardly worse than that with which most humans earn their daily bread. Then comes time off, the leisurely

walk down the mountain toward the shimmering Mediterranean, free
of worry, free of care, with all the tangible goodness of living. Once
Sisyphus gives up the hope of homecoming, of completing his task,
he triumphs over the gods. So Camus concludes: "Il faut considérer
Sisyphe comme hereux."

Might not the same be true of the wayfarer? The Wandering Jew
knows he will never arrive, and so he need not be in a hurry. He is free
with the freedom of those who have nothing to lose and nothing to
gain, free of the strains and anxieties of dwellers. So the Romanies have
opted for the life of the open road, and think it not a curse. It was the
attempt to settle them that produced alcoholism, crime, dereliction.
Their wayfaring ways earned them the hate and fear of the dwellers; I
remember the outcry of my childhood, "Coop up your chickens, the
Gypsies are coming!" Yet that hate and fear were always tinged with a
touch of envy. "Tonight I'll sleep in the wide open field along with the
rag-a-tag-a Gypsy, oh!"

The image of the wayfarer is as persistent in literature and imagination as that of the ploughman. There are the voyagers, plying the
rivers of the virgin West as traders and wanderers, to the wistful tune,
"Shenandoah, I long to hear you, away, you rolling river." There are
the seafarers, Vikings ranging from their Scandinavian homeland to
Greenland's icy mountains and the gates of Byzantium. There is the
romance of rusty tramp steamers in the Pacific, with its latter-day echo
in a radio program called *X Minus One* and its sterilized descendants
like *Star Trek* or Stanley Kubrick's *2001*. Noblest of all, there is the
haunting theme from *Gunsmoke* and William Conrad's voice, "It's a
chancy job. Makes a man watchful—and kinda lonely."

The strategy of the wayfarer is the opposite of that of the dweller.
Dwellers are strong in sinking roots, wayfarers in traveling light.
Dwellers seek to stay with their love. Wayfarers know the task vain
and cut their anchor rope before time and tide can drag them down.
Perhaps their respective ways of experiencing time are the key. The
dwellers' time is as cyclical as the eternal return of the seasons. There
is nothing new under the sun, and unto its circuits the wind returneth.
Here each end is also a new beginning, each death a new birth. The
time of the wayfarer is linear, as the endless open road. There are no
returns; there are no replays. Time is irreversible, ever new. What is
left behind is gone forever. Wayfarers must travel light and never look

back. Their strength is detachment as the strength of the dwellers is rooting.

Stoics understood the strategy of the wayfarer as clearly as the Romantics understood the strategy of the dweller. They knew that time is irreversible and that, if we would not perish with its passing, we need to detach ourselves from what passes and perishes. Epicurean *apraxia* may be the privilege of the fabulously rich and of the dismally poor. Stoic *atharaxia* speaks to every person. It is the strategy of detachment, of the wayfarers who need not fear homelessness because they call no place home, who need not fear loss because they call nothing their own. "Oh, for the life on the rolling sea!"

Consider the literature of your childhood. What images predominated as you formed your conception of the rhyme and reason of the world and of your own place therein? In mine, the metaphor of the dweller all but overwhelmed the wayfarer who, in any case, was viewed with suspicion, much as the passing Romany. Božena Němcová's *Babička*, Karel Rais's *Zapadlí vlastenci*, Alois Jirásek's *F. L. Věk*—and when I learned English, Louise Dickinson Rich's *We Took to the Woods* followed by Willa Cather's *My Antonia*. Furtively, I also read *The Adventures of Marco Polo*, the journeys of Vasco da Gamma, and even some Mika Waltari, but it seemed suspect and somehow immoral. I suppose that the reading that shaped your perceptions was rather more balanced, or, if also slanted, then in favor of the wayfarer. You are, after all, the descendants of the people who went to America, we of those who stayed home. Still, tell me what your metaphors are, and I will tell you who your friends will be. As for myself, I loved *The Vicar of Wakefield* and never finished *On the Road*.

The dweller and the wayfarer are the perennial metaphors of our humanity. One or the other will ever seem suspect, as Parmenides to Heraclitus and vice versa. Yet it would be difficult to assign values of good and bad to the two poles. Both are metaphors of incarnation. Life becomes actual only as it consents to dwell, to commit itself to flesh, to a time and a place. In Christian imagery, God consents to becoming all-too-human, born in a sleepy Palestinian town in the summer of the year 3 B.C.E. Never traveled outside Palestine, never visited Rome, never went to college. In Jewish imagery, God becomes as concrete as a Law which tells cooks what dishes to use for *milchikes* and *fleischikes*. To be is to be in the world, to be a dweller. And yet the opposite is also true: to be actual, life must not become submerged in its embodiment. It must transcend the present in memory and imagination; it must transcend space in love and vision. Were it ever to identify with a state, not a process, it would cease to live. To be is to *ek-sist,* to stand out of this world as a wayfarer. The dweller and the wayfarer, those are the root metaphors of being human. Life is a dialectic of dwelling and wayfaring, in the world yet not of it.

When we approach the metaphor of the master and the slave which so impressed the twentieth century as a metaphor rather than as systematic philosophy, it appears rather as a decayed version of the basic dialectic of dwelling and wayfaring. Mastery is, in any case, a very decayed version of dwelling. It is the mode of the conqueror, subduing the earth. In my Central European imagination, the image of the conqueror reflects our boyhood reading—the Mongol horseman, perhaps Avar, perhaps Magyar or Hun, in peaked felt cap, downturned moustaches and a bent bow, cutting down the ploughman and roping to his saddle the ploughman's fair daughter—who is invariably flaxen-blond, beautiful, and scantily clad. The point, though, is that the conqueror seeks a shortcut to incarnation. Rather than give of himself to the land in love and labor after the manner of the dweller, he seeks to seize by force the wherewithal of his presence upon the earth. He is not a wayfarer, indifferent to fortune. He wants possessions, only has rather idiosyncratic ideas about the best way of acquiring them.

The conqueror's strategy, though, is as self-defeating as seeking to win love by rape. All the conqueror seizes by main force turns dead and loveless in his hands. He can never have enough: since he has not invested of himself in what he possesses, he can find little in it in return. In this respect, an up-to-date image for the conqueror would be the shoppers who simply buy, buy, buy but can never have enough because no love or labor flows into their acquisitions. Alas, a person can build a home but can buy only a house. The bond of love and labor enriches; the cash nexus impoverishes.

When Hegel described the master in his *Phenomenology,* he may have been thinking of Napoleon or of the Prussian Junker, but in some respects his image fits both the conqueror and the shopper. The strategy of the masters is one of subduing their world, of making it conform to their wishes, swallowing it whole and making it a part of themselves. In the terminology we have used to describe the conqueror, masters seek to become incarnate, but go about it counterproductively, killing what they would posses. Superficially, Napoleon succeeded, as masters will, because they are willing to take risks—and incarnation is a risky business. As Alexandre Kojeve would have it, masters do not fear death. Perhaps, on a Lukácsian or Marcusian reading, we should say that they do not fear to overcharge their credit cards. But masters at their leisure, neither spinning nor toiling, lose touch with the world. Hegel stressed the contact with nature which European humanity was setting out to conquer. The masters, commanding rather than carrying out the actual conquest, lack the direct familiarity with nature that makes its conquest—and mastery—possible.

That familiarity is the asset of the slave—or perhaps we should speak of the drudge. Hegel had no familiarity with slavery, American readers with serfdom—there is not even an English word for *courvé*. Yet we all know drudges, plodding along as their masters bid them, in the process acquiring intimate knowledge and mastery of their world, be it motorcars or computers, which bewilder their bosses. As Hegel reads it, the basic motivation of the drudges is fear, their strategy one of giving up all responsibility, all initiative, all freedom. Nothing ventured, nothing lost. Better safe than sorry. Here the slave is a good metaphor in the sense that slaves own nothing, not even their bodies, and so have nothing to lose, like the drudges of Marx's imagination—or like the wayfarers. Whether it would or not, the Hegelian metaphor has to accommodate the two basic modes of being human, dwelling and wayfaring.

Yet surely, the drudge and the shopper, the slave and the master, present a hopelessly degraded conception of the basic human roles of wayfaring and dwelling. The source of their impoverishment is the reduction of all relations among humans and between humans and the world to the one dimension of domination. That reduction may or may not reflect the impoverishment of a world view based on physical theory rather than lived experience. The physical sciences could and at times did set as their goal the explanatory simplicity of one basic force and one basic law. Perhaps, seen through the eyes of a physicist, reality is that simple. In lived experience, though, the nexus is much richer. There are love, compassion, care, and an entire range of possible relations, among which force with its modes of domination and submission is but one—and not a very helpful one at that. Nietzsche's assertion in Aphorism 113 in *Morgenröthe*, that "striving for excellence is striving to overwhelm one's neighbor," is at best an oversimplification. The reality is the irreducible richness of human motivation and of the varieties of human transactions. When we read the dialectic of dwelling and wayfaring in terms of only one of them, domination and submission, the result is inevitably a distortion.

The problem with the metaphor of the master and the slave, however, is not simply that it represents a hopeless oversimplification, but more generally that, perhaps unwittingly, it seeks to resolve the tension between the two poles of being human, dwelling and wayfaring, freedom and incarnation, by subordinating one to the other. Martin Heidegger may claim that terms like "authentic" and "inauthentic" imply no valuation, but the claim is disingenuous. We can similarly claim that the metaphor of the master and the slave implies no valuation, that the master and the slave, the shopper and the drudge, are caught up in the same dialectic of power, but such a claim is again unconvincing. Were we not seeking to capture an experience of a basic inequality, we should hardly choose such metaphors. There is an obvious motivation for the choice: the easiest way to resolve any dilemma is by identifying one of its horns as good, the other as bad. Then there may be a power struggle between them, but there is no contest between good and evil. Good has it hands down.

The problem is that, tempting though it always is, the attempt to rank order the two poles of being human, freedom and incarnation, as good and bad respectively or inversely, cannot be justified. It can be attempted. Some interpreters believe that Paul took this turn in distinguishing between life after the spirit and life after the flesh in Rom. 8:13. Hereafter incarnation is an unfortunate accident; our true being is spiritual. In our terminology, the poetically dwelling human authentically dwells in the earth, the wayfarer inauthentically wanders. To be sure, such a reading ignores Paul's assumption in Phil. 3:20–21, that we shall be incarnate even in glory, but that is another matter. Certainly the literature of my childhood was unambiguous on the point: to dwell is good, to wander is bad. "Opustíš-li mě, zahyneš!" ("if thou leave me, thou shalt perish") Victor Dy warns would-be emigrants in the name of our homeland. A popular patriotic marching song, in a transparent reference to H. G. Schauer, who gave up his Czech and accepted German nationality, recommends thrusting a sword through such a treacherous bosom. "A kdo se adrodí, čepelem v tu zrádnou hrud'!" We have already noted that American literature—but also Jesus according to Matt. 25:15—shows the opposite preference for the ways of way-faring. Either value ordering solves the problem, at least temporarily and regionally. In the long run and globally, though, we run up against the irreducible reality that the two poles cannot be ranked with one as good, true, and *eigentlich,* the other as a defective mode of being human. Both are irreducibly and incompatibly authentic dimensions of being human.

What shall we do then? Give up the quest for metaphor as a lost cause and resign ourselves to life in contradiction? Perhaps so. Before we do, though, we might do well to take a look at one other perennial metaphor, that of the pilgrim. To an English speaker, the term evokes John Bunyan's *Pilgrim's Progress* and perhaps the Pilgrim Fathers, complete with a blunderbuss and a turkey. In the Christian tradition, it has a rich history from Saint Augustine's *peregrinus* through the *homo viator* down to the "pilgrim through this barren land" of Protestant hymnody. To a Czech, it calls up the images of the pilgrim in Jan Amos Komenský's *Labyrinth of the World* and of course of Komenský himself, scooping up a handful of native soil on the way to a life-long exile.

Jan Amos Komenský, known to English speakers, if at all, by the Latin form of his name, Comenius, is a moving figure. In his time, he was as well known as Descartes. The two men represented the two directions which modernity might take—and as recent thought casts ever more doubt on the Cartesian option, some thinkers like Čiževskii and Patočka have taken to rereading the works of Comenius. It is, though, his personal fortunes that lend themselves most readily as a metaphor. Komenský was ordained as a pastor of the Unitas Fratrum, the Czech Brethren Church, shortly before the outbreak of the Thirty Years' War. He had just time to establish himself in his parish, to marry and start a family, when the catastrophe hit. His native Moravia was devastated in the first onslaught of the Catholic armies, his wife and children died in an epidemic, and his church was proscribed by the new masters. After a time in hiding, Komenský left his native land to minister to the thousands of Czech Protestants expelled from their homeland and settled across the border in the Polish Leszno. He re-married, started another family. Amid the fortunes of war, he found himself called to Sárispatak, on the border between present-day Hungary and Slovakia, to found a school. After a brief stay in England, he was called to Sweden, to reform its school system, although he did most of the work across the Baltic Sea in East Prussia. He returned to Leszno only to see it devastated in another round of warfare, in which his second wife and children perished together with many of his manuscripts. He and his third wife found refuge in Amsterdam, where he lived out his life, ministering to the Czech exiles (and, among other things, befriending a young philosopher named Leibniz). To the Czechs, he is an embodiment of the third metaphor, that of the pilgrim.

The pilgrim—or in the less archaic terminology which Albert Camus and Milan Kundera use, the exile—is not a wayfarer in the classic sense. The wayfarer, Ahasuerus, the perennial Wandering Jew, the Flying Dutchman of seafaring lore, have opted for the life of the open road and so of willed homelessness. That is the wayfarer's strategy, escaping the risk of losing by avoiding having. The wayfarer has no home, both by choice and by definition, and seeks none.

The pilgrim and the exile very much have a home. It is, in fact, the love of their homeland that sets them on their way. Komenský did not leave as a wayfarer, opting for the open road, nor as an emigrant, the displaced dweller seeking a more desirable dwelling across the sea. He left because he loved his land and his people so intensely—and could serve them only by leaving them. Had he remained, he would have faced death in prison or on the scaffold. To love his home effectively, he had to leave it. Yet, in an embarrassingly bathetic Czech phrase, "svůj domov v srdci nosíme" ("our homeland is borne in our hearts"). Or more exactly, pilgrims bear the dream of homeland in their hearts, weeping by the rivers of Babylon as they remember Zion. In that they are clearly dwellers, not wayfarers. Their basic posture is one of dwelling, of becoming incarnate in a time and a place, though life has called them to the life of the wayfarer.

This is the double posture that speaks to us from Komenský's writings. They are basically of three kinds. Some are consolatory, written to sustain his countrymen in times of trial. They speak of the homeland we bear within as the *centrum securitatis* while we wander amid the devastation without. Some are emendatory, seeking to lay a more reliable foundation for the age. Some are pedagogical, presenting a grand schema of a reformed school system on which Europe draws to this day. Perhaps most revealing, though, is a collection of autobiographical statements, gathered from all his works, which appeared two years ago as *Komenský o sobě*, "Comenius about himself." The title is not altogether accurate because when writing of himself, Komenský writes mostly about the people and places he loved—and time and again left behind. There is no bitterness in him. Like the wayfarer, he accepts the life on the road. But neither is there any indifference. Rather, there is a ploughman's love for the land, though without the ploughman's clinging. Komenský is *the classic pilgrim, living the life of a wayfarer with the basic posture of the dweller.*

The pilgrim is the exile of Camus's sober and sensitive essays, *The Exile and the Kingdom.* The pilgrim's basic posture is one of dwelling, of reaching out to the land and all the particularity of incarnation in love and labor, yet with the wayfarer's awareness that that home can find only transient instantiations on this earth. Home is not a place; it is a posture, willing to be at home, whose forms in this life are never final and for ever. Like the wayfarer, the pilgrim can never arrive, but for a different reason. The wayfarer cannot arrive because he is unwilling to risk the commitment of incarnation. The pilgrim can never arrive because he has given of himself to too many places and left too much of himself behind at each move.

Granted, here I am again being autobiographical. I left my home at fourteen, an exile, not an emigrant. I bore the posture of dwelling as a deep program within me. I have not traveled light: I sank roots in all the places of my sojourn—and roots nourish. Connecticut, Minnesota, the South Shore, New Hampshire, Vienna, and all through that the halls and classrooms, colleagues and students at Boston University—they were all my homes. At each move, a part of me was left behind. I could never be in one place and one place only. I have buried too many memories in too many places. And now I have come home, to Prague, to Czechoslovakia, to the land of my childhood, the land of my dreams, living and teaching in the language which for so long had been only my private secret. It is all as deeply fulfilling as seeing my books appear in Czech in Prague bookshops. I am home. Yet so much of me did not come along. It stayed at Boston University, in New Hampshire, on the South Shore, with my memories.

And yet, is that biography really only mine? The paradox of pilgrimage, of the exile and the kingdom, is it not for all of us the resolution of the contradiction of incarnate freedom, the synthesis which takes up the dialectic of the dweller and the wayfarer and raises it to a higher level, transforming its destructive conflict into a creative tension? When it is a conflict, it tears us apart—and when one pole of our being triumphs as a master, enslaving the other, it leaves us crippled. Contrary to the prophets of wayfaring, we cannot give up the tangible reality of dwelling. Contrary to the prophets of poetic dwelling, we cannot give up the freedom of wayfaring. As both free and incarnate, do we not need to learn precisely the pilgrim's fusion, the attitude of dwelling, of love and labor, in a life of wayfaring?

That, admittedly, is rather less than a philosophical conclusion at which we could ring bells and clang cymbals. We have traveled the highway home and lo, it is ended. We are no closer to knowing what Hegel really meant; we have not constructed any ingenious arguments. Perhaps we have done no more than acknowledged a paradox: to be human means both to dwell and to wander. But we have gained a metaphor, that of the pilgrim, that of the exile. Comenius, with a tired team and a heavy load of books, fleeing the burning Leszno he had loved and prepared to love the next place of sojourn, knowing fully well that it is not forever. Or should we make that Lillian Gish standing off Robert Mitchum in *The Night of the Hunter?* Comenius is, after all, a bit heavy. Or perhaps we have not reached even that much of a conclusion. We have not yet found the metaphor, though we know now what to look for: the metaphor of the pilgrim.

The Only Henniker on Earth[1]

WERNER GUNDERSHEIMER

IN 1940 THE PASTOR OF THE Congregational Church in Henniker, New Hampshire, was the Reverend Francis S. Tucker. The highlight of a typical week in that quiet village was his sermon every Sunday morning. Services began at 10:45 A.M., and the order of worship rarely varied. First there was an organ prelude, followed by a processional hymn and the minister's call to worship. This was followed by a lesson from the Old Testament and the Doxology, "Praise God from whom all blessings flow." There followed the invocation, the Lord's Prayer, responsive readings, an opening anthem, and a brief talk to the children. After the offertory and the consecration of gifts came an anthem and the reading of the New Testament. Several additional hymns, prayers, and meditations ensued, often culminating in the Sacrament of the Lord's Supper and the communion hymn. The service concluded with the benediction and response and an organ postlude, during which the parishioners went to the vestibule or, in fine weather, the outdoor steps to greet the minister, chat briefly with each other, and head on home for the traditional chicken dinner.

Henniker was a small town, which then as now prided itself on being the only Henniker on earth. In the nineteenth century it had had a shoe factory as well as another establishment which produced paper and woodenware on the banks of the Contoocook River. For decades dry measuring cups, nest boxes, dippers, and barrel covers emanated from this plant, and nice examples still turn up from time to time in places where American antiques are sold and collected. While these factories were the largest buildings in Henniker, the Congregational Church was its most imposing edifice. Placed on a hillside overlooking most of the town, it was (and is) an austere white clapboard structure with an attractive steeple, a typical example of a pleasant northern New England village church of no architectural distinction. Among

47

Henniker's public buildings were also a Friends meeting house and a small public library.

Outside the village, up on Depot Hill to the northwest, a farmer named J. Philip Chase maintained a laying brood of about 12,000 hens through the 1930s and 1940s. The other local farmers were dairymen who came to town to avail themselves of the creamery, to shop in the dry goods store, the food store, and the corner drugstore, with its mammoth five-cent ice cream cones. Railroad tracks ran through town along the river, and freight trains stopped occasionally to pick up Henniker's modest output and convey it to the marketplaces of Concord and Boston.

The Congregational Church formed the social, intellectual, and spiritual center of that little world, still quite isolated from the vast social and technological changes which within a few years would utterly transform it. And in that church on a succession of Sunday mornings from September 1940 to the summer of 1941, I had my first religious experiences as the foster child of Reverend Tucker and his wife, Annah. Church, of course, was only part of it, for I had an opportunity unusual for a Jewish refugee child in America—that of living in a genuinely Christian household at a crucial time in my own development. Francis Tucker—Uncle Frank as I called him—had been well named; though a Protestant to the core, he was a man of Franciscan temperament. Idealistic, gentle, totally forgiving, he trusted in Divine Providence, which in turn brought him many trials. Aunt Annah was more of an activist, forced to cope with the world on a more primal level. The couple had three daughters, the youngest of whom was seven when the family took me in. The peculiar circumstances of my childhood up to that point had decreed that I had had very little contact with other children, and practically none with girls. It was enchanting suddenly to have become the absolute center of the universe for three talented, intelligent, playful children, and all for reasons I couldn't begin to comprehend. After a year of strange and unsettling moves made tolerable by the constant presence and reassurance of my parents, I found that they had disappeared, and that I had a new, but very friendly and caring, family. I couldn't speak German with these people, but they were patient and helpful with my English, and they clearly liked having me around.

In the 1940s, New England villages were not exactly multi-cultural, so the arrival of a diminutive exotic like me was an extraordinary event. In fact, I quickly became a kind of mascot for the whole town, which in all likelihood had never seen a Jewish child before. The place was certainly nothing like my fading memories of Frankfurt and London, or even of the little town in Essex where my mother and I had gone during the frightening days of the previous winter. Henniker was a picture-book village, its rhythms geared to the seasons and the festivals of the American and Christian calendars. There were very few automobiles, and even fewer telephones. Medical care was rudimentary. Beginning in 1933 a visiting nurse came by from time to time. Until the Tuckers came to town in 1937, there was nothing like a kindergarten. In that year, Aunt Annah started one for seven pupils, a fact noted with pride in the town history published in 1980. Nobody in Henniker had much money, but the people I remember certainly did not feel poor.

For the most part that year unfolded for me in the rambling white parsonage a few doors up from the church. There were quite a few toys around, and I was always welcome to "help" Aunt Annah with her ceaseless round of chores. Most of my days were spent in eager anticipation of the girls' return from school. The oldest, and my great favorite, was Helen. Very much a first child, Helen was quiet, thoughtful, and patient. She was willing to read to me, tell stories, and help me figure out how to say things in the new language. The assertive side of her strong and centered personality came out in her trumpet playing. Great blasts of quite unlovely sound could be heard behind her door, and the hymns she played to Aunt Annah's halting accompaniment on the broken-down upright in the dining room were the only painful moments she ever caused anyone. Helen was born with her father's selfless generosity of spirit and her mother's energetic sense of purpose. Just after the war ended, she took the summer of her freshman year at Bates College to work as a volunteer in a refugee camp in the eastern sector of Germany. There this warm and gentle girl, my big sister, contracted polio, and died.

Betty, the middle sister, was ten in 1940, and as cute and bright as could be. Her real name was Janet Elizabeth, but no one ever called her that. Blond and blue-eyed, far more vivacious and outgoing than Helen, Betty was a highly motivated student, and extremely popular. She played the cello, and in time became a talented musician. Though we formed more of a bond later on, she saw me as an amusing house pet during that year. Early on, she had discovered how susceptible I was to tickling, and brought out a capacity for helpless transports of laughter which hadn't been tapped before. After marrying just out of Mount Holyoke, and having a daughter of her own, named Helen, Betty became an elementary school teacher. Later, she had a happy marriage to a kind Jewish man who adored her. They had a few happy years, and then Betty died, her life sadly foreshortened by cancer.

I had less to do with Anne, who was closest to me in age. Perhaps she resented the presence of a new, unbidden sibling, who attracted so much attention from her older sisters. I have few memories of her, except as a brooding presence at the edge of whatever was going on. She grew up differently from her sisters, having difficulties at school, in her personal relationships, and her later life.

This was the cast of characters who suddenly dominated my life, after the odyssey with my poor, beleaguered parents. What an idyllic world to have landed in so suddenly. Family life and village life suited me perfectly. I loved accompanying Aunt Annah on her diurnal round of chores, marketing, chatting with this shopowner or that farmer's wife. Almost all of that was done on foot. Distances were short, there wasn't much gas for the old Plymouth, and what there was was saved for necessary trips to Concord, or to visit parishioners on outlying farms. That was good, because until some years later, when either the cars, the drivers, or my semicircular canals improved, I tended to get carsick after fifteen or twenty minutes on the road.

I have always had the sense that the hours of every day are precious, and I think that started in Henniker. In the barn there lived an old wooden wagon, the Peerless, which I pushed and pulled wherever I was allowed to go. There was the rushing Contoocook, and the great freight trains rumbling by. There were the trees, full of nuthatches and woodpeckers, and the sloping, snow-covered green where, day after day, the girls took me sledding, the most fun I had ever had. At Christmas, I got my heart's desire, a tricycle, which I rode around the downstairs rooms for months, until the snow melted and, free at last, I pedaled off along the empty streets. All through the year, there were visits to the farmers who carved out their livelihoods from the granite-strewn pastures in the uplands surrounding the town. These were lean, flinty, taciturn men with broad, strong wives. Visiting their places was a feast for all the senses. Most of the farmers kept cows, though not, as I recall, the big Holsteins so prevalent in New England nowadays. The barns tended to be connected to the farmhouses by those cozy passageways called ells, and I always wanted, more than anything else, to get out of the clean, spare parlors, with their Victorian settees and antimacassars, and explore those barns, where the smells of hay, grain, manure, and steaming, hulking cow mixed in such glorious richness. Farm dogs appealed to me too. Calm and watchful they seemed, after the yippy irritability of the Tuckers' neurasthenic cocker spaniel, Taffy. Most farmers, and for that matter many other people, kept a few chickens, both as layers and for the occasional festive dinner. It was especially exciting to hunt for the eggs, shooing the red hens from their straw-strewn nests, or finding behind woodpiles or sacks of meal the hiding places they had settled upon. Best of all was to hide oneself in the loft, behind some bales of hay, or in an empty stall. Even in the coldest weather, the barns offered warmth and protection, the comforting sounds and sights of a placidly ordered world that was totally new to me, and seemed totally safe and benign. That world was peopled by such kindred creatures as calves, puppies, kittens, and tiny, fluffy yellow chicks, but it was also furnished with fascinating objects of all kinds and degrees—picks, shovels, and axes; tractors, balers, carts, and sleighs; barrels, buckets, firkins, ladles, scoops, and troughs; three-legged stools for milking; yokes, harnesses, hoses, reins, and bridles; baling wire, barbed wire, kerosene lamps, oilcans, saw-horses, pumps. I had to know about all these things, their names and their uses. The people who owned and used this rich array of creatures and materials seemed to me the most fortunate and powerful of men. I wanted to be one of them, to help and work with them; and occasionally, memorably, it fell to me to scoop some grain from a huge burlap bag or a great, painted slant-topped wooden bin into a wooden bucket or a galvanized pail, and toss handful after handful to the frantically receptive chickens.

It mattered even to the littlest to be useful in some way, for everyone who could worked hard. In the parsonage, a rambling clapboard structure, which still stands at the corner of Maple and Prospect Streets, nothing was wasted. Worn-out adult clothes were cut down and recycled for the children. Everything was darned and mended until it was ready to fall apart. Most of the girls' clothes were produced on Aunt Annah's trusty Singer, the kind with the foot pedal, the only important piece of machinery in the house. Massive efforts went into canning and preserving the ripening harvest of late summer, and every household had a root cellar which by October was crammed with carrots, potatoes, apples, turnips—anything that would survive the cold months without having to be canned. Wood was cut and stacked, hauled and burned; socks, mittens, hats, and sweaters knitted; everything bought large enough to last you through the next growth spurt.

Amidst this routine of drudgery, which in some ways seems closer to preindustrial societies than to our own, the Tuckers maintained a close family, with a warm spiritual life. It was a notable impropriety to raise one's fork before everyone around the table had joined hands for grace, which in deference to Aunt Annah's Quakerism (for this was a mixed marriage!) was always brief, and often silent. Now I wonder whether this quietude might also have embodied a grim foreboding about the impending meal. Boiling was the method of choice for most food preparation, and herbs and spices were unknown frills. This lent Sundays and such occasions as Thanksgiving and Christmas a particular delight, for on those occasions a chicken or turkey would be *roasted*, and one might be able to avoid the otherwise omnipresent beets or turnips. The Tuckers knew a bit about the Jewish dietary laws, and patiently explained to me why the sizzling platter of bacon which occasionally appeared in the mornings never came my way. How happily I would have traded the inescapable (and mandatory) root vegetables and brussels sprouts for a few slices of that forbidden, fragrant meat. The prohibition was, to be sure, merely one of many expressions of the enormous respect the Tuckers showed for the fact that I had come from a different heritage and would one day return to it.

Nevertheless, despite their conscientious efforts, I was drawn like a moth to a flame by the warmth of that loving, very Christian family, the charm of the liturgy, and the power of the unmistakable authority and respect that a clergyman of that era possessed in small-town New England. There was also a wonderful quality to the life of that household. Even the material surroundings held a mysterious charm not much inferior to the magical contents of barns. In the front hall stood a great hairy elephant's foot, wider than I was and almost as tall, a souvenir of the Tuckers' missionary work in black South Africa. I spent hours trying without success to reach my puny little arms all the way around it, while trying to avoid those stiff, prickly hairs. There were few pictures, but I do recall a large sepia photograph —perhaps a reproduction of an Edward Curtis print—of a proud-looking Indian brave on a white horse, his arms raised toward heaven to embrace the Great Spirit. And of course there was a Last Supper, probably Leonardo's, and here and there some saccharine, Sunday-School representations of Jesus, with flowing brown hair and beard, the embodied versions of which unexpectedly and improbably came to life in some of my students in the late sixties.

One of the defining events of my Henniker year took place at Christmas time, when I was to make my first appearance on stage, at the very beginning of the church's Christmas pageant. My job was to walk up to the stage with a teddy bear in my arms, sit down on a little rocking chair, and say, with great feeling, "Today is Christmas, Teddy Bear; the best day of all the year." I had been meticulously groomed for this assignment. As Aunt Annah wrote to my mother a few days after that fateful evening, "the girls had had him say his piece a thousand times, shrieking it from the kitchen into the living room, with all the right inflections and expressions, too." When the great day came, though, in front of all the assembled parishioners and their friends and relations, I inexplicably clammed up. As Annah wrote: "He walked up the stairs, sat down and rocked and rocked without saying a word. Of course everyone thought he was so cute and laughed at him and he just sat. Finally he looked down at me and I told him to start and his teacher tried starting him and finally when he was good and ready he said it. Then he wanted to stay there sitting with his bear! He finally got up and when his teacher told him to bring the chair with him he said in a louder voice than he had said the piece, 'I guess I'll leave it up here'—and he did."

What could it have meant that this exceptionally obedient little boy, normally so compliant and so well schooled in what was expected of him, chose this unusually public and ritually significant moment literally to make a show of independence? The simplest explanation would be stage fright. If so, it served as a childhood vaccination against the disease, for those symptoms rarely recurred. But one could suggest other possibilities. A thoroughly bilingual three-year-old, I may have felt that I had been asked to say something I didn't, or shouldn't, believe. The fact of my difference—that I was in reality something called Jewish, and just on loan as a kind of Christian *pro tempore*—may have been made clear enough to me that I couldn't say those words without some symbolic act of resistance. Moreover, at that point I still had no idea of what Christmas was like; for me, the best day of the year might be some other day, for example, the promised day when I would see my mother again. In the meantime, I would use this moment to show the world that I could be pushed so far, and no further. That little part of me which eventually sustained me through a whole series of adversarial roles I've had to take on in later life seems to have found expression first in the parish hall of the Congregational Church of Henniker, New Hampshire. Years later, I suddenly realized why I always admired that state's slyly reactionary motto, "Live Free, or Die." In my own childish self-fashioning, I had come out as a New Hampshireman.

Long after that event, I felt great inner conflict between the attractions of the Christian festivals, rituals, and songs which had provided my initial place of access to the inner life, and the fierce loyalties which our Judaism required of us and which I, often ungrudgingly albeit idiosyncratically, fulfilled. On the one hand, I was often deeply moved by the Christian promise of redemption, especially as expressed in music—certain hymns, the B-Minor Mass, the Verdi *Requiem*, and so on—and by the cathedral sculpture of the Middle Ages and the paintings of the Italian fifteenth century. On the other hand, once I got to public school, I determined not to sing the carols which I had so loved and which were so embedded in the seasonal routines, alienated as I soon was by the heavy-handed atmosphere of compliance which surrounded those tempting but forbidden rituals. The same misgivings about enforced pieties led me to feel contemptuous of the compulsory but generally innocuous, or even mildly uplifting, morning chapel services at Amherst College in the fifties. By then, of course, the world had taught me a few more things about discrimination, prejudice, and the dehumanizing excesses of orthodoxies. From my high school years on, I refused to join any group, or even knowingly set foot in any social club, which discriminated on the basis of religion, race, or gender. That decision, never regretted, has kept me out of some pretty nice places until quite recently, when most of those places changed. In the meantime, I never missed them for a moment.

For all its pleasures and growth, my year with the Tuckers was not free of pain, and a recurrent sense of loss. Through the frantic days of our departure from Germany, the harried and anxious months in England, the dangerous and protracted crossing of the Atlantic, and the precarious early days in New York, Pawtucket, and Wolfeboro, I had always had the security of being with my mother, and most of the time, my father, too. Life had not been stable, comfortable, or predictable, except in the one way that really mattered. Now, the tables were precisely turned. Outward circumstances presented no troubles or dangers, yet the people I loved most and relied upon completely had disappeared.

Although I felt safe, I had no idea what it meant that my parents had left me indefinitely with these lovable strangers. Everyone tried to assure me, in reply to my constant questioning during the first few weeks, that my parents were fine, and that they would come back some day and take me with them. But I did not understand where they were, what they were doing, and why they had left me behind. If things were all right for them, why couldn't I be with them? As the year went on, and my memories of my mother and father began to fade, I became anxious about what would happen to me if and when they did return. Would we all stay in Henniker, or would I have to leave my wonderful new family? And if so, where would we go, and what would I do? I had begun to feel closer to the Tuckers than to my biological parents, and happier in Henniker than ever before. I loved the girls, the Tuckers' friends, the town. I loved my tricycle, and my little stuffed monkey, Wu-wu. What would happen to them if I had to leave? What would happen to me?

DAYS AND NIGHTS AT OSSIPEE LAKE

Like most New Hampshire townspeople, the Tuckers had a "camp," a rustic summer cottage on the shore of one of the state's innumerable lakes. In fact, when my parents first handed me over to Aunt Annah and Uncle Frank in late August, 1940, my new family was still at the cabin at Ossipee Lake, just beginning to put the place in mothballs for the long winter ahead. That was, as it turned out, an ideal place to begin a foster childhood, for it was strangely and wonderfully different from any place I had ever been before.

It may be hard to believe that a lakeside cabin of absolute simplicity could become a place of enchantment. Yet for decades, that place and the little world around it lived in my imagination as the epitome of life's richness and beauty. The cabin was part of a cluster of four or five summer houses situated along a stretch of shoreline about 200 yards long. It was the last place on the left, isolated from the other places by a swamp, which had to be traversed on foot, using a crude, narrow boardwalk. Since the swamp made it impossible to get to the cabin by car, everything and everybody who came and went either used the boardwalk, waded along the shoreline, or came in by canoe or row-boat. Dense woods surrounded the little clearing in which the cabin stood, although Uncle Frank had cleared enough space over the years for a small pump-house and a chicken coop, whose Rhode Island Red residents supplied us with eggs and, more sacrificially, Sunday dinner.

The cabin was a modest affair. It nestled beneath an enormous pine, and was therefore surrounded by deep beds of fragrant needles, which also covered most of the asphalt roof. The screened front porch was just a step or two off the ground, where a boardwalk led to a small boat dock, perhaps thirty feet away. Sweeping the pine needles off the walk was one of the few chores which could be entrusted to a three-year-old. On the right side of the porch stood a round table, where we ate in all but the worst weather. To the left were two cots for sleeping out. The interior of the cabin was a rectangular space, with a central common area flanked by partitioned cubicles where people slept. The knotty pine walls were eight feet high, and afforded little privacy. A crude wooden ladder led up to a loft, which served as a play area, stor-age facility, extra sleeping space, and vantage point. Under the loft was the kitchen, with its cast iron wood stove, soapstone sink with hand pump, oaken ice box, and open shelving for simple crockery and glass. Fuel for cooking and keeping warm came from the abundant wood which Uncle Frank chopped out back, using as a platform for splitting logs the same massive stump on which, every Saturday, he decapitated the hens who provided our Sunday protein. I was generally not per-mitted to witness this gruesome spectacle, but there were occasions when I caught a glimpse of a headless chicken careening madly around the place on its final approach to the plucking basin.

While the nearest town provided such amenities as a general store, a "filling station," and a pharmacy, there was no such thing as a supermarket in rural America in those days, and most of what we used was locally grown. If we had fish, it was perch or pickerel caught in the weed beds along the lake. Vegetables, meat, butter, and milk were bought from local farmers, and the risk of undulant fever from unpas-teurized milk was always present. (Aunt Annah suffered from this ailment.) Bread, biscuits, and desserts were baked at home, using flour, molasses, and shortening that were bought in bulk. Huckleberries, raspberries, and blueberries were gathered in season, made into jellies, pies, and syrups, and used in pancakes, biscuits, and cobblers. There were few if any restaurants, and no money to spend on them. I cannot remember ever going to a restaurant, or even hearing of anyone doing so, until I was much older.

Rural electrification had not yet extended to the lakes of central New Hampshire, so we lit the place with kerosene lamps. The only entertainment besides books was an old windup Victrola, with a handful of ten-inch records, almost all of them marches by John Philip Sousa. These got hard use on the Fourth of July, and on rainy days.

Vacation, like life in general, was a lot of work. Annah, with the help of the older girls, ran the kitchen, and took care of the laundry and the (constant) mending. The wash had to be done using water heated in kettles on the wood stove. Then it was rinsed and wrung through a hand-turned mangle, and finally hung out to dry. Frank provided the firewood, took care of the chicken coop, and hauled in from the common ice-house the great blocks of ice which provided the only refrigeration available. The ice was cut out of the lake by some local people during the winter and stored in a building behind our nearest neighbor's place. From there, Frank brought it through the swamp in a wheelbarrow, the blocks covered with sawdust to prevent melting. The sawdust was then brushed off, to be recycled into the chicken coop. Frank also took care of all the maintenance and repairs to the house, and every year scraped, caulked, and painted the wooden row-boat and painted the canvas canoe. He also served as guest preacher at one or two of the local Congregational churches, which probably enabled him to recycle a few sermons and maintain a precarious balance of payments. When time permitted, he would sit and read the Bible in a canvas chaise under the great pine tree.

For the children, these were halcyon days. Just beyond the swamp was a long stretch of beautiful white sand beach. That was where most of the days were spent. The older kids could swim out to a raft, or even sail with our neighbors, the Rouners. The Reverend Arthur A. Rouner, also a Congregational minister, and his wife had four children—Betsy, Arthur, Lee, and Louise. All four of the Rouner children were athletic and musical, and just about the same age as the older Tucker girls, who shared those traits. They were together constantly, constituting a tight generational peer group within the larger community of the beach houses. The elder Rouners and Tuckers were also good friends, but there were marked differences between them in social and professional status which must have meant more to them than it did to the younger generation. Although raised in poverty near the stockyards of Omaha, Mr. Rouner was a kind of Horatio Alger of the cloth, a charismatic preacher with a Harvard degree who was on a very fast track within the church. The family was more secure financially, and more urban and cosmopolitan in its orientation.

Frank Tucker made up in idealism and sweetness for what he lacked in ambition and fire. A country boy from a hardscrabble farm, he went through the University of Massachusetts at Amherst when it was primarily an agricultural college, married an alumna of Mount Holyoke of good family but limited means, and set forth on an idealistic but never particularly successful career in the ministry. He was of a retiring, unworldly temperament, and lacked the confidence and panache to lead a big urban church. The disparities between the accomplishments and resources of these two families must already have been apparent in 1940, but that never seemed to affect the children.

Theirs was an endless round of swimming, sunning, talk, parlor games, berry picking, campfires, cookouts, and singing. During my first two summers at Ossipee I was too young for most of this, and very jealous of the others. Just as the last hot dog had been roasted and the first marshmallows were consumed, Aunt Annah would whisk me off to bed. As I lay there, hearing the voices drifting down the beach, I drifted off to sleep keenly feeling my marginality to the enterprise. This, perhaps, contributed to feelings I had for a good part of my life that I was missing out on the real fun, which I was certain was happening to people very close by, but just outside my field of vision.

The Rouners had an old upright piano in their house, and I recall being taken home too early from some musical evenings there. Arthur Rouner, Jr., who himself became a famous Midwestern preacher, played the trumpet, as did Helen Tucker. Betsy Rouner was a pianist and Betty Tucker was studying cello. Louise was a gifted soprano, and later became an opera singer. With this array of talent, there must have been some classical music from time to time, but what I remember are the pop tunes of a vanished era, sung in three-part harmony, with Uncle Frank's reedy tenor carrying the descant—"Love's Old Sweet Song," "There's a Long, Long Trail A-Winding," "His Grandfather's Clock," and so on. The glimpses of the pleasures of music which I caught at Ossipee and Henniker brought me, a few years later, to the violin, which I proceeded to play badly, and with diminishing satisfaction, for a long time thereafter.

A half-century ago, the smaller New England lakes were places of extreme tranquillity and beauty. Summer cottages were few and far between, and motor boats practically nonexistent. There was no joy-riding, and no water skiing. Herons and egrets waded in the shallows, while loons and ospreys fished the silent coves. On shore and from the lily bed, a cacophony of frogs kept up an almost continuous barrage of sound, ranging from the deep, rumbling croaks of the big bullfrogs to the shrill squeaks of the spring peepers. Huge, warty, brown toads slowly patrolled the paths where snakes of various sizes and hues stretched languidly to catch the sun. The Rouner boys once killed a big female black snake, which turned out to be full of wriggling young. Another time, running along, I stepped on a fat brown one (probably the harmless creature New Englanders call the adder), and have been a cautious walker of paths ever since.

Most of these memories survive from the summer of 1941, my first full summer at Ossipee. At the end of that season, my parents came to reclaim me and take me back to Philadelphia, where my father had found what was to be his permanent job teaching the history of art at Temple University. The Tuckers had done everything they could to preserve my memories of my biological parents, reassuring me of their love, sharing their letters, showing me pictures, and referring to the day when we would be reunited. But as my bonds with Aunt Annah and Uncle Frank grew stronger, and the girls came to feel more and more like my sisters, I missed and talked about and thought about my parents less and less. This is clear from Annah's weekly letters to my mother, though she made little of it.

While I cannot recall any of my feelings when my parents appeared at Ossipee in August of 1941, they cannot have been uncomplicated. My sole comment upon meeting my father was "You are a monkey." This was the only thing I was willing to say to him during his first day there, although I repeated it whenever he said anything to me. Apparently I said and reiterated it in an utterly matter-of-fact tone, while carrying on quite normally otherwise. What on earth could I have meant by it? While my parents often recalled my surprising behavior, they never speculated on its possible significance. Perhaps they were content to believe that this was a term of endearment, identifying my father with my prized possession, the stuffed monkey, Wu-wu. Clearly, though, it was not being used as a term of endearment but rather as an identification, as if seeing Dad as a monkey somehow served to label and domesticate what had presented itself as an alien presence. For in addition to actually being an alien in the technical sense, my parents had become aliens to me, especially my father, with whom I had spent much less time, and who, perhaps, was to blame for taking my mother away. It also became clear very quickly that her English was much better than his, more colloquial and less accented. She had a gift for languages, so that her English conversation, while less vivid and complex, quickly became and always remained more fluent. I suppose I sensed how separate and how different from them I had become, not only through the natural individuation of a four-year-old, but through membership in a new clan to which I had had to adapt and then come to love. Now, having been at the center of that richly peopled world, I would be moving to the margins again, giving up my new family to become an only child—a lonely child—under circumstances I couldn't begin to imagine. Yet this was to be a fulfillment, the happy ending everyone had been hoping for. What was this stranger going to do to me? Maybe he would be as nice as Monkey Wu-wu, and let me control him and get my own way. Maybe he would just sit quietly in the corner while I rekindled the central relationship of my life, with my mother.

That, of course, is not exactly how things worked out. Both of my parents had been raised in traditional Central European families, where the authority of the *pater familias* was absolute and unchallengeable. My father's upbringing embodied this heritage perfectly. His father had left school at sixteen to support his widowed mother and his siblings. On his own, he had built a successful business in Wurzburg, as a merchant in the wines of Franconia. Largely self-taught, he prided himself on his knowledge of Latin and Greek. He brought a certain perfectionism to his personal and professional life, which included a meticulous observance of the Jewish dietary laws and exacting standards of behavior for his own two children. My father, the firstborn, was encouraged in his academic pursuits and his scholarly goals. His sister, born two years later, was just a girl; no hopes were pinned on her, other than that she would find someone to marry and support her. This she eventually did, recognizing only too late, having demonstrated little aptitude for motherhood, that her own fine mind might have been channeled in any number of interesting and productive ways.

My mother's situation was not unlike my aunt's. Her father was also a wholesaler in the wine trade, working in Landau, a town in the Rhineland-Palatinate, near the French border. He had married a woman of slightly higher social position, and the Siegels practiced their Judaism far more casually than the Gundersheimers. Mother was the middle child of three, following a very gifted sister and preceding that most coveted of offspring, a boy. Accordingly, her claims to being taken intellectually seriously were brushed aside, and after being sent abroad to learn French as an *au pair*, she was taken on as a shopgirl in one of the men's clothing stores owned by her mother's five brothers. Nothing more was expected of her than that she marry and have a family, nor did she receive any encouragement to conceive of her role in life in other, let alone larger, terms.

Having already spent more than three years with my parents, I may already have been aware of the power relations they had naturally come to accept. Perhaps it was clear to me that my father was the final arbiter of all things, that he was regarded as the learned and wise one, that it would be his foibles and whims that would be tolerated or at least forgiven. All through his life, his promise had been recognized and cultivated, his needs and interests acknowledged. Even after Hitler, it was his choice of an alternative career path within the Jewish community which had reconciled my parents to remain in Germany, and perhaps emboldened them to have a child. Having emigrated, every major decision they made was driven by his professional goals and needs, including the decision to place me in foster care. Surely that was power. If I could make a monkey of this titan just by saying the words, that would be real magic.

But of course, my magic failed. My father wasn't a monkey. He was a newly minted assistant professor at Temple University, hired for a one-year appointment at a salary of $1,400. So, as Labor Day approached, I had what I was sure were my last hugs from the Tuckers, and then our little nuclear family took the Boston and Maine Railroad to North Station in Boston, found our way to South Station, and rode the Pennsy to 30th Street Station in Philadelphia, the jumping-off place for the next chapters of my life.

NOTE

1. This text is part of a longer work tentatively titled *Coming Across: Reminiscences of a Refugee Childhood*. It addresses the topic of "The Return Home" in terms of my heart's earliest remembered way station. For in reality, my primal home—if it exists at all—lacks spacial coordinates. My birthplace was Frankfurt, a medieval river town which in all its splendid variety and beauty was obliterated. A necessary loss, to be sure, but still

gone, forever a part of "the world we have lost," in Peter Laslett's poignant phrase. A faceless concrete office slab rises over the site of the sixteenth-century house where I was born, and I have little recall of the thirteen other places where I stayed with my parents before coming to rest in Henniker at the age of three years and four months. That is the place and time where my memories begin, where my compass finds its true north.

The Longing for Home

FREDERICK BUECHNER

"Home, sweet home." "There's no place like home." "Home is where you hang your hat," or, as a waggish friend of mine once said, "Home is where you hang yourself." "Home is the sailor, home from sea,/ And the hunter home from the hill." What the word *home* brings to mind before anything else, I believe, is a place, and in its fullest sense not just the place where you happen to be living at the time but a very special place with very special attributes which make it clearly distinguishable from all other places. The word *home* summons up a place—more specifically a house within that place—which you have rich and complex feelings about, a place where you feel, or did feel once, uniquely *at home*, which is to say a place where you feel you belong and which in some sense belongs to you, a place where you feel that all is somehow ultimately well even if things aren't going all that well at any given moment. To think about home eventually leads you to think back to your childhood home, the place where your life started, the place which off and on throughout your life you keep going back to if only in dreams and memories and which is apt to determine the kind of place, perhaps a place inside yourself, that you spend the rest of your life searching for even if you are not aware that you are searching. I suspect that those who as children never had such a place in actuality had instead some kind of dream of such a home which for them played an equally crucial part.

I was born in 1926 and therefore most of my childhood took place during the years of the Great Depression of the thirties. As economic considerations kept my father continually moving from job to job, we as a family kept moving from place to place with the result that none of the many houses we lived in ever became home for me in the sense I have described. But there was one house which did become home for me in that sense, and which for many years after the

63

last time I saw it in 1938 or so I used to dream about, and which I still often think about, although by now I am old enough to be the grandfather of the small boy I was when I first knew it.

It was a large white clapboard house that belonged to my maternal grandparents and was located in a suburb of Pittsburgh, Pennsylvania, called East Liberty, more specifically in a private residential enclave in East Liberty called Woodland Road which had a uniformed guard at the gate who checked you in and out to make sure you had good reason for being there. For about twenty years or so before he went more or less broke and moved away in his seventies with my grandmother to live out the rest of their days in North Carolina, my grandfather was a rich man and his house was a rich man's house, as were all the others in Woodland Road, including the one that belonged to Andrew Mellon, who lived nearby. It was built on a hill with a steep curving driveway and surrounded by green lawns and horse chestnut trees which put out white blossoms in May and unbelievably sticky buds that my younger brother and I used to stir up with leaves and twigs in a sweet grass basket calling it witches' brew. It also produced glistening brown buckeyes that you had to split off the tough, thorny husks to find and could make tiny chairs out of with pins for legs or attach to a string and hurl into the air or crack other people's buckeyes with to see which would hold out the longest.

The house itself had a full-length brick terrace in front and lots of French windows on the ground floor and bay windows above and dormers on the third floor with a screened-in sleeping porch in the back under which was the kitchen porch which had a zinc-lined, pre-electric icebox on it that the iceman delivered ice to and whose musty, cave-like smell I can smell to this day if I put my mind to it. To the right of the long entrance hall was the library lined with glassed-in shelves and books, some of which I can still remember like the slim, folio-sized picture books about French history with intricate full-page color plates by the great French illustrator Job, and my great-grandfather Golay's set of the works of Charles Dickens bound in calf like law books with his name stamped on the front cover. To the left of the hall was the living room which I remember best for a horsehair settee covered in cherry red damask which was very uncomfortable and prickly to sit on and a Chinese vase almost large enough for a boy my size to hide in, and an English portrait done in the 1840s of a little girl named Lavinia Holt, who is wearing a dress of dotted white organdy with a slate blue sash and is holding in her left hand, her arm almost fully extended to the side, a spidery, pinkish flower that might be honeysuckle. In the basement there was a billiard room with a green baize table which as far as I know was never used by anybody and a moose head mounted on the wall that my brother and I and our cousin David Wick used to pretend to worship for reasons I have long since forgotten as the god of the dirty spittoon and several tall bookcases full of yellow, paper-bound French novels which ladies of the French Alliance, of which my half-French-Swiss grandmother was a leading light, used to come and borrow from time to time.

At the end of the entrance hall a broad white staircase ascended to a landing with a bench on it and then turned the corner and went up to the second floor where the grown-ups' bedrooms were, including my grandparents' which had a bay window and a sun-drenched window seat where I used to count the pennies I emptied out of a little penny bank of my grandmother's made like the steel helmet of a World War I French *poilu*. The stairway then continued on up to the third floor where you could look down through the banister railing to the carpeted hall which seemed a dizzying distance below. The third floor was the part of the house that for many years I used to go back to in my dreams. My brother's and my bedroom was there with a little gas fire that on winter mornings Ellen, the maid, used to light for us before we got out of bed, and the servants' rooms, and other rooms full of hump-backed trunks covered with steamship labels and tied-up cardboard boxes and round Parisian hat boxes and all sorts of other treasures which my brother and I never fully explored, which is perhaps why for all those years my dreams kept taking me back for another look. The smell of the house that I remember best was the smell of cooking applesauce. Out in the kitchen paneled with dark match board, Williams, the cook, put cinnamon in it for flavoring, and the fragrance as it simmered and steamed on top of the stove was warm and blurred and dimly pungent and seemed somehow full of enormous comfort and kindness.

What was there about that house that made it home in a way that all the other houses of my childhood never even came close to being? The permanence of it was part of the answer—the sense I had that whereas the other houses came and went, this one was there always and would go on being there for as far into the future as I could imagine, with Ellen bringing my grandmother her glass of buttermilk on a

silver tray just at eleven every morning, and my grandfather going off
to his downtown office and returning in time for a cocktail before
dinner with the evening paper under his arm and maybe something
he'd bought at the bakery on the way home, and the Saturday night
suppers when the cook was out and the menu, in honor of the New
England half of my grandmother's background, was always mahogany-
colored beans baked with salt pork and molasses and steamed Boston
brown bread with raisins in it and strong black coffee boiled in a pot
with an eggshell to settle the grounds and sweetened with lumps of
sugar and cream heavy enough to whip.

And beauty was another part of the answer, beauty that I took in
through my pores almost before I so much as knew the word *beauty*—
the paintings and books and green lawns, the thunder of water falling
in a long, silver braid from the goose-neck spigot into the pantry sink,
the lighting of lamps with their fringed shades at dusk, the knee-length
silk mandarin's coat which my grandmother sometimes wore in the
evenings with a coral lining and embroidered all over with flowers and
birds, and out behind the house by the grassed-over tennis court the
white stables which were used to garage, among other cars, the elegant
old Marmon upholstered in salmon-colored leather that had belonged
to my mother in her flapper days and hadn't been used since.

But more than all of these things that made that house home, or
at the heart of all those things, was my grandmother, whom for reasons
lost to history I called Naya. How to evoke her? She loved books and
music and the French language of her father, who had emigrated from
Geneva to fight on the Union side in the Civil War and eventually died
of a shoulder wound he received from a sniper's bullet at the siege of
Petersburg. She loved Chesterfield cigarettes and the novels of Jean
Ingelow and a daiquiri before dinner and crossword puzzles and spoke
the English language with a wit and eloquence and style that I have
never heard surpassed. She loved to talk about the past as much as I
loved to listen to her bring it to life with her marvelous, Dickensian descriptions, and when she talked about the present, she made it seem
like a richly entertaining play which we both of us had leading roles in
and at the same time were watching unfold from the safety and comfort of our seats side by side in the dress circle. The love she had for
me was not born of desperate need for me like my mother's love but
had more to do simply with her interest in me as a person and with the
pleasure she took in my interest in her as the one grandchild she had

who was bookish the way she was and sat endlessly enraptured by the spells she cast.

On my thirty-fourth birthday when she was going on ninety-one, she wrote me a letter in which she said, "[This] is to wish you many and many a happy year to come. And to wish for you that along the way you may meet someone who will be to you the delight you have been to me. By which I mean someone of a younger generation." For all its other glories, the house on Woodland Road could never have become home without the extraordinary delight to me of her presence in it and the profound sense of serenity and well-being that her presence generated, which leads me to believe that if, as I started by saying, the first thing the word *home* brings to mind is a place, then the next and perhaps most crucial thing is people and maybe ultimately a single person.

Can it really, that home on Woodland Road, have been as wonderful as I make it sound at least to myself, or has my memory reshaped it? The answer is that yes, of course, it was every bit that wonderful and probably even more so in ways I have omitted from this account, and that is precisely why my memory has never let go of it as it has let go of so much else but has continually reshaped it, the way the waves of the sea are continually reshaping the shimmering cliff, until anything scary and jagged is worn away with the result that what has principally survived is a sense—how to put it right?—of charity and justice and order and peace that I have longed to find again ever since and have longed to establish inside myself.

All of this makes me wonder about the home that my wife and I created for ourselves and our three daughters, both of us coming from the homes of our childhood and consciously or unconsciously drawing on those memories as we went about making a new home for the family that we were becoming. For thirty-odd years the five of us lived in the same house, at first just during vacations but eventually all year round, so that there was never any question as to where home was. It was a much smaller white clapboard house than my grandparents' but built on a much higher hill and surrounded not so much by lawns as by the meadows and pastures and woods of our corner of southern Vermont. The house had a number of small bedrooms in it with a smallish, rather narrow living room which all the other rooms more or less opened into so that to sit there was to be aware of pretty much everything that was going on under our roof. For me as the ever-watchful and ever-anxious father this had the advantage or disadvantage of letting me keep an eye on my children's comings and goings without, I hoped, giving them the sense that I was perpetually keeping tabs on them, but as they began to get bigger and noisier, there were times when I yearned for a place to escape to once in a while so we built on a wing with a large living room paneled in the silvery gray siding of a couple of tumbledown pre-Revolutionary barns. I don't think that it was in conscious emulation of the Woodland Road library that I filled the new room with shelves full of wonderful books—a few of them copies of some of the same ones that Naya had had, like the Job-illustrated French histories—but I'm sure that the memory of it was in the back of my mind somewhere. Like Naya, and almost certainly because of her, I was fascinated by the past of my family—the mid-nineteenth-century German immigrants on my father's side and the mixture of English, French, Pennsylvania Dutch, old New England and almost everything else on my mother's—and I became in a way the family archivist, the keeper of the family graves, and collected in the cupboards beneath the bookshelves as many old photograph albums, documents, letters, genealogies, and assorted family memorabilia as little by little came my way through various relatives who knew of my interest and sent them to me. It was in that silvery gray room too that for some twenty years I both read my books and wrote them. It was there that I listened to music and to what I could hear of the longings and fears and lusts and holiness of my own life. It was in that room that our best Christmases took place with a nine-foot tree that we would all go out together and cut down in the woods and then trim with decorations of our own making.

What my wife brought to the home we were creating was entirely different. The chief delight of her childhood in New Jersey had been not indoor things like me but outdoor things. She had loved horses and animals of all kinds and growing things in gardens and almost by nature knew as much about trees and birds and flowers as most people have to learn from books and then struggle to remember. She planted a fifty-by a hundred-foot vegetable garden and flowers all over the place. She saw to it that each of our children had not only horses to ride but other animals to love and take care of—Aracana chickens who laid eggs of three different colors for Sharmy, and for Dinah a pig who grew to the size of a large refrigerator and didn't suffer fools gladly, and for Katherine some fawn-colored Toggenberg goats who skittered around the barnyard dropping their berries and gazing out at the hills through the inscrutable slits of their eyes.

Like everybody else, what we furnished home with was ourselves, in other words. We furnished it with the best that we knew and the best that we were, and we furnished it also with everything that we were not wise enough to know and the shadow side of who we were as well as the best side because we were not self-aware enough to recognize those shadows and somehow both to learn from them and disempower them.

It became home for us in a very full sense. It was the place where we did the best we knew how to do as father and mother and as wife and husband. It was the little world we created to be as safe as we knew how to make it for ourselves and for our children from the great world outside which I more than my wife was afraid of, especially for our children's sake because I remembered so vividly the dark and dangerous times of my own childhood which were very much part of me still and continue to be. In that Vermont house I found refuge from the dark, as I always had, mainly in books, which, unlike people, can always be depended upon to tell the same stories in the same way and are always there when you need them and can always be set aside when you need them no longer. I believe my wife would say that her refuge from the dark has always been the world of animals and growing things.

Did this home we made become for our children as richly home as my grandparents' home had been for me as a child? How would they answer that question if I were ever brave enough to ask it? Did I hold them too close with my supervigilance? Did my wife perhaps not hold them close enough? Were our lives in deep country away from any easy access to town or neighbors too intense and isolated for our own good? Did they find in our house on the hill anything like the same sense of charity, justice, order, peace that I had found on Woodland Road? As they grow older, will they draw upon what was best about it as they make homes of their own with their husbands and children? I don't know any of these answers. Maybe they themselves don't entirely know them. Maybe even in their early thirties they are still too close to their childhood to be able to see it with the detachment with which I see mine in my late sixties. It was almost not until I found myself putting these thoughts together that I fully realized that my own true home had not been any of the places my brother and I had lived both before and after our father's suicide when I was ten years old, not even the places where we were happiest, but had been instead that house in East Liberty where we never really lived in any permanent sense but only visited. Will our children remember the house in Vermont as their true home? Or are the words *true home* perhaps too much to apply to even the happiest home that lies within our power to create? Are they words that always point to a reality beyond themselves?

In a novel called *Treasure Hunt* that I wrote some years ago, there is a scene of homecoming. The narrator, a young man named Antonio Parr, has been away for some weeks and on his return finds that his small son and some other children have made a sign for him which reads WELCOME HONE with the last little leg of the M in *home* missing so that it turns it into an N. "It seemed oddly fitting," Antonio Parr says when he first sees it. "It was good to get home, but it was home with something missing or out of whack about it. It wasn't much, to be sure, just some minor stroke or serif, but even a minor stroke can make a major difference." And then a little while later he remembers it a second time and goes on to add, "WELCOME HONE, the sign said, and I can't help thinking again of Gideon and Barak, of Samson and David and all the rest of the crowd . . . who, because some small but crucial thing was missing, kept looking for it come hell or high water wherever they went till their eyes were dim and their arches fallen. . . . In the long run I suppose it would be to think of everybody if you knew enough about them to think straight."[1] The reference, of course, is to the eleventh chapter of the Epistle to the Hebrews, where, after listing some of the great heroes and heroines of biblical faith, the author writes, "These all died in faith, not having received what was promised, but having seen it and greeted it from afar, and having acknowledged that they were strangers and exiles on the earth. For people who speak thus make it clear that they are seeking a homeland" (Heb. 11:13–14).

If we are lucky, we are born into a home, or like me find a home somewhere else along the way during childhood, or, failing that, at least, one hopes, find some good dream of a home. And, if our luck holds, when we grow up, we make another home for ourselves and for our family if we get married and acquire one. It is the place of all places that we feel most at home in, most at peace and most at one in, and as I sketched out in my mind that scene in my novel, I thought of it primarily as a scene that would show Antonio Parr's great joy at returning to his home after such a long absence. But then out of nowhere, and entirely unforeseen by me, there came into my mind that sign with the missing leg of the M. I hadn't planned to have it read "hone" instead of "home." It was in no sense a novelistic device I'd contrived. It's simply the way I saw it. From as deep a place within me as my books and my dreams come from, there came along with the misspelled sign this revelation that although Antonio Parr was enormously glad to be at home at last, he recognized that there was something small but crucial missing which if only for a moment made him feel, like Gideon and Barak before him, that he was in some sense a stranger and an exile there. It is when he comes home that he recognizes most poignantly that he is at a deep level of his being homeless and that whatever it is that is missing, he will spend the rest of his days longing for it and seeking to find it.

The word *longing* comes from the same root as the word *long*, in the sense of length in either time or space, and also the word *belong*, so that in its full richness *to long* suggests to yearn for a long time for something that is a long way off and something that we feel we belong to and that belongs to us. The longing for home is so universal a form of longing that there is even a special word for it, which is of course *homesickness*, and what I have been dealing with so far is that form of homesickness which is known as nostalgia or longing for the past as home. Almost all of the photographs that I have managed to find of my grandparents' house in Pittsburgh show simply the house itself. There is a view from the front with the long brick terrace and the French windows, and another from the rear with the sleeping porch over the kitchen porch beneath it and the bay window of my grandparents' bedroom and the tall, arched window on the first landing of the central staircase. There is an interior shot of the living room with Lavinia Holt gazing out over the grand piano which has a fringed shawl draped over it and which, as far as I can remember, Naya was the only one of us ever to use, picking out tunes with one finger every once and so often because that was as near as she ever came to knowing how to play it, and another shot of the library with the wicker peacock chair at one side of the fireplace and the white sofa at the far end where Naya used to let me help her do the Sunday crossword puzzle. But there is one photograph that has a person in it, and the person is Naya herself.

It is winter and there has been a thaw. Wet snow clings to the bare branches of the trees, and the air is full of mist. Naya is standing on the front terrace in profile. She is looking pensively out toward the lawn. She is wearing a short fur jacket and a fur hat with her hands in the jacket pockets. She has on galoshes, or arctics as they were called in those days. The terrace is covered with snow except in the foreground where it has melted away in patches and you can see her reflection in the wet brick. When I look at that photograph I can almost literally feel the chill air of Pittsburgh on that winter day in 1934 or whenever it was and smell wet fur and the smell of wet wool mittens and hear the chink of arctics when you walk in them without doing the metal fasteners all the way up. I can almost literally feel in my stomach my eight-year-old excitement at having the ground deep in snow and at being in that marvelous house and at Naya's being there. If it's true that you can't go home again, it is especially true when the home in question has long since gone and been replaced by another and when virtually all the people who used to live there have long since gone too and are totally beyond replacing. But sometimes I can almost believe that if I only knew the trick of it, I could actually go back anyway, that just some one small further movement of memory or will would be enough to transport me to that snowy terrace again where Naya would turn to me in her fur jacket and would open the front door with her gloved hand and we would enter the cinnamon, lamp-lit dusk of the house together. But it is a trick that I have never quite mastered, and for that reason I have to accept my homesickness as chronic and incurable.

The house in Vermont, on the other hand, is still very much there, but about seven years ago we moved out of it into what used to be my wife's parents' house down the hill a few hundred yards so that now it has returned to being the guest house that it originally was before we became the permanent guests. Our children still use it from time to time, but I don't go back to it very often myself. Not long after we moved out, I remember apologizing to it for that. The house was empty except for me, and I stood in the living room and told it out loud not to be upset that we don't live there any more and rarely return to visit. I said it must never think that it failed us in any way. I told it what wonderful years we had had there and how happy we'd been and tried to explain that we would always remember it with great gratitude and affection, all of which is true. But what keeps me from going back except on rare occasions is that it is so full of emptiness now—the children's rooms still littered with their stuffed animals and crayons and books and pictures but the children themselves the mothers of their own children now so that it is as if the children they themselves used to be simply ceased to exist along with the young man I once was. There is no telling the sweet sadness of all that—of the Woodland Road house gone as completely as a dream when you wake up and as haunting as a dream, and the Vermont house still there but home no longer.

Where do you look for the home you long for if not to the ir-recoverable past? How do you deal with that homesickness of the spirit which Antonio Parr speaks of, that longing for whatever the missing thing is that keeps even the home of the present from being true home? I only wish I knew. All I know is that, like Antonio, I also sense that something of great importance is missing which I cannot easily name and which perhaps can never be named by any of us until we find it, if indeed it is ever to be found. In the meanwhile, like Gideon and Barak and the others, I also know the sense of sadness and lostness that comes with feeling that you are a stranger and exile on the earth and that you would travel to the ends of that earth and beyond if you thought you could ever find the homeland that up till now you have only glimpsed from afar. Where do you go to search for it? Where have I myself searched?

I have come to believe that for me the writing of books may have been such a search although it is only recently that I have thought of it that way. For forty years and more I have been at it, sitting alone in a room with a felt-tip pen in my hand and a notebook of unlined white paper on my lap for anywhere from three to five hours a day on the days when I work. Whether it is a novel I'm writing or a work of non-fiction, at the start of each day I usually have some rough idea of where I plan to go next, but at least as often as not that is not where I end up going or at least not in the way I foresee or at the pace I intend. Time slows down to the point where whole hours can go by almost without my noticing their passage and often without writing anything at all. Sounds tend to fade away—somebody running a power mower, a dog barking in the driveway, voices speaking in another part of the house. Things that have been bothering me disappear entirely—the television set that needs to be repaired, the daughter we haven't heard from for over a week so that I am certain some terrible disaster has befallen her, my wretched defeat in a political argument at a dinner party the evening before.

In between periods of actually writing down words on the white page before me, my eyes almost always glance off to the left toward the floor, but it is not the floor that I am seeing. I am not really seeing anything or doing anything in the usual sense of the term. I am simply *being*, but being in what is for me an unusually intense and unfocused manner. I am not searching for the right way to phrase something, or for the next words to have a character speak, or for how to make a graceful transition from one paragraph to another. As nearly as I understand the process, I am simply letting an empty place open up inside myself and waiting for something to fill it. And every once and so often, praise God, something does. The sign that reads WELCOME HONE. The character who speaks something closer to the truth than I can imagine having ever come to on my own. A sentence or two in a sermon, perhaps, that touch me as usually only something I haven't seen coming can touch me or that feed me as if from another's hand with something that I hadn't realized I was half starving for. I think it is not fanciful to say that among the places I have searched for home without realizing what I was doing is that empty and fathomless place within myself and that sometimes, from afar, I may even have caught a glimpse of it in the shadows there.

Sometimes, I suspect, the search for home is related also to the longing of the flesh, to the way in which, both when you are young and for long afterward, the sight of beauty can set you longing with a keenness and poignancy and passion, with a kind of breathless awe even, which suggest that beneath the longing to possess and be possessed by the beauty of another sexually—to "know" in the Biblical idiom—there lies the longing to know and be known by another fully and humanly, and that beneath that there lies a longing, closer to the heart of the matter still, which is the longing to be at long last where you fully belong. "If ever any beauty I did see, / Which I desir'd, and got, 'twas but a dream of thee," John Donne wrote to his mistress,[2] and when I think of all the beautiful ones whom I have seen for maybe no more than a passing moment and have helplessly, overwhelmingly desired, I wonder if at the innermost heart of my desiring there wasn't, of all things, homesickness.

Finally, as I ask myself where I have searched, I think of another winter—not the winter of 1934 in East Liberty but the winter of 1953 in New York City when I was a twenty-seven-year-old bachelor trying to write a novel which for one reason or another refused to come to life for me, partly, I suspect, because I was trying too hard and hadn't learned yet the importance of letting the empty place inside me open up. Next door to where I lived there happened to be a church whose senior minister was a man named George Buttrick, and depressed as I was about the novel and with time heavy on my hands, I started going to hear him preach on Sunday mornings because, although I was by no means a regular churchgoer, somebody told me he was well worth hearing, as indeed he proved to be. What I discovered first was that he was a true believer, which in my experience a great many preachers are not. Maybe in some intellectual, theological way they believe everything I do, but there is no passion in their belief that either comes through to me or seems to animate them. Buttrick couldn't have been less of a pulpit pounder, but his passion was in his oddly ragged eloquence and in the way he could take words you had heard all your life and make you hear them and the holiness in them as though for the first time. These were also the days before ministers were supposed to be everybody's great pal and to be called by their first names from the word go, the trouble with which, at least for me, is that it's not another great pal that I go to church looking for but a prophet and priest and pastor. Buttrick for me became wonderfully all three, and although I have never met a warmer, kinder man, we never became pals, for which I am grateful, and if there was anybody in his congregation who called him George, I never happened to hear it.

It was toward the middle of December, I think, that he said something in a sermon that has always stayed with me. He said that on the previous Sunday, as he was leaving the church to go home, he happened to overhear somebody out on the steps asking somebody else, "Are you going home for Christmas?" and I can almost see Buttrick with his glasses glittering in the lectern light as he peered out at all those people listening to him in that large, dim sanctuary and asked it again—"Are you going home for Christmas?"—and asked it in some sort of way that brought tears to my eyes and that made it almost unnecessary for him to move on to his answer to the question, which was that home, finally, is the manger in Bethlehem, the place where at midnight even the oxen kneel.

Home is where Christ is was what Buttrick said that winter morning, and when the next autumn I found myself to my great surprise putting aside whatever career I thought I might have as a writer and going to Union Seminary instead, at least partly because of the tears that kept coming to my eyes, I don't believe that I consciously thought that home was what I was going there in search of, but I believe that was the truth of it.

Where did my homeward search take me? It took me to the Union Seminary classrooms of four or five remarkable teachers as different from each other as James Muilenburg of the Old Testament department, who was so aflame with his subject that you couldn't listen to him without catching fire yourself, and John Knox of the New Testament department, who led us through the Gospels and Paul with the thoroughness and delicacy of a great surgeon, yet who were alike in having a faith which continues to this day to nourish mine although it has been almost forty years since the last time I heard their voices. When I was ordained in Dr. Buttrick's church in 1958, the search set me on a path that has taken me to places both in the world and in myself that I can't imagine having discovered any other way.

It took me to Phillips Exeter Academy in the sixties where I tried to teach and preach the Christian faith to teenage boys, a great many of whom were so hostile to the idea of religion in general and at the same time so bright and articulate and quick on their feet that for nine galvanizing, unnerving years I usually felt slow-witted and tongue-tied and hopelessly square by comparison. It took me and continues to take me every now and then to people in the thick of one kind of trouble or another who because they know of my ordination seek me out for whatever they think I may have in the way of comfort or healing, and I, who in the old days would have shrunk with fear from any such charged encounter, try to find something wise and hopeful to say to them, only little by little coming to understand that the most precious thing I have to give them is not whatever words I find to say but simply whatever, spoken or unspoken, I have in me of Christ, which is also the most precious thing they have to give me. All too rarely, I regret to say, my search has taken me also to a sacred and profoundly silent place inside myself where it is less that I pray than that, to paraphrase Saint Paul, the Holy Spirit itself, I believe, prays within me and for me "with sighs too deep for words" (Rom. 8:26).

In recent years the homeward search has taken me as a writer to distant worlds which I never before would have guessed were within the range of my imagination. In eleventh-century England I have heard an old hermit named Godric, aghast at how he has come to be venerated, say, "To touch me and to feel my touch they come. To take at my hands whatever of Christ or comfort such hands have. Of their own, my hands have nothing more than any man's and less now at this tottering, lame-wit age of mine when most of what I ever had is more than mostly spent. But it's as if my hands are gloves, and in them other hands than mine, and those the ones that folk appear with roods of straw to seek. It's holiness they hunger for, and if by some mad chance it's mine to give, if I've a holy hand inside my hand to touch them with, I'll touch them day and night. Sweet Christ what other use are idle hermits for?"[3]

I have stood by the fifth-century Irish saint, Brendan the Navigator, as he preached to some ragged bog people he had just converted and have heard him "tell them news of Christ like it was no older than a day. . . . He'd make them laugh at how Christ gulled the elders out of stoning to death a woman caught in the act of darkness. He'd drop their jaws telling them how he hailed Lazarus out of his green grave and walked on water without making holes. He'd bring a mist to their eyes spinning out the holy words Christ said on the hill . . . and how the Holy Ghost was a gold-eyed milk-white dove would help them stay sweet as milk and true as gold."[4]

And I have traveled back to that day somewhere in the second millennium B.C.E. perhaps, when Jacob stole Esau's blessing from their blind old father, Isaac, and heard him say, "It was not I who ran off with my father's blessing. It was my father's blessing that [like a runaway camel] ran off with me. Often since then I have cried mercy with the sand in my teeth. I have cried "ikh-kh-kh" to make it fall to its knees to let me dismount at last. Its hind parts are crusted with urine as it races forward. Its long-legged, hump-swaying gait is clumsy and scattered like rags in the wind. I bury my face in its musky pelt. The blessing will take me where it will take me. It is beautiful and it is appalling. It races through the barren hills to an end of its own."[5]

Those are some of the places the search has taken me, and what can I honestly say I have found along the way? I think the most I can claim is something like this. I receive maybe three or four hundred letters a year from strangers who tell me that the books I have spent the better part of my life writing have one way or another saved their lives, in some cases literally. I am deeply embarrassed by such letters. I think if they only knew that I am a person more often than not just as lost in the woods as they are, just as full of darkness, in just as desperate need. I think if I only knew how to save my own life. They write to me as if I am a saint, and I wonder how I can make clear to them how wrong they are.

But what I am beginning to discover is that, in spite of all that, there is a sense in which they are also right. In my books, and sometimes even in real life, I have it in me at my best to be a saint to other people, and by saint I mean life-giver, someone who is able to bear to others something of the Holy Spirit whom the creeds describe as the Lord and Giver of Life. Sometimes, by the grace of God, I have it in me to be Christ to other people. And so of course have we all—the life-giving, life-saving, and healing power to be saints, to be Christs, maybe at rare moments even to ourselves.

I believe that it is when that power is alive in me and through me that I come closest to being truly home, come closest to finding or being found by that holiness which I may have glimpsed in the charity and justice and order and peace of other homes I have known but which in its fullness was always missing. I cannot claim that I have found the home I long for every day of my life, not by a long shot, but I believe that in my heart I have found, and have maybe always known, the way that leads to it. I believe that Buttrick was right and that the home we long for and belong to is finally where Christ is. I believe that home is Christ's kingdom which exists both within us and among us as we wend our prodigal ways through the world in search of it.

NOTES

1. Frederick Buechner, *Treasure Hunt* in *The Book of Bebb* (San Francisco: Harper Collins, 1990 reprint ed.), p. 529.

2. John Donne, "The Good Morrow," lines 6–7.

3. Frederick Buechner, *Godric* (San Francisco: Harper, 1983), p. 43.

4. Frederick Buechner, *Brendan* (NY: Atheneum, 1987), pp. 49, 48.

5. Frederick Buechner, *The Son of Laughter* (San Francisco: Harper, 1994 reprint ed.), pp. 85–86.

PART II

The Meaning of Home

Home Is Where We've Never Been: Experience and Transcendence

LEROY S. ROUNER

THE WORLD'S GREAT RELIGIOUS traditions think of the self as not being at home in this world. In Confucian China the goal to be achieved is "humanness," but even the great Confucius confessed that it lay beyond him. True humanness is a transcendent ideal. We are not yet truly human. In India most schools of Hinduism insist that human fulfillment is present to each of us if we could only perceive it, but even those who gain insight must wait for a final moment of *moksha*, freedom, or spiritual release when their souls unite with the transcendent Holy World Power. In the West, Judaism waits for the Messiah before all will be well with its people, and Christianity is blatantly nostalgic for this home where we have never been, most notably perhaps in that tradition, so much celebrated by Protestant orthodoxy, which runs from Saint Paul through Augustine to Luther and Calvin, Kierkegaard and Barth. The most memorable text of that nostalgia is surely Augustine's famous prayer at the opening of his *Confessions*, "O Lord thou has made us for thyself, and our hearts are restless till they find their rest in thee."[1]

The philosophical treatment of this theme is not quite so consistent, but in the history of Western thought the issue is central. Plato makes the same point: the self is not at home in its present historical situation. The death of Socrates is marked by his longing to leave existence for the transcendent world of true essence, and this longing is completely in keeping with his previous arguments about how we know what we know. To know something, for Plato, is not simply to assess its various empirical characteristics, but to know the *eidos*, or "idea," of the thing. One knows a thing truly only when one knows the "kind" in which it participates. And the *eidos* of that kind is

81

not an empirical reality which is part of our experience. It is "beyond" our world of immediacy, not as individual psychological projection, or common social assumption, but as a real thing in a reality which is "transcendent."

But what do we mean by *experience*? And what do we mean by *transcendence*? I do not use the word *we* in the academic magisterial sense. By *we* I mean you and me, because my argument is not going to be some counterintuitive logical case. It is going to be an appeal to our common experience. My question is always: "This is my experience. Is it yours also? Does it have something of our common humanity in it?" John Dewey, that great philosopher of experience, was honest enough to say that experience is a "weasel word." And indeed it is. We will never get a complete definition of experience on which we can all agree, but perhaps we can agree on some preliminaries.

One is that *experience*, in the sense of human experience, is both broader and deeper than the category of "empirical" truth. Empiricism validates truth in terms of sense experience. If you can see it, touch it, taste it, then it must be real. Much philosophy in the modern period has limited itself to empiricism and rationalism as touchstones for the truths of experience. But when we talk of "human experience" we talk of things that we all know and share but which are neither empirical nor rational. Love, for example, is not an empirical fact, and it is certainly not rational, but it is a real part of our experience. So I intend to use the term *experience* in this wider and deeper sense. With James and Whitehead, and against Hume, I will argue that causal connection, value, and certain intuitions which go with them are all part of our experience. But the test of seriousness in this discussion is common agreement, not irrefutable logic. When dealing with human experience in this broad sense, counterintuitive arguments are almost always dead ends.

The argument for solipsism—the view that the only things we can know are the states of our own individual minds—is my favorite "dead end" case. It is logically irrefutable, as far as I know. The problem is that no one really believes it, and only the mentally ill use it as a model for behavior. So, along with T. R. V. Murthi of Banaras, I will argue for "a reasonable use of reason" in exploring human experience.

Transcendence is also difficult. For dualists like Plato and the Christians, transcendence means a different metaphysical order of things. Just as the *eidos* of a thing is in a different Platonic realm than the particular to which it gives meaning, so God, in the Christian tradition, is always in some sense different from us and our world. This is a strong view of transcendence. But even for Confucians in their determined humanness, the Mandate of Heaven is always other than social convention or psychological projection, even though its metaphysical status is never clear. Buddhist "nothingness" is also embedded in the way things are, and is nondualist. But it is still a dimension of reality which is not immediately apparent to unaided consciousness, and is thus beyond ordinary human experience. This is what I shall call a weak view of transcendence.

The "home where we have never been" is clearly going to be transcendent, since experience is where we *have* been, and my reading of at least some of the great traditions of human reflection on this issue suggests that we are not entirely at home in our experienced world. On this reading, transcendent meaning holds the key to who we really are, and we will need only a weak view of transcendence to establish this. We long for home because we sense in ourselves at least a lack, and often a wrongness, that we anticipate will be fulfilled or made right when we "come home." But the longing, as I understand it, is not simply psychological or moral; it is also metaphysical. In our present experience of ourselves we sense that we are not always truly who we really are. In common speech we occasionally say, "So and so is not himself today," or "She is acting out of character." The universal human experience of "conscience" is testimony to this metaphysical disjointedness in our experience of ourselves. Who among us has never felt bad about doing "the wrong thing"? And who among us has ever been thoroughly satisfied that what we did to make up for the wrong, really *did* make up for it? Where is the man or woman without at least some spiritual or psychic loose ends in their life, keeping them from being who they want to be, who they sense that they really are? So home is both the "place" from which we have come, and the "place" to which we go. Life is a journey home to this transcendent meaningfulness. This is part of what has been called "The Myth of the Eternal Return."

But is there any evidence for real transcendence—in either the weak or the strong sense—in our ordinary human experience? I stress the word *ordinary* because, in the same sense that we are not looking for a purely logical case, we are also not looking for something esoteric. The Hindu tradition of Advaita Vedanta argues that transcendence is indeed a dimension of experience, but that it is covered over by the exoteric ordinariness of things. Only a long intense discipline of body, mind, and spirit enables one to see that ordinary experience is *maya*, "illusion." But the commitment to ordinary experience rejects that route. What we can hope for must be something which has always been part of ordinary experience.

But then, in what sense will it be a discovery? If it has always been there, why don't we already know it? The answer lies in James's observation that the primal ground of our experience (to which he gave the unfortunate name "pure experience") is a "booming, buzzing confusion" from which the mind selects those elements which, for its own reasons, it chooses to focus on. In any given moment, there is a lot going on in our experience to which we are not paying any attention. Our good hope, then, is that we will find what we are looking for in something that has always been right here, but which we have not noticed.

So we need to take some area of human experience and examine it to see if a deep reading of our experience inevitably points beyond itself to some transcendental meaning. Is there something in our experience of our world which bespeaks transcendence?

The question is significant to me as a Christian philosopher because I believe that the world is a creation of God which has the marks of the Creator on it. Therefore I should be able to find some evidence of those marks in our common human experience. This is not to suggest a natural theology in the Catholic medieval tradition, but only a typically American attempt, combining both pragmatism and idealism, to seek out hints and guesses of the transcendent in our ordinary human experience.

Stating my belief makes me open to the naive criticism that such belief prejudges the issue. The criticism is naive because examining beliefs is what philosophy is all about. We come to philosophy with a whole host of experiences and beliefs. Philosophy is the way we sort them out. A good working definition of philosophy is that it is "the examination of belief." While my belief may not be totally dependent on my philosophy, the question here is whether or not a persuasive case can be made. And I would agree that if it cannot be made, then I need to rethink my belief.

There are three fundamental areas of human experience open to us: ourselves, other selves, and the natural world. Everything we experience can be listed under one or the other of these categories.

Theoretically we should be able to explore any one of these areas and find those philosophical hints and guesses which, if my belief is correct, ought to be there. I've chosen our experience of nature because I have long needed to reflect on why people expose themselves to the extreme dangers of nature in mountain climbing, wilderness exploration, and the like.

I suggest that we begin with the scientific notion of objectivity regarding facts of nature. Scientific fact is publicly verified. A fact becomes objective, not when observed by an isolated individual mind, but when confirmed by a community of those concerned about, and expert in, the same field. So Crick and Watson's discoveries about DNA were not science at the point where they completed their lab experiment. They became science when they published their results and others in the field did the same experiment and got the same results. This illustrates John Dewey's point about the relationship between science and democracy. Both are public, open, exoteric. Expertise is indeed required in science, but it is always verified by the community of experts.

But when I am alone in my back meadow, looking to Mount Chocorua, I do not need another person to confirm my belief that the mountain is really there. This is not just because I have empirical evidence, since that *could* be deceptive. Hindu philosophy never tires of pointing out that the stick in the water which looks bent is not really bent; and the coil of rope in a dark corner which looks like a snake is not really a snake. No, I am confident in my belief that the mountain is really there because I do not see it in my capacity as an isolated, atomistic individual. *I see it as also being seen by an other.* Or to put it somewhat differently, I experience this conglomerate of natural objects as a presence.

This idea seems passing strange to us moderns, since modernity invented the idea of the "thing," and has persuaded us that nature is the realm of "things"—inanimate objects. But the notion of nature as a *persona* was the norm in the prephilosophical world of the great Greek epics, the Hebrew Bible, *Gilgamesh*, the *Enuma Elish*, and even in Aristotle, for whom natural entities all had a final purpose, a notion which we now credit only to persons. And it has continued to be the norm for most poets, so that we moderns find our philosophical preconceptions pitted against our poetic sensibilities. Since philosophical sophistication tends to regard poetic sensibility as sentimental, it is dangerous to defend one's view by quoting a nineteenth-century poet like Wordsworth, or a twentieth-century poet like Mary Oliver. Nevertheless, in his *Lines Composed a Few Miles Above Tintern Abbey*, Wordsworth writes of his experience of Nature:

> For I have learned
> To look on nature, not as in the hour
> Of thoughtless youth; but hearing oftentimes
> The still, sad music of humanity,
> . . . And I have felt
> A presence that disturbs me with the joy
> Of elevated thoughts; a sense sublime
> Of something far more deeply interfused,
> Whose dwelling is the light of setting suns,
> And the round ocean and the living air,
> And the blue sky, and in the mind of man:
> A motion and a spirit, that impels
> All thinking things, all objects of all thought,
> And rolls through all things. . . .[2]

This is, I admit, a "picture window" view of nature: the Anglo-Saxon gentleman in his tweed suit strolling through his manicured meadows, thinking high thoughts. My own perspective may be subject to the same criticism. But lest we become too scornful too soon, we need to be reminded that this is part of a great tradition in Western accounts of our experience of nature. Our contemporary Mary Oliver is more sparse in her language, and less pretentious in her claims, but her feeling is equally powerful in her poem "Wild Geese."

> You do not have to be good.
> You do not have to walk on your knees
> for a hundred miles through the desert, repenting.
> You only have to let the soft animal of your body
>   love what it loves.
> Tell me about despair, yours, and I will tell you mine.
> Meanwhile the world goes on.
> Meanwhile the sun and the clear pebbles of the rain
> are moving across landscapes,
> over the prairies and the deep trees,
> the mountains and the rivers.

Meanwhile the wild geese, high in the clean blue air,
are heading home again.
Whoever you are, no matter how lonely,
the world offers itself to your imagination,
calls to you like wild geese, harsh and exciting—
over and over announcing your place
in the family of things.[3]

But it still seems to most of us that, while our experience of nature is constant, even in deep sleep, our social experience is intermittent. After all, we spend time alone. Our companions do, indeed, come and go. But surely if experience is ever to be social it must *always* be social. In order for any two people to establish communication with one another they must already share some common ground. They must trust their real knowledge of the other self, and the connection which already exists between them. This makes communication possible. We have to trust the reality of one another, and trust that we are already "wired" for communication—that the other person can "hear" us when we "speak" to them—before any substantive communication is possible.

We are already prepared for this prospect by the experience of our own self-transcendence. Humankind is distinctive not just for its capacity to "reason" in the sense of figuring things out, but in its capacity to stand off from itself, and to view itself from above, so to speak. It is this capacity which is recognized in the popular definitions of humankind as the animal who thinks, or laughs, or goes to school. These all require the capacity to stand off from oneself, to look at oneself, to make judgments about oneself, to plan for oneself, to criticize oneself, and so forth. But then who is the self that is doing all this? Who is this "No. 2 Self" who is observing "Self No. 1"? It is the No. 2 Self, the self-transcendent self, who is the source of what is distinctive about human rationality. It is also the self which is moral and spiritual. It is the No. 2 Self which hopes and dreams and longs for home.

And, of course, it is this capacity which makes humankind "little lower than the angels" and distinctive from other animals, like my dear German Shepherd, Maya, who is very good at figuring some things out, but who is completely un-self-critical. This point is very unpopular with my students, because I take Maya to the office and to class with me, and the students love her, and they think me arrogant when I say, "The difference between me and Maya is that I know that I am a man, and she doesn't know that she is a dog." But, alas, that is the special grace of being human. We are self-transcendent creatures, so our experience of ourselves is already a social experience—the experience, as Paul Ricoeur puts it in a recent book, of *Oneself as Another*.

Now, is Self No. 2 a psychological projection? I don't see how one could argue that, since it is a universal experience and therefore clearly part of what it means to be any and all possible selves. But are we then inherently divided against ourselves? Is selfhood dualistic? Well, yes and no. I think we are all ambivalent about ourselves, and that ambivalence is metaphysically imbedded in us. I am more like Maya than I want to admit. When she wants something she just goes for it, whether it is the right thing to do or not; and I sometimes do that myself. Yet I know it is wrong, and when I do it I am ashamed. I know myself to be greedy. She, on the other hand, is a totally happy warrior, completely shameless. I can't tell you how much I envy her. She has no idea of what it means to do the wrong thing. There are just some things she gets away with, and other things she gets whomped for. But you and I need integrity; and duality is, for us, something to be overcome. So our reach always exceeds our grasp, because our No. 2 Self yearns for an integrity which our No. 1 Self doesn't know how to achieve. In the meantime, however, our experience of ourselves is always of this conversation between Self No. 1 and Self No. 2. So we instinctively conceive of our relationship to the world as comparably social.

This sociality is sensed in our earliest experience of not being alone in the world. Child psychologists point out that an infant's cry is not just an expression of inner pangs; it is also an instinctive "crying out" to someone. From the very beginning we know ourselves to be part of a community. But the popular mind doesn't recognize that. Most folk you and I know are both individualistic and relativistic, in spite of their yearning for community. They speak of "my" view of this and that. And, on their side, Ernest Hocking once pointed out that the "best fruit of modernity" was the idea of the free-standing individual standing on his or her rights. Yet these rights were recognized as rights for *everyone*, so there is a universalism presupposed in our most fundamental individualism.

But what do we make of the existentialist argument that we are all incurably lonely, fraught with angst, confronted with decisions which inevitably focus on our personal moral integrity? I think the existentialist analysis of loneliness is defective. I don't think any of us is ultimately alone. (The only people who are totally alone are people in Hell. I commend to you Charles Williams's *The Descent Into Hell*, which is a description of what it means to have chosen to be totally alone.)

For us, loneliness is not the experience of being totally alone in the world. It is the experience of being in the world and suffering the *absence* of those whom we want to be with, and whom we need to have pay attention to us. To be lonely is not to experience a world in which there is absolutely no one else. To be lonely is not to have anyone else in *our* world. To be lonely is to have people who *were* in our world *go away*. To be lonely is to have people for whom we cared, and who once cared about us, or who should have cared about us, not care about us, or no longer care about us, even though we continue to care for them; which is why we are lonely. To be lonely is to need *attention* from others which they will not or cannot give.

To my mind, the loneliest cultural antihero of our time is Willy Loman in Arthur Miller's play *Death of a Salesman*. He keeps saying, "They love me in Providence," but of course they don't even remember him in Providence. The only one who realizes how desperately lonely he is is his wife Linda, who says: "Attention must be paid. He's not to be allowed to fall into his grave like an old dog. Attention, attention must finally be paid!"[4]

Without wanting to sound too much like Bishop Berkeley, I think *attention* may be the philosophical translation of what the theologians mean by love. This was Josiah Royce's view and there is much to commend it. To be lonely is to be unloved because no one is paying attention to you. To be rejoined in a community of hope and love is to know that at least someone, somewhere, is attentive to who you are and knows what is happening to you. Our deepest inner longing may well be for the attention of a Knowing Other: someone who is different from us, who really knows us, and who cares enough about us to pay attention to who we are and what is happening to us.

But do we have any of that in our experience of nature? My lonely experience of the mountain elicits belief in its objectivity because I intuitively experience it as also known by others, as part of the constant immovable world space which we all inhabit. I may have particular memories of having taken in this same view in the company of another person, and discovered that I understood something of the mind of that particular person through this shared experience. Nevertheless, my lonely experience of the mountain—while occasionally mindful of having been there with X or Y—is always larger than those particular memories, or the felt presence of those particular people. Those memories flit in and out of my mountain-viewing reverie, but what remains constant is the sense of some larger presence which is admittedly vague and unspecific.

The reason I can describe the mountain scene as "awesome" is not just because the mountain is so big, but because I experience it as set in a "world." The blue sky above it is endless, and I am dimly aware that this presently cherished space is part of the infinite, total context of Space Itself, the Whole of things. *That* is what is overpowering. I often don't notice this at the time because this sense of the Whole of things is not something I am thinking *of*, but a notion I am thinking *with*. And one vague dimension of that awe is the sense that this infinite Whole is somehow self-aware.

I realize that this is a hard saying, but think about your experience. I have not promised rational proofs, but only hints and guesses of the transcendence in the midst of my experience which I hope may appeal to yours. This method could easily become intellectually sloppy and emotionally sentimental. But I persist in my appeal to your own experience because I am persuaded that we have been divorced from much that we instinctively believe to be true by the presuppositions of our modern culture.

When you imagine the farthest reaches of outer space, isn't it with the sense that while you and I have never seen it, *someone knows what it is like there*? Way out beyond the Milky Way, where eye hath not seen nor ear heard, there is a realm which has come to be. Can we really help thinking that Whatever or Whoever caused it to be, knows what it is like to be there? I'm not asking you whether that is true or not. I'm just asking you whether, in your heart of hearts, that isn't what you really believe. And if that is what you really believe, then our philosophical conversation ought to start with that belief, and examine it, and see if it holds up, rather than beginning with counterintuitive propositions which no one believes.

This awesome presence in the face of nature elicits the longing for home just because it is Whole, and we are not. We want to be whole. We know somehow that we are intended to be whole, but we are too much aware of our fragmentariness. We never quite "get it together." Our secret, innermost sense of the human condition is one of incompleteness, if not actual tragic brokenness.

The casual experience of viewing the mountain during a walk through the meadow is much intensified if you have actually climbed the mountain, and seen the whole world spread out before you from the summit. Try that with a friend, and then notice what you talk about. I climbed Mount Washington with my brother last summer, and I offer this report on our conversation. First, "Wow! What a view!" Then aches and pains, followed by self-congratulation that a couple of old guys had made it in the guidebook time. But then the interesting part: expressions of humility in the presence of the whole wide world spread out below us—and then philosophical reflections on life and death.

This raises the question: in our culture of expertise, to whom should we look for a definitive view of our experience of nature? My response has been that we should look first to ourselves, on the ground that our culture has deceived us about what we actually experience, and we need to recover our own truth. But the question takes us back to William James, and the odd assortment of folk whom he regarded as expert witnesses to *The Varieties of Religious Experience*. His argument was that the people who had had intense religious experiences were the people who really knew about religion. By the same token, I suggest that people who have had intense experiences of nature are the people who really know about nature. These are those mountain women and men, our contemporary crop of rock climbers, wilderness explorers, and nature crazies, like the hero of the film *The Man Who Skied Down Everest*.

There are two elements in the mountaineering literature about these people which are significant for our purposes. One is that, when alone, climbers regularly report an experience of not being alone, but being in the presence of what I have called a Knowing Other. The second element in the literature is even more important, and that is in response to the question, Why do people climb? In his *Mountains of the Great Blue Dream* Robert Leonard Reid notes:

> To nonclimbers' regret, we keep our insight to ourselves. When called upon to explain why we climb, we turn to our more expressive friend love for an answer. Why, it's the beauty of the mountains, we say. It's the adventure, the exhilaration, the chal-

lenge, the camaraderie, the quest for our limits. It's . . . the view from the top! We climb because climbing is a joy, we say; we climb because climbing takes us closer to God.

All of which is true, but none, save possibly the last, suggests the full truth, that more than love animates our affairs with the high peaks.[5]

Reid goes on to say that the real issue is not love, but death. He rejects the idea that climbers are unconsciously suicidal. No one is trying to die, but the serious mountaineers are there to *taste* death, and thereby momentarily to be made whole. In one sense climbing these high peaks is a purification ritual. I've done a little climbing myself, and most of the time you are scared to death. Knowing you could die any minute fixes the mind. Everything else in your life falls away. For those brief, ecstatic moments, the human condition is radically changed. You are *not* ambivalent about *anything*, because you cannot possibly think about anything else. At that moment there is only one thing in the whole world you want, and that is to make the next move. Søren Kierkegaard wrote a little book on Christian spirituality entitled "Purity of heart is to will one thing."[6] He was speaking of total faith in God, but in our exploration of the hints and guesses of transcendence which we find in experience, "to will one thing" in climbing is a foretaste of that transcendent unity with God, because in that ecstatic moment one becomes whole, and therefore pure.

My son Timmy wrote a poem to his brother Rains about their climbs together which ends:

> Hanging between sky and earth,
> we revel in lofty halls
> of mountain majesty
> and cleanse our dusty souls
> in frozen purity.

Because, together, they had been scared to death.

And Reid tells of his friend Dina Lombard who froze to death on a winter climb of Mount Shasta in California. He writes,

> Those who had known her might well have decided never to climb Shasta, or at least never to climb it in winter. For me, per-

haps, like Ariadne, confused between love and death, the effect of this tragedy was precisely the opposite. My love for Shasta was deepened; so enraptured, I needed to know her better. I believed that in Shasta's winds I would feel something of the peace of Dina Lombard, in its swirling mists *catch a glimpse of the place where she had gone.* So it was that in a later winter I made the arduous ascent of the mountain. On an afternoon of such splendor and clarity that I seemed to be moving through timeless space, I came at last onto Shasta's icebound summit and saw the sky go black and the earth fall away at my feet. The cold air bristled with the scent of galaxies and nebulae. . . . It came to me that I had climbed to the center of the universe. I stood for a moment, taking it in, and then I began to weep. My tears were born of ecstasy and heartbreak alike—tears for the beauty of the world, tears for the gentleness of death.[7] (Italics added)

"To catch a glimpse of the place where she had gone." Without necessarily implying any religious doctrine, I think Reid would not object to the suggestion that she had gone home. He argues that the mountaineer's fascination with death is a mystical quest for that transcendent meaning of life which alone can give us a sense of being at home. His climb to what he called "the center of the universe" was a journey to the secret heart of things, where ecstasy gave him a fleeting moment of infinite wholeness, and peace; and heartbreak reminded him of his loss, and of the finite brokenness of human life.

NOTES

1. Augustine *Confessions* 1.1.
2. William Wordsworth, "Lines Composed a Few Miles Above Tintern Abbey . . ." in *Wordsworth: The Poems,* ed. John O. Hayden, vol. 1 (London: Penguin Books, 1977), p. 358.
3. Mary Oliver, "Wild Geese," in *New and Selected Poems* (Boston: Beacon Press, 1992), p. 110. Reprinted by permission of the author.
4. Arthur Miller, *Death of a Salesman* (New York: Viking Press, 1949), p. 56.

5. Robert Leonard Reid, *Mountains of the Great Blue Dream* (New York: Harper Collins, 1992), pp. 4–5.

6. Søren Kierkegaard, *Purity of Heart Is To Will One Thing*, trans. Douglas V. Steere (New York: Harper and Brothers, Publishers, 1938).

7. Reid, *Mountains of the Great Blue Dream*, pp. 10–11.

Are We at Home in the World?

RÉMI BRAGUE

THE TITLE OF THIS BOOK refers to the idea of home, being at home vs. feeling homeless. A philosopher cannot tackle such a question in the same way as specialists of other disciplines. Unlike the historian, who can tell us how different places on earth came to be considered as homelands for people who went to live in them; unlike the theologian, for whom our permanent abode is not of this world; the philosopher must first discard any precise reference to a definite place on earth, and ask what being at home means. Furthermore, the philosopher must discard, at least at the beginning of his or her reflection, any call from outside of the world, and ask what it means to be at home *in the world* as such. Hence my title: are we at home in the world?

I. ARE WE IN THE WORLD?

Before I can deal with this question, however, a preliminary question should be asked. Clearly, we may feel more or less at home in the world if, and only if, we are in the world. But are we really in the world? Such a question looks weird, and its answer obvious. Nevertheless, I think it should not be skipped and its answer taken for granted, for three reasons, that correspond each to a different way to stress the question.

A. *Are We in the* World?

Is that, in which we are, a world? Now humankind has not always conceived of something like the world. The idea, and the word for it, had to wait for the second half of the history of the race. If we stick to the traditional distinction between prehistory and history, according to which history begins with the invention of writing, we can say that human history is not older than five millennia, since writing was found about the beginning of the third millennium before our era. The first word meaning "world," the Greek *kosmos*, appeared in that sense around 500 B.C.E. For that reason, humankind could do without the idea of world during the first half of its career in history. Before that date, being in its totality was divided into two halves, heaven and earth. What God is said to create in the first line of Genesis is not the world, but heaven and earth. Such a view thwarted any interrogation about our being in the world. There was no word to express that in which we are. Furthermore, the question was not only impossible; it was superfluous, too. For any question about our place could immediately be answered by referring, not to that in which, but to that on which, we are, namely, the earth that we tread, the ground of all our doings.

B. Are *We in the World?*

On the other hand—this is my second reason—it is not enough, for us to ask the question of our presence in the world, to have a linguistic expression of what contains us. For although the word *kosmos* had been available for several centuries, the phrase "in the world," functioning as a description of human existence on earth and under the heavens, is not to be found at an early date. Let alone do we find phrases that are at present common parlance such as: "to come into the world," meaning "to be born." Such phrases hardly turn up before the second century of our era, for instance, in the famous prologue to the Fourth Gospel: according to the various interpretations, either "every man" or "the divine Logos" "comes into the world" (John 1:9). There, the source is Jewish: the world is less a merely "physical" container than a situation, the present eon, as distinguished from the world to come.

C. Are We *in the World?*

Who is *we?* We will have to do justice to the first person. One can make a whole array of third-person statements on what the human is and where he or she is. For instance, contemporary science can show that the human body consists of particles that came into being even earlier than our planet, so that we are sort of children of the heavens. But this hardly tallies with the experience that we can make of our relationship with the universe. The question implies a reflection on the nature of our self, too. What do we mean by the pronoun *we*, when we ask: are we in the world? It is evident that our body is a part of the world. But our soul can escape, can find that the world is too narrow. What is at stake here, nevertheless, is something far humbler in nature, that is, the way in which our self feels or experiences its presence in the world.

II. WORLD VS. HOME

As for the question I chose as a title, it may look irrelevant at first blush. To be in something and to be *at home in* something are two different things. On the one hand, when we ask where we are, *wherein* we are, we implicitly mention the world. We are in a certain place, in a certain city, in a certain country, etc. For example: "Stephen Dedalus /Class of Elements / Clongowes Wood College / Sallins / County Kildare / Ireland / Europe / The World / The Universe."[1]

We may wonder, however, whether this shift from what is near us to the remotest confines of the universe is a legitimate one. In particular, we can hardly apply the idea of home to the universe in its entirety. What we are at home in can hardly be the world. We are at home first and foremost in our house, where we feel we belong, "at our place," as the idiom has it. By extension, we can call "our home" our city of birth, our province, our country—our homeland. We can even go further and say that the earth in its entirety is the home of humankind. In any case, however, we would not think of calling by the name of "home" the total show, the universe—what we commonly mean by "the world."

Furthermore, the difference between home and world is not merely linguistic in nature. There is a concrete dimension to it. Home and world simply exclude one another. Home is the part of reality that we hedge from the onslaught of exterior elements: most simply, from wind and precipitation. Home is defined by a limit, be it a fence or a wall. Our country is separated from neighboring countries by a boundary. The wide world, on the other hand, extends beyond all limit, and is perhaps infinite. It even seems *unheimlich* ("not-homelike"); we feel it as endangering our comfort.

However, we are compelled to ask the question, because of the very nature of humankind. We are not at home at home only. Human beings possess what Thomas Aquinas called, in another context, *affi-*

nitas ad totum, a kinship, more precisely a neighborhood, *vis-à-vis* the Whole.

This is to be seen at several levels, beginning with biology. Unlike other living beings, humans do not possess a definite place in the ecosystem. Bugs are said to be snug on rugs; animals are essentially snug somewhere. They have a natural place of sorts—not only their den, their nest, etc., but a whole system of places that they unconsciously organize around them: the place where they sleep, their hunting field, the pond where they slake their thirst. On the other hand, however, this whole system is forced upon them by the surrounding area: climate, food, and water supply. Some animals depend so much on their environment that they simply die if they can't find it at hand. Human beings can live in any surroundings, because they create their own surroundings instead of merely adjusting. Consequently, they can turn the whole world into a home: the earth, the moon, not to mention projects of making other planets habitable.

Furthermore, whereas our body is confined in narrow limits, our thought can outsoar the bonds of the world and scan light-years. This is a very old idea. The ancients harped upon it already: Lucretius, Philo, and Seneca could be quoted here.

The question arises, then: what does it mean for us that we are committed to this wide world, if we are in it, nay, in for it?

III. PREMODERN HOMELINESS AND MODERN HOMELESSNESS

For late antique and medieval thought, or at least for the main stream in it, the question received a qualified answer: we live on the surface of the earth, under the system of heavenly bodies that revolve around it. Contrary to a common opinion, this was not a place of honor. Far from being the throne that becomes the king of creation, the earth was the worst place of all, a cosmic dustbin of sorts. But this was a place all the same. Humankind knew where it was. More importantly, it knew what it was expected to do in order really to become what it was. Ethics and cosmology, care of the self and care for the world, were connected to one another. Ethics consisted mainly in adjusting to the world order. We could lift our eyes and soul toward the most beautiful spectacle there is: the orderly array of the stars. We could even model our lives on the pattern they afford. According to Plato's *Timaeus,* for instance, the world itself has a soul, and the heavenly bodies express and make visible its regular motions. By imitating them, we can bring some order into the disorderly movements of our own puny individual souls.

> God devised and bestowed upon us vision to the end that we might behold the revolutions of Reason in the Heaven and use them for the revolving of the reasoning that is within us, these being akin to those, the perturbable to the unperturbable; and that, through learning and sharing in calculations which are correct by their nature, by imitation of the absolutely unvarying revolutions of the God we might stabilize the variable revolutions within ourselves.[2]

By this token, humankind could give the question a coherent answer, so coherent that it accounted for the very nature of the self, of the "we" that lives in the world: we are not at home where we live, but we are definitely citizens of the world, cosmopolites. This was no escapism, for the place where we really belong, the place where we really are at home, is not a rear-world *(Hinterwelt),* but what is worldly in the world, what truly deserves to be called a *kosmos,* that is, the heavens.

For us, this answer is no longer possible. We know that the heavens do not follow ethical rules. Planets revolve around the sun, not to pay homage to the king of the heavens, nor to produce a musical harmony, but to escape its greed. For the ancients, the way in which fishes eat one another was the paradigm of the brutal law of the jungle: bigger fishes eat the smaller ones. We know that the heavenly bodies behave hardly better than fish; the bigger draw the smaller and would swallow them if they were not swift enough to flee. The apparent harmony of the solar system is only a compromise between greed and the will to survive. The planets do not peacefully circle. They simply scoot away from the sun's jaws.

Therefore, we cannot rely on the world to become ourselves. This is the cosmological dimension of the modern predicament. We are, to quote Walker Percy's "last self-help book," "lost in the cosmos."

IV. POSSIBLE ANSWERS

As we face that shift in paradigm, several ways are open to us. Among these, some are a modern version of ancient answers given to my question. I will sketch them first. The late antique world view was mainly Platonic in nature, with Stoic elements. Its medieval version added some Jewish and Christian elements to the melting pot. This synthesis won out over rival trends, Epicureanism and gnosis. The collapse of the late antique and medieval cosmology set them free, enabling a comeback of sorts of those alternative views. And indeed, large parts of modern philosophy could be interpreted as more or less conscious revivals of Epicureanism and Gnosticism.

A. *Epicureanism*

For Epicurus, the external world is, literally speaking, uninteresting: *non inter-est*. We don't have to go through it to come to ourselves. We don't have to pay much attention to it. We have to do physics for negative reasons only, that is, in order to get rid of whatever fear could ruffle the smooth surface of our mind. We simply have to arrange ourselves as well as possible and try to get on together as best as we can. This is highly respectable and, at least, harmless.

There is a modern equivalent to that Epicurean idea. This is comfort. Exceptionally, the popular meaning of the adjective "Epicurean" does not betray its original, philosophical meaning. Morally speaking, comfort is discreet and temperate; it looks for tranquillity. Sociologists will describe it as the bourgeois equivalent of the former luxury of the nobility. Feeling comfortable means feeling at home. But our idea of comfort captures only a part, and a puny part into the bargain, of the original meaning of the word. Think of Thomas More's *Dialogue of comfort and tribulation*. Comfort is not the opposite of tribulation. It enables one to face tribulation, to bear it with courage, hence, to endure it as such. On the contrary, what we mean today by comfort is a total lack of tribulation: privacy, pleasant furniture, whatever can help us forget the outer world in favor of a feeling of coziness and security. But can the good life consist of forgetting what is outside the cave?

The idea of comfort (without using the word) occurs first in Aristotle's version of—and answer to—the Platonic allegory of the cave as exposed in his lost treatise *On Philosophy*. Some people are said to live below the surface of the earth as in Plato's cave. But they are not fettered in moist dungeons; they move freely in well-furnished subterranean lairs. The point of the whole story, however, is that they are awakened from their slumber by an earthquake that compels them to look at the heavens and the stars and to realize how parochial their former existence was.

B. Gnosis

Gnosis went the other way. We are absolutely not at home in the world, since we belong to another place. Some Gnostics even coined for this world a term of art, *to anoikeion*,[3] which we can translate, perhaps too literally, by "that in which we are *not* at home." Our true home is elsewhere; it is the place whence we once fell. Our presence in this world is not natural, but violent. As a matter of fact, we were thrown into it by some act of supernatural violence. We are aliens, or prisoners, or exiles, etc.

We can find in our modern world strains that remind us of the basic attitude of gnosis towards reality. This is the case first of all among people who were influenced by Schopenhauer, who very consciously rehabilitated the Gnostic outlook. Let us quote, for instance, a character in Joseph Conrad's *Lord Jim*, the German planter Stein, an entomologist by hobby:

> Man is amazing but he is not a masterpiece. . . . Perhaps the artist was a little mad. Eh? What do you think? Sometimes it seems to me that man is come where he is not wanted, where there is no place for him; for if not why should he want all the place?[4]

We find the same theme even in writers who, probably, would have loathed any association with gnosis, such as Kierkegaard:

> Where am I? What does it mean to say: the world? What is the meaning of that word? Who tricked me into this whole thing and leaves me standing here? Who am I? How did I get into the world? Why was I not asked about it, why was I not informed of the rules and regulations but just thrust into the ranks as if I had been bought from a peddling shanghaier of human beings? How did I get involved in this big enterprise called actuality? Why should I be involved? Isn't it a matter of choice? And if I am compelled to be involved, where is the manager—I have something to say about this. Is there no manager?[5]

For us, the trouble with this outlook is that we cannot say where we came from. We fell; we were thrown into the world; but from nowhere. On the other hand, we can hardly say, either, whither we go. Modern thought retains Gnostic imagery, but removes its axis, namely the existence of another world. An empty longing for a lost home that never was and never will be regained boils down to sulks.

C. Technology

A third, more active trend is more specifically modern. This is the project that is involved in technology. It is a paradoxical synthesis of Epicureanism and Gnosticism. Like Epicureanism, it rejects teleology and looks for efficient causes only. Unlike Epicureanism, it does not content itself with adjusting to a world that is radically indifferent to our pursuits, but endeavors to correct it. Like Gnosticism, it considers that the world as it now stands is not good and needs mending. Unlike Gnosticism, it does not dream of flying off. The catchword of technology could be: since the world is not our home, let us build us a home in it, or, more radically, let us build the world into a home of our own, in the same way as we call our home a world of our own.

Such a stance arose first in the context of poetry. The poet as creator is supposed to create a "heterocosm," to quote Abrams' *The Mirror and the Lamp*. Vico has enlarged this view to the whole realm of human action, that is said to produce another world, the historical world, created by humankind, to be distinguished from God's creation, the physical world. Karl Marx then conceived of human work as creating a world that is properly human. We should conceive, says Marx, "the sensuous world as the total living sensuous activity of the individuals composing it."[6]

Yet what is called here "the world" is scarcely more than the earth as the *oikoumene*, as the home of humankind—which begs the question. Technology has a tendency to reduce the world to what is feasible and to discard what escapes human influence. An extreme form of this is presented in George Orwell's *Nineteen Eighty-Four*, when O'Brien, who is reeducating Winston Smith, contends that the stars are only light specks.

—But the whole universe is outside us. Look at the stars! Some of them are a million light-years away. They are out of our reach for ever.

—What are the stars? . . . They are bits of fire a few kilometers away. We could reach them if we wanted to. Or we could blot them out. The earth is the center of the universe. The sun and the stars go round it.[7]

V. A NEW WORLD

We want, however, to do justice to reality and at the same time find another way of being at home in the world. In what follows, I will venture some steps in that direction. Let me first look for some advice in three philosophers.

A. *Plotinus*

I will take my bearings from Plotinus. He will help me to formulate my basic question. He does that in a text that probably reaches and transcends the limits of his philosophy.

> But if this All (*tode to pan*) is of such a kind (*toiouton*) that it is possible to have wisdom (*sophia*) in it and to live according to things there (*kat'ekeina*) when we are here, how does it not bear witness that it depends on the realities There (*ta ekei*).[8]

Plotinus is criticizing the Gnostics. Now the presence in the world of Wisdom, the fallen Sophia, is a well-known Gnostic myth. Her presence is the consequence of a fall from a higher world. Plotinus accepts the basic tenet, but he cunningly turns the tables: there is wisdom in the world, but this is *our* wisdom. He then asks a transcendental question, in the precise meaning of this word, since it deals with the conditions of possibility of phenomena: what must the world be if moral action is to be possible in it? Our action proves that the world is a world. We must not only contemplate the order, but bring it out by our action. For Plotinus we have, literally speaking, to make ourselves at home.

This argument is not clearly formulated, and it is not dominant in Plotinus's work, let alone in the treatise from which I have just quoted. The keynote is a plea for the moral dignity of the Greek *kosmos*. Plotinus lived in an epoch in which the orderliness and beauty of the world still coincided with its alleged greater moral worth. How can we restate his thought after modernity?

B. Kant

Since a transcendental question has been asked, let me now turn toward Kant. On the one hand, he takes up a very old idea, an idea that is to be found in Plotinus: we are amphibious creatures; we live in two worlds, a sensible one and an intelligible one. But he gives it a decisive twist. The presence of the moral law in me

> exhibits me in a world which has true infinity but which is comprehensible only to the understanding—a world with which I recognize myself as existing in a universal and necessary (and not, as in the first case, merely contingent) connection, and thereby also in connection with all those visible worlds.[9]

The two worlds are not on the same footing. In the physical world, our presence is merely contingent in nature. It so happens that we are in the physical world. But there is another, moral world, of which we are necessarily citizens.

Now this moral world is the true one. The physical one is not really a world. Practical reason

> leads to the concept which speculative reason contained only as an antinomy, and the solution of which it could base only on a problematical, though thinkable, concept whose objective reality was not provable or determinable by speculative reason. This is the cosmological idea of an intelligible world and the consciousness of our existence in it. It leads to this by means of the postulate of freedom (the reality of which practical reason exhibits in the moral law, at the same time exhibiting the law of an intelligible world, which speculative reason could only indicate but whose concept it could not define).[10]

The strength of Kant's position is that he sets the world free from physics. The attempt at looking for the predicates of the idea of a world in the physical realm leads us to antinomies. The concept of world is not a physical concept any longer. We commonly distinguish a proper use of the term *world* and a metaphorical one. The first one designates the Whole, whereas the second one refers to the earth, insofar as it is inhabited, or even more narrowly to society. But Kant's revolution does not consist in privileging the metaphorical sense over the proper, physical one. More radically, he shows that our physical concept of the world is not original, but derivative. The physical use of *world* is the metaphor, exactly in the same way that reason is primarily practical, and secondarily only theoretical. Nature cannot bear the weight of the idea of a world—for this is an idea. Nature, so to speak, is not "worldly" enough.

C. Heidegger

A third step will lead us through Heidegger who, for that matter—strange bedfellows—is in the wake of Kant. His is an attempt to take seriously the subjective character of the idea of world. *Being and Time* begins with an analysis of "Being in the World" (*In-der-Welt-Sein*). Being in the World is not a category, that is, a feature of what is at hand (*vorhanden*); it is what Heidegger calls "an existential," a feature of *Dasein* itself. Therefore, we have to draw a line between world and nature. Previous ontologies jumped over the phenomenon of the world. They mistook it for nature, as its Ariadne's clue. Now nature is not the world. It is a being that is to be found inside the world. On the other hand,

> ontologically, "world" is not a way of characterizing those entities which Dasein essentially is *not,* it is rather a characteristic of Dasein itself.[11]

Let me restate what can be of interest for us. Kant showed that totality must remain an idea of reason, that cannot be presented in experience as long as we stick to the domain of physical nature. Heidegger takes his bearings from the idea of the world as a totality and asks in which experience totality is given as such. This is not perception, for perception looks out on this or that object. On the other hand, usage—handling implements—is not only the most basic way of getting in touch with what is; it implies that we are located in a world of tools, that we look at the whole world as being *something for*. This experience of a world is not perceptive in nature; it has more to do with living in, with abiding.

Furthermore, we never live without our feeling good or ill. In mood (*Stimmung*), everything receives a definite color. We see everything through rosy or through gray glasses. Presence is total, an every-thing or nothing. Instead of entering the windy path of Heidegger's analysis, let me borrow two examples from Solzhenitsyn: Nerzhin, a prisoner, has just received the news that his wife will visit him in jail.

> In keeping with an astonishing human characteristic *everything* had instantly changed inside Nerzhin. Five minutes ago . . . his *whole* thirty-year-old life had seemed a meaningless and painful chain of failures from which he had not had the strength to extri-cate himself. . . . Then had come the announcement of a visit . . . and his thirty-year-old life appeared in the light of a new sun: a life taut as a bowstring, a life full of meaning in both big and small things, a life striding from one bold success to another. . . .

In the same novel, a young officer of the secret service is arrested:

> Twenty minutes ago his past life had appeared to him as a single harmonious *whole*, every event evenly illuminated by the light of other events, all of them well ordered and linked up by brilliant bursts of success. But those twenty minutes had passed, and here in this narrow little trap his past life seemed to him, just as con-vincingly, a clutter of mistakes, a black heap of refuse.[12]

In mood, the whole world is seen in a definite light. When we are sad, we feel as if the world in its entirety is a sad thing. When we are happy, everything in the world, including the lark, the snail, and God, are where they belong.

Heidegger insisted on the subjective character of the concept of the world throughout his work of the twenties. *Vom Wesen des Grundes* (1929) deepens the analysis and adds some elements on the history of the concept of world:

> *Dasein*, then, is not Being-in-the-world because and only because it exists factically; on the contrary, it *can* only *be* as ex-isting, i.e. as *Dasein*, *because* its essential constitution lies in Being-in-the-world. . . .
>
> It is wrong then, to use the expression "world" either as a name for the entirety of natural things (the natural concept of world) or as a title for the community of men (the personal concept of world). Metaphysically essential to the meaning of *kosmos* (*mundus*, "world")—however clearly that meaning can

be defined—is that it aim at explaining human *Dasein* in *Dasein*'s relationship to being in its totality. . . . World belongs to selfhood; it is essentially related to *Dasein*. . . .[13]

Nevertheless, the text in which Heidegger goes farthest in his analysis of the phenomenon of the world might be his lecture course of the winter 1929–30, which explicitly takes up the reflections he developed in *Vom Wesen des Grundes*. He does that on the basis of a comparison between the mineral, the animal, and the human that articulates a triple thesis:

1. stones (material objects) are worldless (*weltlos*); 2. animals are poor in world (*weltarm*); 3. Man is world-framing (*weltbildend*).[14]

Unfortunately, the last point never was submitted to as careful an analysis as the second one. It seems to have remained merely programmatic. Heidegger never turned his mind again to the question of the world. Or, if he did, he did it only indirectly, at another level, or in another style that need not detain us here. Therefore, Heidegger leaves us somewhat in the lurch as to the precise elaboration of the concept of world.

VI. TOWARD A SUBJECTIVE WORLD

This concept is already extant. It corresponds to what we more or less explicitly mean when we call the *world* that to which a child comes when it is born, or that which a dying person leaves. Some languages borrowed from this experience terms for *world* which do not stem from the idea of *kosmos*, but from the idea of *aion*, "duration of life." *World* stems from the ideas of "humankind" (see Latin *vir*) and "age" (see the adjective *old*). As a rule, we use "coming to that world" to mean entering human community. Nevertheless we more or less consciously perceive that our coming into the world leads us to a totality, and that, conversely, we leave a totality.

Some thinkers gave this impression a full-fledged formulation. This is the case in Montaigne: "As our birth brought us the birth of all things, so shall our death the end of all things."[15]

As often happens, Pascal places himself in the wake of Montaigne and reformulates the same idea: "Chaque homme est un tout a soi-même car, une fois mort, le tout est mort pour soi" (Each man is all in all to himself, for when he is dead, all is dead to him).[16]

Pascal pays attention to mortality only and keeps silent on what Hannah Arendt called human "natality." Nevertheless, his formula has the merit of a greater pregnancy. And, what is more, it has the great virtue of placing the idea of totality on the side of the subject. Montaigne mentioned "all *things*"; Pascal deals with the whole that we are, thanks to which things are for us a totality, the total show. The total character of things, a feature that makes of them the world that they constitute, comes from our mortality.

We can't speak of a world without referring to a totality. Those passages do contain the idea of totality. However, the totality that is at stake is highly unusual in nature. It is not reached through a synthesis of elements. It is given from the outset. Its total character is not quantitative. The unity that binds the elements into a totality does not result from our mustering the multiplicity till we exhaust it. This unity precedes every going through and makes it possible. And it subsists in every point of this path. By this token, the total character of our presence in the world or of the presence of the world around us has nothing to do with how many objects we experience, a quantity that, be it as large as possible, is only a tiny part of whatever is contained in the world. Hence, the world is not a world because of itself. Its worldliness does not stem from itself, but from our presence in it.

This does not mean that we create the universe. None of the authors I mentioned ever contended that what is exists because we are conscious of it, a so-called "idealistic" thesis that was probably never expounded by any real thinker. What they implicitly contend is that the things constitute a world, that is, a totality, only because of the total character of our presence among them. By this token, placing the idea of world in a relationship with the subject does not amount at all to jettisoning the infinity of the universe in favor of the warm intimacy of our immediate surroundings. When we entered the world, at our birth, we entered something that contains, as decidedly and as indifferently, our cradle as well as the remotest galaxy. More radically, we do not have to take refuge in subjectivity by forsaking the world of concrete objects. On the contrary, conceiving of our subjectivity amounts to acknowledging that our presence does not add anything to what is and that our absence does not detract anything from it.

If this holds true, we can give our initial question an answer, but a paradoxical one. The very nature of subjectivity implies the phenomenon of the world. The world is at home in us. But we are not at home in the universe. Both are two sides of the same coin. Insofar as we are subjects, we cannot be parts of what is. Being at home and not feeling at home cease to exclude one another. On the contrary, the very fact that we feel hardly at home in the world gives evidence for the fact that we are world-bearers, *kosmophor*, if I may mint such a term.

CONCLUSION

A last question: how are the two, the world as a dimension of our subjectivity and the universe of things, to be reconciled? This question remains for me. It remained for better people, too. In particular, it remained for the three I have just been drawing upon: Plotinus, Kant, and Heidegger. In the latter, for instance, we can wonder how the *Dasein* can have a body. This is a well-known blind spot in Heidegger's thought. Kant had the merit to face the difficulty explicitly, when trying to bridge the gap between the first two *Critiques*. This is all the more difficult for him since he stands at loggerheads with the worldview I sketched a moment ago, according to which humans' ethical nature is linked up to their imitating the world or to their adjusting to it. For him, morality not only does not consist in imitating the world or adjusting to it; it consists in *not* imitating it. Any influence of the world must be carefully avoided, for it would be, to quote his term, "pathological"; it would damage our freedom. It is as if the pietist Kant took seriously Paul's injunction "not to be conformed to this world" (Rom. 12:2).

We should find a way of being at home in the world while abiding by the interdiction to adjust to it. This will remain an open task. Let me conclude with the well-known chapter of Kant's third *Critique* on "beauty as a symbol of morality."[17] I won't explain it, but I will pick up one phrase only, as a program—or a symbol—for further research. This phrase is the title itself. Kant was no philologist. He had better things to do than learning languages. He does not allude to the etymology of "symbol." I will. In ancient Greece, there were no hotels or identification cards. When two families decided to enter a bond of hospitality, they would break some piece of earthenware into two parts, one for each family. Each would keep its half and bequeath it from father to son, so that a traveler would be able to identify himself by means of it. For it was enough for two scions of those befriended families to show that both halves fit perfectly for them to make sure that, though they had never seen one another, they belonged to families between which links of hospitality had obtained for a long time. The act of putting together the two broken halves—word for word, of *throwing* them together—was called in Greek *symballein*. As a consequence, this token was called a *symbolon*. This is our word "symbol." In the same way, the very fact that we can identify natural beauty as a symbol of what is most human in us—that is, ethics—shows that we are, in this world, neither parts and parcels, nor strangers, but guests.

NOTES

1. James Joyce, *A Portrait of the Artist as a Young Man* (1916; reprint ed., New York: Viking Press, 1964), p. 15.

2. Plato *Timaeus* 47bc.

3. Clement of Alexandria *Excerpts from Theodotus* 33.3.

4. Joseph Conrad, *Lord Jim* (New York: Penguin Classics, 1989), p. 195.

5. Søren Kierkegaard, *Repetition*, ed. and trans. with introduction and notes by Howard V. Hong and Edna H. Hong (Princeton: Princeton University Press, 1983), p. 200, letter of 11 October.

6. Karl Marx, *Deutsche Ideologic* (Moscow, 1932), pp. 41–43.

7. George Orwell, *Nineteen Eighty-Four* (New York: Knopf, 1992), pp. 111, 3.

8. Plotinus *Enneads* (trans. A. H. Armstrong; modified) 2.9. 43–46.

9. Immanuel Kant, *Critique of Practical Reason*, trans. Lewis White Beck (New York: Liberal Arts Press, 1956), p. 169.

10. Ibid., pp. 139f.

11. Martin Heidegger, *Sein und Zeit*, 3.14; trans. John Macquarrie and Edward Robinson (New York: Harper & Row, 1962), p. 92.

12. A. I. Solzhenitsyn, *The First Circle*, trans. Thomas P. Whitney (New York: Harper & Row, 1968), pp. 156, 525.

13. Martin Heidegger, *The Essence of Reasons* (*Vom Vesen des Grundes*), trans. Terrence Malick (Evanston, Ill.: Northwestern University Press, 1969), pp. 45, 81–83, 85.

14. Martin Heidegger, *Grundbegriffe der Metaphysik* 2.2.42; trans. William McNeill and Nicholas Walker (Bloomington, Ind.: Indiana University Press, 1995), p. 177.

15. Michel de Montaigne *Essais* (trans. John Florio) 1.20.

16. Blaise Pascal, *Pensées*, trans. H. F. Stewart (New York: Pantheon Books, 1950), p. 81.

17. Immanuel Kant, *The Critique of Judgement*, trans. James Creed Meredith (Oxford: Clarendon Press, 1952), par. 59, p. 221.

Places Of Experience
and the Experience of Place[1]
KATHERINE PLATT

I THOUGHT ABOUT CALLING this essay "The Inside of the Inside and the
Outside of the Inside" because I want to explore the culturally and
experientially lively boundary between the inside and the outside
which transforms space into place. Anything that we would call a place
has some kind of an inside. The inside of a meaningful place, as Victor
Walter has said, is a container of experience; hence the term "places of
experience," which I borrow from the introductory chapter of his book
Placeways: A Theory of the Human Environment.[2] Places capture experience and store it symbolically. Its collective meanings are
extractable and readable by later inhabitants. This symbolic housing
of meaning and memory gives places temporal depth. But not only
do places of experience store meaning about the past; they also are
platforms for visions and plans about the future. Places of experience
provision us with identity to venture forth out of this place into less
certain or orderly spaces. Places of experience provide categories for
managing new adventures and new cycles of old adventures. Places of
experience connect the past to the future, memory to expectation, in
an invigorating way. Places of experience give us a sense of continuity
and energy.

Home, of course, is the penultimate place of experience, second
only to the body. Gaston Bachelard has said that the house is "one of
the greatest powers of integration for the thoughts, the memories and
dreams of mankind."[3] The home is a tool for the process of creating or
becoming an identity. It has both a hidden, private, recuperative aspect
and an open, presentational, hospitable aspect. It conceals and it reveals. Perla Korosec-Serfaty has written of attics and cellars in rural
France, part of the hidden aspect of home and the self. It is easy to see
the marriage of memory and expectation symbolized in the home

simply by looking at the contents and categories of cellars, attics, pantries, closets, and drawers.[4] Many past experiences and prospects for future experiences are stored in such places. Sometimes the past and the future are linked in a cherished object, such as a rocking horse or a wedding dress, waiting patiently for its next designated user.[5] Childhoods are archived; seasons are anticipated; tonight's sleep is staged. One can test this idea by doing a quick mental inventory. Homes are contexts in which the self is accounted for in many concrete ways and the boundaries and curtains of the self can be drawn.

A rather different way of looking at the home is suggested by the anthropologist Mary Douglas, who sees it in terms of its moral dimension. She argues that, among other things, home can be seen as the presentation of a general plan for meeting future needs. Its *de facto* budget of material resources, time, and attention is an instrument for structuring collective effort. Underlying such a plan is a working concept of the collective good which is vigilantly protected with complex rules and rituals for the coordination of activities and long-term reciprocities. The home is a very complex embryonic moral community whose primary purpose is to perpetuate itself. In its determination to achieve this purpose, the home is remarkable in its ability to "muster solidarity and demand sacrifice."[6] Douglas is interested in the moral and social aspects of the home as a model of distributive justice.

In the same vein as Mary Douglas, James Duncan has written about the home as a symbol of the social structure. "The built environment, in addition to providing shelter, serves as a medium of communication because encoded within it are elements of the social structure. It speaks in the language of objects about the moral order of that culture. It serves as the stage set for the morality play, the backdrop for that collection of stories that a people tell themselves about themselves, in order that they may better know who they are, how to behave and what to cherish."[7]

I can think of numerous examples of this from my own field research in Tunisia where the structures of gender stratification and the associated prescribed and prohibited behaviors are built into the stage set. An earthy example is the absence of bathroom facilities for women in what might be called the public domains of the city. The built environment instructs women about where they should be: in the domestic domain. The presence of very grand washing facilities for men in the mosques communicates not only an invitation to men into this place, but also a message about their capacity for ritual and moral purity. On the other hand, the domestic domain has many types of interior gathering and working spaces for women which are centers of intense sociability and cooperation, not isolated seclusion.

I like putting these ideas of home together because, looked at in combination, they allude to the relationship between what I referred to earlier as the inside of the inside and the outside of the inside. Korosec-Serfaty's interest in the personal, private, even hidden meanings and values of the home is the inside of the inside. It is about home as a centripetal energy which encloses and turns inward. Douglas's interest in the idea of home as an embryonic community and Duncan's interest in home as a symbol of social structure is the outside of the inside. They are about home as a centrifugal energy which extends its meanings outward into the world.

Many different thinkers from a variety of disciplines have written about the dynamic energies of the boundary between the inside and the outside. Edward and Mildred Hall, pioneers in the study of nonverbal communication and the cultural meanings of time and space, have introduced us to the idea that some kinds of places, such as outdoor cafes, are what they call "sociopedal." They gather people. Other places, such as railway stations, they tell us, are "sociofugal."[8] They scatter people, turning their attention away from each other. The Halls are analyzing what Walters calls the "energies of places." It is this liveliness that I am interested in discussing.

Yi-Fu Tuan, the phenomenological geographer and author of *Space and Place: The Perspective of Experience* and *Topophilia,* to name just two relevant titles, writes about how spaces are turned into places through the courage of experience.[9] Experience, he tells us, is the overcoming of perils in order to venture forth into the unfamiliar and unknown.[10] Through this venturing, we come to learn and know the meaning and value of the centers and objects which give space its "geometric personality."[11] Through experience, venturing outward, meaningful places become visible and "legible" in the blur of unfamiliar space.[12] To use my idiom of the inside and outside, the venturing energy which sends us bravely outside expands our experience of belonging, of being inside, making us more at home in a larger world. It takes a lot of courage, for example, for students to overcome the perils of the unknown when first moving onto a college campus. It is disorienting and strange and, worst of all, empty of one's own experience.

But once one has discovered the gathering places of other members of one's species, eaten a meal in the same place a few times, and performed the housewarming ritual of watching one's favorite television show in one's new room, the place begins to have an inside, which was the inside of one's own experience. And in this wonderful process, one's experiential world gets larger.

Gaston Bachelard, the poet of space, is another thinker who meditates on the dynamic relationship between freedom and security, dancing on the inside/outside boundary. He says, "Outside and inside form a dialectic of division, the obvious geometry of which blinds us. . . . Outside and inside are both intimate—they are always ready to be reversed, to exchange their hostility."[13] His famous thoughts about doors illustrate this dynamism.

> How concrete everything becomes in the world of the spirit when an object, a mere door, can give images of hesitation, temptation, desire, security, welcome and respect. If one were to give an account of all the doors one has closed and opened, of all the doors one would like to re-open, one would have to tell the story of one's entire life.
>
> But is he who opens a door and he who closes it the same being? The gestures that make us conscious of security or freedom are rooted in a profound depth of being.[14]

In these reveries, Bachelard emphasizes two important points. One is that we create and recreate ourselves out of our experiences. A second is that the boundary between the outside and inside is vital and active; it expands and contracts. It is permeable and plastic.

I now want to discuss these two ideas, the connection of identity to the experience of home place and the liveliness of the inside/outside boundary, with reference to three specific cases. I am going to describe how the experience of three very different home places has been mobilized as a vehicle for identity formation, survival, and transformation. The three examples I am going to use are the Eastern European Jewish shtetl or ghetto of the early twentieth century, the childhood home places of women in rural Iran, and the Arab peasant villages of pre-1948 Palestine.

All of the episodes of experience that I am going to explore are situations in which a home place has become dislocated, disoriented, or relocated for some reason or another. In each of these conditions of dislocation, the strategy for reestablishing identity involves some manner of symbolically externalizing the inside meanings of the former home place. One might expect that in a time of identity crisis, dislocation, loss, or uprootedness an individual or group might submerge rather than display the meanings of the inside. This dynamic is partly about the cultural energy which compels us to name ourselves rather than to be named; hence the trajectory of names for the colored, Negro, black, Afro-American, African-American population. This energy is also part of a bigger energy in the human race which I find both heartening and heart-breaking. This is our creative genius for making, and our creative desperation to make, the world meaningful. We cannot and will not live without meaning, and the meanings of place are one of our special passions.

My first example is taken from the anthropological study that Barbara Myerhoff did of a group of elderly Eastern European Jews in a senior citizens' center in Venice, California, which resulted in a film and a book called *Number Our Days*.[15] Almost all the elders in this center originated from the Jewish ghettoes of Eastern Europe. These, of course, are places which no longer exist. Although the members of the center mostly left these ghettoes for the United States in the teens and twenties of this century, nearly all of the remaining populations were exterminated in the Holocaust. Much of Myerhoff's study is a discussion of the strategies the members of the center employ to fight cultural invisibility. Their identities are at risk from the outside and the inside. They need to remind the world that they are still there and they need to tell themselves who they are. In the case of these triply marginal people—marginal as immigrants, Holocaust survivors, and, finally, elderly Americans—the struggle against cultural invisibility is profoundly connected to the poignant task of carrying the experiential meanings of places which no longer exist in the symbolism of themselves.

The tailor, Shmuel, speaks of this task born of loss:

> As long as my eyes are still open, I'll see those beloved people, the young, the old, the crazy ones, the fools, the wise, and the good ones. I'll see the little crooked streets, the hills and animals, the Vistula like a silver snake winding in its beauty. . . .
> In that little town, there were no walls. But we were curled up together inside it, like small cubs, keeping each other warm,

growing from within, never showing the outside what is happening, until our backs make up a stout wall. It is not the worst thing that can happen for a man to grow old and die. But here is the hard part. When my mind goes back there now, there are no roads going in or out. No way remains because nothing is there, no continuation. . . . For myself, growing old would be altogether a different thing if that little town were still there. I carry with me everything—all those people, all those places, I carry them around until my shoulders bend. . . . Even with all that poverty and suffering, it would be enough if the place remained, even old men like me, ending their days, would find it enough. But when I come back from these stories and remember the way they lived is gone forever, wiped out like you would erase a line of writing, then it means another thing altogether for me to accept leaving this life. If my life goes now, it means nothing. But if my life goes with my memories, and all that is lost, that is something else to bear.[16]

The problem which Shmuel describes is shared by all of the elders. They need to remember, to describe, to bear witness, but they have no obvious audience to listen to them. The strategy they have developed in their collective life is to dramatize their identities *for themselves* in a series of rituals which Myerhoff calls definitional rituals. These are rituals which allow for the maximum degree of participation and the maximum degree of visibility. As Lee Rouner emphasized in his essay for this book, "Attention must be paid!" In ritual, attention is paid.

The symbolic content for these rituals comes from a variety of threads of identity—American patriotism, secular education, loyalty to the state of Israel, formal Judaism—but most powerful and resonant are the symbols which evoke shtetl life, the culture of childhood, what Myerhoff calls "Yiddishkeit." And among this category of symbols, the single most powerful is the Yiddish language itself.

However temporarily, the Yiddish language is the vehicle of redemption for Shmuel and his peers. It provides the possibility of a kind of continuity which transcends history and geography. As such it is a symbol of enormous depth and emotion. And as speakers of Yiddish, each elder is a symbol of a whole world, which through their speech is made to exist again.

Shmuel again:

> Jewish (Yiddish) we call the mama-loshen. That means
> more than the mother tongue. It is the mother's tongue because
> this was the language the mother talked, sweet or bitter. It was
> your own. It is a language of the heart. This the Jewish writers
> knew, and they used it with love.
>
> It had another aspect. It was not only that Jews from every-
> where could talk with this language. Also, it had words in it that
> could be used differently for the inside sweet world and the hard
> world outside. Now this mama-loshen kept apart the Jewish and
> Polish worlds. . . .
>
> So Jewish gave us unity. In Hebrew you couldn't sing songs
> except for those Psalms. You couldn't amuse yourself in Hebrew.
> We could sing the personal, lyrical songs in Jewish. Lullabies, love
> songs. A boy likes a girl. He couldn't go up to her and say, "I like
> you." This would not be permitted. So how could he approach
> her and capture her attention? He would make up a song, and
> sing it to himself, naturally in Jewish, but so that she could hear
> it. This is the sweet grass from which our language grew. Young
> boys singing songs. The language was our republic.[17]

Now in old age on the California coast, Yiddish is the visceral
link with the lost home places. The very act of speaking Yiddish,
no matter what the subject, carries the lost places into the present.
The experience of place transcends the place of experience. But the
speaking of Yiddish is not just a means of maintaining identity with
the past. Myerhoff describes how many of the survival strategies of
shtetl life, so minutely remembered in the storytelling of the center,
are called upon to meet the challenges of old age in the youth-crazed
culture of southern California. These strategies consist of taking the
meanings of what Shmuel called "the sweet inside" and calling them
up against a different hard outside world.

Myerhoff explains why these meanings—decades and worlds
away—remain so accessible. "Survival comes in cultural inflections.
The infant is fed particular foods, lulled with particular words and
songs, wrapped in particular garments. Desire, appetite, fundamental
feelings are inflected in local, household idioms that once acquired are
not interchangeable. . . . When sacred symbols are employed in rituals,
when the two poles (the abstract, ideal and the particular, physiologi-

cal) fuse, a single experiential reality is created and the individual becomes the embodiment of certain of the collectivity's beliefs. The beliefs are laid upon and empowered by the original mixture of household odors, habits, gestures, sounds, tastes, and sentiments, the accumulation of historical moments—perhaps no longer consciously remembered but nonetheless effective. These first experiences of domestic life, transmuted into Domestic Religion, are permanent and powerful, for their roots have been set down in the deepest layers of the heart."[18]

Basha's experience of lighting Sabbath candles at the center illustrates this effect. "Do you know what it meant to me when I was called to the Candles last Friday? I'll tell you. When I was a little girl, I would stand this way, beside my mother when she would light the candles for Shabbat. We were alone in the house, everything warm and clean and quiet with all the good smells of the cooking food coming in around us. We were still warm from the mikva (communal baths). My braids were tight, to last through the Shabbes, made with the best ribbons. Whatever we had, we wore our best. To this day, when the heat of the candles is on my face, I circle the flame and cover my eyes, and then I feel again my mother's hands on my smooth cheeks."[19]

The inside meanings of childhood nurturing and an as-yet-unbroken world are symbolized, condensed, and externalized in the Yiddish language. Contained within it is the shared cultural knowledge of how to be poor with dignity, with always a penny for philanthropy, how to make something meager and plain into something special and elegant, how to laugh at adversity, and how to elevate the menial tasks of caring for oneself and others into domestic religion. No wonder as Basha prepared to move from her own apartment into an old folks' home she said, "I'll tell you what is the worst that could happen. If no one speaks Yiddish, I don't know how I'll manage. Somehow, no matter how bad things are, when I hear Yiddish, something in me goes free, and everything changes around. Without this I think I would just dry up."[20] Speaking Yiddish is her way of tapping into the energies of her places of experience and of using this energy to make a new home place.

My next example is about women and the experience of place in rural Iran. There is much discussion in the ethnography of the Middle East of gender domains, the division of the world into public and private, and the banishment of women from the public, presumably male domain. One of the problems with these spatialized theories of social organization in the Middle East is that the metaphorical boundaries between the inside and the outside, the private and the public, are too high and too hard. That is, these prosaic theories immobilize something that is plastic and permeable and better described in terms of action, performance, process, and experience than in terms of a concretely bifurcated world. The work of Susan Wright on the Iranian women of Doshman Ziari gives us a very interesting example of gendered space to examine.[21] This is a patriarchal, patrilineal, virilocal society, which means that the socio-religious ideology, the inheritance system, and the place of marital residence put women in a very contingent position relative to all the dominant structures of this society. Due to this contingent position, women, Wright argues, have a very different view of kinship, experience of place, and strategies for functioning than men. Their dependence on the dominant modes of the society means that in some way they are in a condition of displacement and discontinuity from the very beginning. I would argue that, like the elderly Jews of Venice, California, they have created a way to mobilize their idea of home, to externalize it symbolically and in so doing to transform it into a strategy for generating an identity which is vital, and while adaptive, *not* contingent. In other words, in an important way, they are naming themselves, not being named. They are actors, not re-actors. Because of their relationship to the institutions in this society, they are actors in a somewhat different play than men. They have different scripts, but interestingly they share the same stage set which they employ and experience differently. Inside and outside mean very different things to a man whose childhood, work life, marriage, and old age all take place in exactly the same location than to a woman who grows up knowing that she will soon leave her father's home and be relocated in a new role in a strange household, often in an unfamiliar village.

The inside/outside boundary for men is very clear, relatively hard, and impermeable. The inside/outside boundary for women who have relocated as brides is more mobile and fluid. For men, the people with whom they share property, labor, blood, trust, name—and most important, a reputation—are also the people who live within or nearby the same residential enclosure. The self-reliance of the minimal patrilineage (father and married sons), which includes an ability to defend the residential group against insults or theft, is a primary social value.

Many behaviors reflect this value of self-reliance and ethic of distrust: cooperation where possible only among sons or brothers, secrecy about the household's affairs, and vigilant avoidance of any situation or appearance of subordination. These values and behaviors make for a hard physical and symbolic boundary around the patrilineal household.

For women such boundaries are much more complex and porous. To begin with, women's affective bonds of kinship and loyalty are scattered in many locations. A woman is attached to her father's household and her mother in particular, but she leaves in early adulthood. She is attached to her husband's household, but she still has bonds of loyalty to her brothers. The women are emotionally attached to their sisters and other female kin who are scattered all over the countryside in different households. What this means is that they experience the literal and social landscape very differently than men. They have a different experience of place than men. Their ideas about kinship, trust, and cooperation are different. We could say that males view kinship in a lineal and vertical way, with a narrow but deep generational focus. The female view of kinship, on the other hand, is horizontal. It is spread out, wide and flexible, and situational as a guide to behavior. This arrangement also means that the mother-in-law, sisters-in-law, and immediate neighboring wives with whom a woman is in daily contact through cooperative work and visiting rituals are most likely not kin and not even known to her before her marriage. Out of this difference emerge interesting possibilities for women. Because of their cross-cutting ties, women have access to information from a multitude of households to which men would not be privy. Women also, because of the complexity of their ties, are not so locked into a rigid hierarchy of honor which makes wider networks of cooperation and interdependence so problematic for men. In other words, their affective bonds, personal identity, interests, and reputation are not all concentrated in one lineal system. These differences have many repercussions in the daily life of women. Women often pool their resources and work cooperatively with unrelated women at cooking, baking bread, dairy processing, weaving carpets, water collecting, milling wheat, and child care, achieving economy, efficiency, networks of long-term reciprocity, and sociability along the way.

The Middle Eastern trope of the public and private domains has been turned inside out in this example. If women are confined in some ways to the domestic realm, they are inside a wide range of such realms. In this sense, they have a kind of mobility and breadth of experience (which might be a way of talking about public life) that men who belong to only one group cannot have. Also, a woman's inside knowledge of the concerns and strategies of a variety of households to which she has links is significant in two ways. First, it gives her a multifaceted perspective on public issues and the merits of a variety of positions, and in fact, her sense of a good outcome might be quite different from her husband's. Second, her specialized knowledge of other households is an invaluable resource to her husband's household in its struggle to compete with other patrilineal households for resources, influence, and honor.

While the power structures of this society are certainly male-dominated, women have a kind of power which ironically rises from their subordinate and displaced position, but this power is not a mirror or a miniature of male power. This is a power unique to their position. Once again, in a condition of displacement, the experience of place becomes a source of identity. And once again the resources of the inside, the centripetal energy of the home place, can shift into its centrifugal mode to create experiences of home in challenging circumstances. For the women of Doshmen Ziari, pushed out of their fathers' hard-boundaried, inside-of-the-inside, patrilineal homes, home becomes a diffuse, expanding, multicentric, outside-of-the-inside experience with many possibilities for cooperation, connection, and solidarity.

The third place of experience and experience of place is that of Palestine and the Palestinians who left and became refugees in 1948. Whereas gender was the determining distinction in the experience of place in the last example, generation transforms the experience of place in this example. The meaning of home place to the original generation of Palestinian refugees is profoundly and qualitatively different from the meaning of home place to the children and grandchildren of those people.

What is the difference? For the original refugees of 1948, the home place is a very specific, literal, minutely remembered piece of land. It is remembered in terms of the categories and values of peasant agriculturists: the quality of the soil, the types of vegetation, the location of each and every fruit tree, what the fruit tasted like. Correspondingly, disconnection from the land was a source not only of personal pain but of social shame. To quote Simon Shamir, "Even though they had not lived on the land for some twenty years, they still

adhered to the value system of an agrarian society in which landless-
ness is regarded as unforgivable. They often repeated the dictums such
as 'the landless is despised' and 'he who has no land has no religion and
no homeland.' The refugees claimed that their loss of landed property
had marked them indelibly; their painful inferior status, they believed,
'will follow them wherever they go' and will plague them 'even after
one hundred years.'" [22] Their identity was tied to the land, so without
their land their identities were in crisis.

A seventeen-year-old schoolgirl, interviewed by Rosemary Sayigh, reflects on the pain of the older generation, "Once at home . . . the
conversation changed to the past, and how they used to live. And when
they spoke, they wept, because of their attachment to their country.
Whoever sits with them can understand more about Palestine than
from going to meetings, because they lived the life . . . but what
affected me most was their weeping, because their land was so dear
to them."[23]

The social relations of their old way of life, rooted in the land,
were organized concentrically in terms of clan and village solidarity.
The first-generation refugees, uprooted from the land, tenaciously
reproduced this system of peasant social relations in the camps by
grouping themselves again in the same village communities and naming their section of the camp by the old village name. They met every
day in groups of kin and neighbors, not to plow the fields, but to plow
the fields of memory, going over and over the same territory with
minute detail of recollection.

Sayigh points out that this not only helped them survive in their
condition of dislocation, but also created a cultural inheritance in the
form of a rich oral history to replace or hold the place of what they considered to be the rightful inheritance of their children. Their daily
remembrance ritual has all of the attributes of the definitional rituals
performed by the elderly Jews in Venice, California. They remembered the land in order to remember who they themselves were and to
transmit this knowledge to their descendants. Edward Said, in his book
After the Last Sky, reflects on this process of remembering and symbolizing: ". . . intimate mementos of a past irrevocably lost circulate
among us, like the genealogies and fables of a wandering singer of
tales. Photographs, dresses, objects severed from their original locale,
the rituals of speech and custom: much reproduced, enlarged, thema-
tized, embroidered, and passed around, they are the strands in the web

of affiliation we Palestinians use to tie ourselves to our identity and to each other."[24]

The first generation had two modes for thinking about their home place: one was to remember and grieve. Sayigh again: "The village with its special arrangement of houses and orchards, its open meeting places, its burial ground, its collective identity—was built into the personality of each individual villager to a degree that made separation like the obliteration of the self. In describing their first years as refugees, camp Palestinians use metaphors like 'death', 'paralysis', 'burial'. . . . Thirty years after the Uprooting, the older generation still mourns, still weeps as it recalls the past. The passion of their attachment is shown in the way old people make their children promise to re-bury their bodies in Palestine, after the return. The same word, *hajj*, is used for visits to Palestine/Israel as for the pilgrimage to Mecca."[25]

The second mode for thinking about the home place was to plan for the full return to their place of origin, the *'awda*. For the first generation the Return was imagined to be a direct and literal return to the exact land they had left. Proportionate to their disbelief at what had happened to them was their belief in the literal *'awda*. To them it was not possible that they would not be restored to their land.

Edward Said illustrates this mode of thought. "When A.Z.'s father was dying, he called his children . . . into his room for a last family gathering. A frail, very old man from Haifa, he had spent his last thirty-four years in Beirut in a state of agitated disbelief at the loss of his house and his property. Now he murmured to his children the final faltering words of a penniless, helpless patriarch. 'Hold on to the keys and the deed,' he told them, pointing to a battered suitcase near his bed, a repository of the family estate salvaged from Palestine when Haifa's Arabs were expelled."[26] Because of this belief in the Return, many refugees refused to be settled in new circumstances and to give up their UNRWA (United Nations Refugee and Works Agency) refugee status. They believed that in holding on to the internationally recognized status and symbols of being a refugee, they were holding on to their land. As Shamir says, "The ration card that refugees hold was thus seen as a promissory note on this right (to return). Hence the conviction that he who sells his card, sells his honor, or that 'selling the card is like selling one's land.'"[27] The language they used to talk about the camps emphasized their impermanence. They lived in "shelters," not houses, even though they lived in these shelters for decades.[28] These domiciles could not be experienced as home places for that would betray and abandon the claim on the original home place.

The relationship to the home place and the meaning of the Return became very different for the descending refugee generations, and now there have been nearly two. The literal places of origin so copiously mourned by the older generation became generalized and symbolic. Peasant class position and consciousness was replaced by working class position and consciousness. Clan and village solidarity gradually crumbled and has slowly been replaced by a Palestinian nationalist identity. Stunned disbelief at what is called the Catastrophe or the Uprooting has been replaced by a determined militancy. The literal Return, *'awda*, has become the idea of self-determination. In the terms of this paper, the inside meanings of the Palestinians' experience of the home place have been externalized and turned into outside political meanings. The specific, remembered home place which faced south and had two lemon trees has become the collective, imagined Homeland. The experience of the home place turned the energy of the original refugees inward toward remembering and trying to recover the past. The yearned-for experience of the Homeland has turned the energy of the younger generations outward toward the future, imagining and perhaps now even building a Palestinian state.

This transformation is a protracted rite of passage, as conceived by Arnold van Gennep and Victor Turner.[29] The Catastrophe or Uprooting is the stage of separation from "normal society." Being a refugee has been the state of liminality, a time of *communitas*, disorder, structurelessness, and status reversal. Out of the experience and symbols of liminality, social reaggregation and the formulation of a new kind of identity, with new structures, statuses, and symbols, is emerging.

The Palestinian refugee experience of place was transformed through a process in the course of which the crisis of identity was passed from one generation to the next. In this process the definitional rituals of minute remembrance were transformed in the next generation into political rituals of self-determination. The personal rituals of mourning were transformed into rituals of protest and militance. The centripetal gathering of the inside meanings of home was transformed into the centrifugal expression of the outside meanings of nation building.

There is almost an infinite number of conditions of rootlessness, marginality, and homelessness in the modern world. The percentage of the world's population designated as refugees is staggering and growing. These are grim facts. The grimmest fact is that it is human beings who, through many means, create these conditions of displacement at the cost of their fellows. But these are not the only facts about displacement. Less grim is the human ability to hold onto home meanings when home has vaporized. Less grim is the human ability to mobilize the energy housed in these home meanings for the purpose of structuring new experiences, for creating new order out of chaos. Less grim is the human symbolizing skill of turning ourselves inside out to create new places of experience.

NOTES

1. This essay is dedicated to Larry Platt, whose poignant and articulate sensitivity to places of experience and the experience of place has been an inspiration to me.

2. Victor Walter, *Placeways: A Theory of the Human Environment* (Chapel Hill, N.C.: University of North Carolina Press, 1988).

3. Gaston Bachelard, *The Poetics of Space*, trans. Maria Jolas (Boston: Beacon Press, 1969), p. 6.

4. See the fascinating work of Perla Korosec-Serfaty on this subject in rural France: "The Home, from Attic to Cellar," *Journal of Environmental Psychology* 4 (1984): 303–21.

5. Carol Werner, Irwin Altmann, and Diana Oxley, eds., *Home Environments* (New York: Plenum Press, 1985), p. 18.

6. Mary Douglas, "The Idea of a Home: A Kind of Space," in *Home,* ed. Arlen Mack (New York: New York University Press, 1993), p. 271.

7. James Duncan, "The House as a Symbol of Social Structure," in *Home Environments*, p. 148.

8. Edward T. Hall, *The Hidden Dimension* (Garden City, N.Y.: Doubleday, 1969), pls. 13–14.

9. Yi-Fu Tuan, *Space and Place: The Perspective of Experience* (Minneapolis: University of Minnesota Press, 1977); and *Topophilia* (Englewood Cliffs, N.J.: Prentice Hall, 1974).

10. Tuan, *Space and Place*, p. 9.

11. Ibid., p. 17.

12. Kevin Lynch, *The Image of the City* (Cambridge, Mass.: MIT Press, 1960).

13. Bachelard, *Poetics of Space*, pp. 211, 217–18.

14. Ibid., p. 224.

15. Barbara Myerhoff, *Number Our Days* (New York: Touchstone Press, 1978).

16. Ibid., pp. 73–74.

17. Ibid.

18. Ibid., pp. 257–58.

19. Ibid., p. 256.

20. Ibid., p. 253.

21. Susan Wright, "Place and Face: Of Women in Doshman Ziari, Iran," in *Women and Space*, ed. Shirley Ardner (New York: St. Martin's Press, 1981).

22. Simon Shamir, "West Bank Refugees: Between Camp and Society," in *Palestinian Society and Politics*, ed. Joel Migdal (Princeton: Princeton University Press, 1980), p. 150.

23. Rosemary Sayigh, *Palestinians: From Peasants to Revolutionaries* (London: Zed Press, 1979), p. 12.

24. Edward Said, *After the Last Sky: Palestinian Lives* (New York: Pantheon Press, 1985), p. 14.

25. Sayigh, *Palestinians*, p. 107.

26. Said, *After the Last Sky*, p. 14.

27. Shamir, "West Bank Refugees," p. 152.

28. Ibid., p. 161.

29. Arnold van Gennep, *Rite of Passage*, trans. M. B. Vizedom and G. L. Caffee (London: Routledge and Kegan Paul, 1960); and Victor Turner, *The Ritual Process* (Ithaca, N.Y.: Cornell University Press, 1991).

The Man Who Committed Adultery with His Own Wife

WENDY DONIGER

I. RUSHDIE AND THE WIZARD OF OZ

Why did Dorothy want to leave Oz and return to Kansas? This question, one of the enduring mysteries of the American cinema, always bothered me (I am a New Yorker, with a New Yorker's scorn for everything west of the Hudson). I was not surprised to learn that it bothered the author himself, who later reworked the story much as Melina Mercouri reworked the Greek tragedies in *Never on Sunday*: in the end, they all went to the seashore. For in subsequent Oz books by Frank L. Baum,

> Dorothy, ignoring the "lessons" of the ruby slippers, went back to Oz, in spite of the efforts of Kansas folk, including Auntie Em and Uncle Henry, to have her dreams brainwashed out of her . . . ; and, in the sixth book of the series, she took Auntie Em and Uncle Henry with her, and they all settled down in Oz, where Dorothy became a Princess. So Oz finally *became* home; the imagined world became the actual world.[1]

So Rushdie, too, was bothered by Dorothy's choice of Kansas over Oz. But he does not let us rest with the happy ending:

> The real secret of the ruby slippers is not that "there's no place like home," but rather that there is no longer any such place *as* home: except, of course, for the home we make, or the homes that are made for us, in Oz: which is anywhere, and everywhere, except the place from which we began.[2]

128

Indeed, Dorothy's choice of Kansas over Oz is at first inexplicable to anyone immersed in Indian mythology. If, however, we look more closely at South Asian mythology—and, indeed, at world mythology—we will find a powerful precedent for Dorothy's apparent preference for a real home over the seductive world of fantasy.

For there is a widespread, cross-cultural (if not universal) mythological theme of a woman who, faced with a choice between her mortal lover or husband and an immortal god who resembles him in every way but his mortality, chooses the mortal. I would like to examine a few examples of this theme and to ask what it tells us about the longing for home.

II. WILL THE REAL MORTAL PLEASE STAND UP?

But before we can tackle these texts, we must distinguish between the masquerade of a deity as a mortal, and that of one mortal or immortal as another, for the logic of the choices that the victims of these masquerades must make vary greatly. In the first type, which involves both mortals and immortals, the victim must discover the generic criteria that distinguish any mortal from any immortal. In the second type, which involves either nothing but mortals or nothing but immortals, the victim must discover the specific criteria that distinguish one from another, criteria of identity that lie at the heart of all myths of sexual masquerade. Let us postpone the larger philosophical problem of human identity raised by this second group and begin instead with the first group of texts. This is a more circumscribed corpus that raises the equally important mythological and theological problem of telling a mortal lover from a masquerading god or goddess.

There is another distinction that is useful to make at the start. In most myths of this corpus, a single god impersonates a single mortal. For example, Zeus impersonates Amphitryon in order to seduce Amphitryon's wife, Alkmene, and to beget Herakles.[3] A close parallel is offered by the Hindu myth in which the god Indra impersonates the sage Gautama in order to seduce Gautama's wife, Ahalya.[4] But there is also a subcorpus of this theme in which a number of gods present themselves in a form identical to the human lover, and the victim must choose between them all. In this subgroup, the issue of individualism, already made generic by the contrast between one entire species and another, is made even more generic by the existence of a whole group of gods. The criteria of choice are correspondingly even more sharply focused on the properties of immortals in contrast with mortals.

Within this more extreme form of the identity crisis, divine lineups prevail; there are relatively few myths in which the human imposter, who is often an identical twin, proliferates into triplets or larger groups. Multiplicity, in contrast with mere doubling, seems to be primarily a divine prerogative. But multiple lineups do sometimes occur in real life. Thus, in the trial of Martin Guerre, "The commissioners arranged a theatrical test. The newcomer [the old Martin Guerre] was placed among a group of men all dressed alike. Pierre recognized his nephew, wept, and rejoiced that at last his fortune was changing."[5] But "dressed alike" hardly constitutes a convincing replication; and police lineups seldom match anything beyond the approximate size and color of the suspects. Our myths are often more subtle, though occasionally a most approximate double does the trick, as when Indra merely changes into Gautama's clothes to seduce Ahalya.[6]

III. DAMAYANTI'S DILEMMA

The paradigmatic divine lineup occurs in the story of Nala and Damayanti, first told in the *Mahabharata* and retold throughout Indian history, with many interesting variations. It is also a paradigmatic text for Western Indologists, in part because the standard Sanskrit Primer begins with it, so that the opening lines (*asid raja nala nama*, "There was a king named Nala") plays the same role in Indology that the opening lines of Caesar (*gallia omnis divisa est in partes tres*, "All Gaul is divided in three"—another myth of splitting) played for earlier generations of classicists.

It is a very long story, but the central episode may be summarized for our purposes as follows:

> Nala and Damayanti were in love, but four gods—including Indra—were also in love with Damayanti. They gave Nala the power to enter the harem unnoticed, to plead for them. As soon as he saw Damayanti, Nala's desire grew, but he mastered his love, keeping his promise to the gods. Damayanati said to him, "Who are you? You have come like an immortal. How did you

enter here unobserved?" He said, "I am Nala, and I have come here as the envoy of the gods. It is by their power that I have entered here unobserved." She bowed to the gods and said to Nala, smiling, "I am yours, and I love you." Nala said to her, "How can you want a mortal man, when the World Guardians are here? I am not worthy of the foot dust of these world-makers. Incline to them, for a mortal who displeases the gods, dies. Save me; choose the gods."

She told him that she had a plan by which no guilt would attach to him: she would choose him from among them at the ceremony at which she was to choose her husband. Nala reported to the gods, "By your power, no one saw me enter, except Damayanti. I told her about you, but she has set her heart on me, and she will choose me."

On that day, Damayanti saw five men standing there, entirely identical in appearance; any one of them she looked at seemed to her to be Nala. She wondered, "How can I know which are the gods, and which is Nala?" She remembered that she had heard, from old people, of the signs (*lingani*) of the gods, but still she saw none of them on the men standing before her. Then she prayed to the gods, by her faithfulness to Nala, begging them to point Nala out to her and to display their own forms so that she could recognize him. The gods were moved by her pitiful request, and demonstrated their divine signs. She saw all the gods without sweat, with unblinking eyes, with unwithered garlands, without dust, and standing without touching the ground, and she saw Nala revealed by his shadow, his withered garland, his dustiness and sweatiness, his blinking eyes, and his feet on the ground. She chose Nala for her husband.[7]

Damayanti recognizes her lover by the signs of his mortality, the normal human flaws that all of us share with him. She recognizes the divine impersonators by their (abnormal) lack of those signs, such as sweating.[8] The gods, however, can manipulate those signs; sometimes they have them, sometimes they do not. Here, at first, they do not, and Damayanti is ultimately able to identify her husband, not by her powers of recognition, dwelling within herself, but by virtue of her faithfulness *to him*, the ultimate power of a woman in India, which persuades them to reveal themselves to her. She knows him because she knows herself.

What is the meaning of the signs by which she recognizes the gods? Some are particularly Indian; others occur as criteria in other cultures as well. It is interesting to note a minor lapse in the text: though the gods are not said to lack shadows, Nala is said to *have* one; that gods have no shadows may have been such a truism even at this early period that shadowlessness didn't even have to be listed among their defining criteria.

As for the five main criteria, "both feet on the ground" is one of the official signs of mortality throughout the world. (Recall Achilles' heel, and the bruised heel of Eve as she leaves Eden.) But "some of these points may be uncertain, as contradicted by other accounts."[9] For instance, the garlands of the gods fade when they are frightened.[10] So too, the feet of the metaphysically gifted mortal woman Cudala do not touch the ground.[11] The blinking of the eyes is a symbol of the fact that we mortals cannot always see straight—especially in matters of the heart or groin—as well as a reference to the eyes of Brahma, each blink of which represents a night for mortals. It is also a prefiguration of that moment in which, unlike the gods, we will close our eyes forever. The *Rg Veda* says that the gods do not experience the need to close their eyes, for they never sleep.[12]

The shadow is quite a shifty indicator in mythology throughout the world. Below the simplest material level, on which the shadow is a shadow, *tout court*, is a complex symbolism which may equate the shadow with the immortal soul or the mortal soul, with death or with the mother, with the self or with the enemy of the self. Being a play of darkness and light, the shadow is therefore inextricably bound with the mythology surrounding night and day, the rising and setting of the sun, and the eye. Otto Rank spoke of "the odd representations of the double as a shadow, mirror image, or portrait, the meaningful evaluation of which we do not quite understand even though we can follow it emotionally."[13]

In European thought in general, the shadow or the mirror reflection represents precisely the *immaterial* part of the self, the immortal soul. In Christian mythology, people who have no souls have no shadows or reflections. In Bram Stoker's *Dracula*, for instance, vampires have no mirror image because they have no souls, but also because they themselves are nothing but mirror images. Nor do they cast shadows, since, like gods and fairies, they *are* shadows of other creatures. Moreover, where gods (and fairies) cast no shadows because they are made of light, vampires cast no shadows because they are creatures of darkness. Count Dracula casts no reflection in Jonathan Harker's shaving mirror.

In India, gods cast no shadows, presumably because they are made of light, like the sun. Charles Malamoud, in an article entitled, "The Gods Have No Shadows," says, "This is the weakness of the gods: they are altogether light/clear (*clairs*). When they are forced to reveal their nature, they reveal their affinity with the light of the sun: it does not change them, it does not burn them, they don't have to shelter themselves against it, and the material of their bodies does not constitute an obstacle for it that engenders (and that is indicated by) an attached shadow."[14] It is precisely this quality of light and insubstantiality that Damayanti rejects.

IV. WHY PREFER A MORTAL?

These myths of choice send several different messages. Humans are double in this respect, too: some prefer their own kind, but others prefer creatures from another world. One group of texts, typified by Damayanti, argues that the human woman prefers her mortal lover or husband; another group, typified by some variants of the Alkmene and Ahalya myth, argues that she prefers an otherworldly lover. Each of these types has its male analogue, too. The human man who longs for an otherworldly woman appears in the genre of the Swan Maiden, best known in India as the story of the goddess Urvasi and the mortal Pururavas, and best known in the West from the ballet *Swan Lake*. And the mortal man who prefers his mortal woman appears in the myth of Undine, whom the mortal man prefers only for a while but ultimately rejects, as well as in a closely related corpus of stories in which a man prefers his wife to the *demonic* female who replaces her, the myths of *succubi*. Indeed, it might almost be said that when a man prefers a human woman to a nonhuman substitute, that substitute is usually therefore *defined* as demonic—or, at least, whorish—rather than divine.

Why does the human woman, such as Damayanti, prefer her human lover? Not, presumably, for sexual reasons. Is the gods' sexuality different from ours? In most cultures it is (Siva can make love for as many years as he likes without releasing his seed),[15] though in other cultures the gods are entirely anthropomorphic in this respect.

Indeed, in general what endears the humans is not their inferiority but, rather, safety and familiarity. The clue of revelation is often a sign of intimacy, an endearing flaw that is the true trigger of love. Damayanti loves her human husband, with all his imperfections, and recognizes him by the imperfections that she loves: sweaty, blinking, earth-bound, dusty, shadowy Nala. In Hindu mythology, the gods are twenty-five years old forever.[16] To some of us over fifty, this might appear an attractive alternative; but to most of us, it would not.

Barbara Fass Leavy has commented on this peculiar pattern of women in folklore and myth who prefer mortal husbands to other-worldly suitors:

> Of primary importance is the nature of the otherworld itself, a land of dreams-come-true, where man is forever young and pleasures forever available. It is a static realm, lacking the earthly cycles of birth and death, a point worth stressing, for if the other-world is, as the Irish put it, the Land of the Living, that is, a world in which no one dies, it also appears that it is a world in which no one is born. . . . La Belle Dame sans Merci and the land in which she dwells are not creative. What they supply instead is perpetual bliss, and bliss, when it is its own end, inevitably palls.[17]

And Angela Carter, in her retelling of "Beauty and the Beast," has imagined the heroine's reasons for rejecting divine perfection when she contemplates her beast:

> I never saw a man so big look so two-dimensional. . . . He throws our human aspirations to the godlike sadly awry, poor fellow; only from a distance would you think The Beast not much different from any other man, although he wears a mask with a man's face painted most beautifully on it. Oh, yes, a beautiful face; but one with too much formal symmetry of feature to be entirely human: one profile of his mask is the mirror image of the other, too perfect, uncanny. . . .[18]

The god, who may become the mirror image of the human whom he impersonates, is himself his own mirror image, too perfect and symmetrical to be real. The mirror, which, like the shadow, is a common vehicle of a double, here takes on a new function, which is to make possible a symmetry and perfection that is inhuman.

The choice made in these stories is the choice of real life, how-ever brief, in preference to infinite nonlife, misleadingly referred to as immortality. What does this mean? What does it mean to choose death? Is this a move from Eros to Thanatos? I think not. A closely related theme is that of the *inadvertent* choice of death, a choice made as the result of a trick or a riddle. This is the point of an In-donesian myth:

> The natives of Poso, a district of Central Celebes, say that in the beginning the sky was very near the earth, and that the Cre-ator, who lived in it, used to let down his gifts to men at the end of a rope. One day he thus lowered a stone; but our first father and mother would have none of it and they called out to their Maker, "What have we to do with this stone? Give us something else." The Creator complied and hauled away at the rope; the stone mounted up and up til it vanished from sight. Presently the rope was seen coming down from heaven again, and this time there was a banana at the end of it instead of a stone. Our first parents ran at the banana and took it. Then there came a voice from heaven saying, "Because ye have chosen the banana, your life shall be like its life. When the banana-tree has offspring, the parent stem dies; so shall ye die and your children shall step into your place. Had ye chosen the stone, your life would have been like the life of the stone, changeless and immortal." The man and his wife mourned over their fatal choice, but it was too late; that is how through the eating of a banana death came into the world.[19]

They chose the banana, because it was luscious, a symbol of life, while the stone was a symbol of death. But in making this choice, they fool-ishly and unwittingly threw away their chance of being immortal, never changing, like the stone (the stone which is the curse, in Indian mythology, inflicted on those who have been too much alive). But were they in fact so foolish to choose, instead of the sterility of an eternity of stone, the luscious, phallic banana of death? Did they really make the "wrong" choice? They made the same choice that Prometheus made for mankind: the flesh, instead of the smoke.[20] So, too, Eve chose the apple, and sex, and death, a choice that made the Romantics regard Satan as the great benefactor of humankind.

This choice is not conscious in these myths; it is the result of a trick or a mistake. But a *conscious* preference for the human is what we find in the myth of Damayanti. The logic behind these apparently "wrong" choices is one that opts for a kind of continuous connectedness[21] which is our symbolic immortality, the fragile, ephemeral, conditional, dependent, emotional intensity of real life, the emotional chiaroscuro,[22] the sense of impending loss that makes what we have so precious while we have it, more precious than the security of an eternity without that immediacy and intensity.

Stepping back outside the text, for a moment, we might suggest another reason for the choice of a human lover. One of the many functions of a myth is to affirm the status quo. For instance, in addition to those myths that we have just considered, which explain why we chose death, some myths imagine what the world was like when there was no death, in order to affirm either that we must settle for what we have, or that we really would not be happy if there were no death.[23] And some folktales depict a man and woman who exchange roles for a day, the woman working in the fields, the man in the house, with hilarious and disastrous results, confirming that a woman's place is in fact in the home. In the same way, when our stories imagine that a woman might be able to make love with a god, they do so in order to encourage her to imagine that she would rather keep the human husband she has. The myths in which the woman chooses a mortal husband combine the choice of her own role with the choice of her own mortality, and thus doubly affirm the status quo.

What of those men who preferred their wives to goddesses? This is the pattern of all the stories of succubi and demonic women that we have seen. Indeed, it might almost be said that when a man prefers a human woman to a supernatural substitute, that substitute is usually therefore *defined* as demonic rather than divine, or at least as whorish rather than divine. As for rejected goddesses, famous examples are supplied by Enkidu, who rejects Ishthar, Odysseus, who rejects Calypso, and Arjuna, who rejects Urvasi.[24] Men do sometimes reject goddesses, but only when the goddess, too, is depicted as a whore, and she brings the man nothing but trouble—or, indeed, death.[25] Thus the myth of death meets itself coming in at the door, like the myth of the appointment in Samarra: women choose mortal husbands, and death, while men who choose immortal wives also, inadvertently, choose death.

V. HOW TO TELL A HUMAN FROM A GOD

The most basic sign of mortality is, of course, death. Indeed, the Four Noble Signs that appeared to the future Buddha to pre-cipitate his enlightenment were simply a sick man, an old man, a dead man, and a renouncer—three problems and their proposed solution.[26] But these signs on all other occasions appear only in the course of time, and the protagonists of our myths must look for more immediate, and generally more subtle, signs.

Some of the criteria of differentiation apply only to women. Indian texts suggest other ways out of dilemmas such as Damayanti's, ways far less dramatic than divine intervention. Descending from the divine to the banal, there is a most down-to-earth criterion in a Ben-gali story:

A ghost seized a woman and hid her in the trunk of a tree. She put on the clothes of the woman and returned to the home of her husband, a Brahmin who lived with his mother. The Brahmin thought his wife returned from the tank. . . . Next morning the mother-in-law discovered some change in her daughter-in-law. Her daughter-in-law, she knew, was constitutionally weak and languid, and took a long time to do the work of the house. But she had apparently become quite a different person. All of a sudden she had become very active. She now did the work of the house in an incredibly short time. Suspecting nothing, the mother-in-law said nothing either to her son or to her daughter-in-law; on the contrary, she only rejoiced that her daughter-in-law had turned over a new leaf.

One day she observed her daughter stretching her arm from one room to another to get something. The old woman was struck with wonder at the sight. She said nothing to her, but spoke to her son. Both mother and son began to watch her. One day she went in, and, to her infinite surprise, found that her daughter-in-law was not using any fuel for cooking, but had thrust into the oven her foot, which was blazing brightly. The old mother told her son what she had seen, and they both concluded that the young woman in the house was not his real wife but a she-ghost. Eventually the ghost was exorcized, after which the Brahmin and his wife lived many years happily together and begat many sons and daughters.[27]

The divine imposter does housework dramatically better than the mortal woman—but the mother-in-law is so pleased by this that she does not question its implications; she allows herself to be fooled. The abnormal stretching of limbs, however, is not such an attractive sign and thus begins the process of exposure. It is when the woman's foot *fails* to be injured, like the tell-tale foot that is the sign of mortality, that her supernatural status is revealed.

But cleaning the house is the normal task of the European heroine in many fairy tales and, more generally, in women's tales.[28] (See the Stith Thompson motif "N 831.1: The Mysterious Housekeeper.") Ahalya is cleaning the house when Indra comes to her in one text.[29] And the signs of domestic skills are often what distinguish the human woman from the supernatural masquerader, or else what allow the human woman to discover (and reject) her supernatural lover. In a related manner, it is often Cinderella's ability to cook a particular dish in a particular way that identifies her to the prince when she is disguised in his kitchen. And in a story from *The Arabian Nights*, the heroine recognizes her man from the way he cooks.[30]

Stith Thompson baptizes an entire motif "H 119.2: needle left in garment of husband by abducted wife as sign." A Japanese tale is a variant of this motif:

> A . . . woman thrusts a needle and thread into the clothing (serpent skin) of her mysterious nightly lover to follow him and discover his identity. She follows the thread to his daytime abode, to find a snake dead of the needle which she unwittingly had thrust into his skin.[31]

By treating the apparently human lover as a domestic partner (sewing his clothes), she inadvertently pierces the true skin of the nondomesticated demon lover. As Barbara Fass Leavy comments on the Japanese tale of the woman who unwittingly puts a needle into her snake lover, "Does the Japanese woman . . . outwit a demon or destroy her own chance for personal happiness? The Japanese tales suggest that these are not necessarily mutually exclusive possibilities."[32]

Housework is also the criterion in a Native American story in which a man must pick his wife out from a group of seemingly identical women. The characteristic that allows him to recognize her is, as Barbara Fass Leavy remarks, "a sign of her mundane and domestic life": "This one, Chief, is my wife because I recognize the tiny mark of a needle here in the center of her smallest finger."[33] Apparently the Native American gods do not sew—although in Bengal they are better housewives than some human women.

Small domestic signs are often what betray masquerading male demons, too. In a Telugu myth, a mortal who impersonates a god is unmasked when the two strip down to their underwear to fight: the mortal wears a light orange loincloth, the god a green loincloth. The god's wife knows this, and identifies her man.[34] According to the Babylonian Talmud,[35] when the demon Ashmedai took the form of Solomon, Solomon's wife noticed the difference because the demon's feet converged and he transgressed the menstrual taboo, making love to her when she was menstruating. We know the criterion of the feet from the Indian tradition and from Christian mythology. This story combines the generic aspect of feet and the specific aspect of the menstrual taboo—which in this particular context is a Jewish inspiration, the Jewish answer to a green loincloth. In the film *Maxie*, where Glenn Close plays a rather dull woman whose body is intermittently possessed by the soul of a wild, sexy movie actress flapper who died in the twenties, her puzzled husband manages to tell when it is his real wife (whom he prefers to the sexy lady) by asking her her maiden name, where she was born (Kankakee), and her social security number—just as banks and credit cards ask you to identify yourself. This is the ultimate bathos of the longing for home in the divine masquerade.

VI. THE MAN WHO COMMITTED ADULTERY WITH HIS OWN WIFE

In the Telugu story of the loincloths, the test arises because a human man has impersonated a god in order to sleep with that god's wife. But, at the same time, the man's wife has impersonated the goddess in order to sleep with the god. The two masqueraders meet, fail to recognize one another, and make love; only later do they discover that they had gone to all that trouble only to end up in bed with one another. The round trip to the marital bed via the attempted adultery is a voyage to the longed-for home via a fantastic odyssey. It is the longing for the self that can only be found via the detour of the Other.[36]

This theme of the man who commits adultery with his own wife is one of the enduring themes of world mythology. It arises when the two aspects of the sexual masquerade are collapsed together: someone wants not to be with one person and to be with another; the trickster wishes to disappear secretly from one bed in order to appear secretly in another. The wife wishes to masquerade as her husband's mistress, or the mistress as the wife; she wants to be with one man, but to be *a different woman* to that man. The story is widespread; Stith Thompson lists it as "AT 891.D: The Rejected Wife as Lover." The pattern occurs in both genders: a woman may, though much more rarely, be tricked into committing adultery with her own husband.

This myth is the inverse of myths such as the masquerade of Indra as Gautama, in which the victim thinks (wrongly) that he is with his legitimate partner; in the myths under discussion, the victim thinks (wrongly) that he is with his illegitimate partner. It is also the inverse of such masquerades as Leah for Rachel, in which the victim thinks that he is with one woman but is really with two. In the myths we are going to encounter, the victim thinks that he is with two women but is really with one. But here we encounter one of the basic variations on our chart: is another person present or not? That is, does the husband mistake his wife for a woman whom he knows and desires, or does he simply fail to recognize her as his own wife? Sometimes the wife may masquerade as a nonexistent Other Woman, as Tamar, in Genesis 38, masquerades as the harlot, where no other person is actually present; and in others she may replace another woman who does exist, as Helena masquerades as Diana in *All's Well That Ends Well*. How basic is the difference between *As You Like It*, where the woman pretends to be her nonexistent brother, and *Twelfth Night*, where she masquerades as her real brother? The key to this variant is not how many people are present but whether duality is masquerading as unity or unity is masquerading as duality.

The theme, complex as it is, attracts further complications. If the man double-crosses his wife when he sleeps with his mistress, and his wife double-double-crosses him when she substitutes for the mistress, then we may see a double-double-double-cross when a husband and wife meet by mistake in the dark, both of them presumably bent upon separate illicit assignations. This is the situation that prevails in the Telugu myth of the loincloths, and it is a favorite in Indian poetry. Here is a Telugu version:

> A married woman failed to find
> the place of rendezvous;
> she was standing there, in the dark,
> when her husband came
> and embraced her, certain
> she was someone else.
> Great was their passion
> as they made love,
> each of them thrilling to a lover
> not there, while the God of Desire
> screamed with glee.[37]

This poem is used as an example of one of a number of rationalizations for the adultery of Ahalya; this is #3, "Unconscious violation." As David Shulman comments on it: "The poet characteristically lets the violation in disguise succeed as such, without 'regressing' to a state of marital propriety. Violation is its own reward."[38] In the myth of the underwear, the tricksters only find out who they have been in bed with afterwards. In the Telugu poem, they never find out at all; only God (Kama, Eros) sees the truth, and laughs.

The relatively straightforward case of the man who simply double-crosses his chaste wife, who impersonates her husband's mistress, flourishes in Indian literature, with and without variants. In a Sanskrit play composed by King Harsa c. 750 A.D., called *Priyadarsika*, a king falls in love with a young woman in his court, much to his queen's distress. To renew their dying passion, the queen stages a play about their courtship, casting the young girl in the role of herself, the queen; but, unknown to her, the king takes the place of the woman playing *his* role, and uses this as an opportunity to make love to the girl right under the queen's nose. He impersonates himself.

One of the most famous instances of the story in English literature, Shakespeare's *All's Well That Ends Well*, is based upon a Sanskrit text, which found its way to him via Islam and Boccaccio. At the end of the play, when the king asks Helena if it is really she (he thought she was dead), Helena replies, "No, good lord, 'Tis but the shadow of a wife you see, the name and not the thing." The shadow of a wife indeed: in pretending to be Diana, she has become her own shadow, and is recognized only in the dark. The theme that Shakespearean scholars christened "the bed trick" also occurs in *Measure for Measure*, and in Mozart's *Marriage of Figaro*, in which the Countess, knowing that the Count has an assignation with her maid, Susanna, takes Susanna's place. When the Count makes love to "Susanna," he is making love to a woman, the Countess, who is masquerading as herself—as the wife of her husband.

VII. CONCLUSION: WOMEN IMPERSONATING WOMEN, MEN IMPERSONATING MEN

For very different sorts of reasons, people often masquerade as themselves in sexual situations, especially in stories about sexual situations. The wives who impersonate themselves in bed are seldom in search of sexual pleasure, as are the men who impersonate themselves. Often, the women do it in order to fulfill a bet or to get a child—usually two sides of the same coin. Sometimes the man does not recognize his wife until she dresses in the clothing of his mistress. Only then, perhaps, does she become an erotic object to him, someone who catches his attention long enough for him to notice who she is. But often he cannot recognize her when she plays the whore precisely because he cannot imagine her as an erotic partner.

Often these masquerades involve gender. Richard Strauss's *Rosenkavalier*, in many ways a variation on *The Marriage of Figaro*, takes up another theme of the Mozart opera: the masquerade of the page, Cherubino, as a young girl. Since the part of Cherubino is in fact written for a woman's voice, the situation requires a woman to pretend to be a man pretending to be a woman; in the Strauss opera, the Marshallin's lover, Oktavian, is situated on the same cusp between the true woman singer and the "fake" impersonated girl. The inverse of this situation recurs in Shakespeare, in *As You Like It* and *Twelfth Night*, where male actors play women playing men. A further twist occurs in *As You Like It*, in which a male actor plays Rosalind playing Ganymede. In one scene, Ganymede pretends to be Rosalind, so that a male actor is playing a woman playing a man playing (the same woman).

Oscar Wilde remarked, in *The Importance of Being Ernest*, that it is every woman's tragedy that she comes to resemble her mother, and every man's tragedy that he doesn't. Underlying his characteristic wit is an equally characteristic insight into some of the messier human problems, including, in this case, aging and homosexuality. Angela Carter takes Wilde's insight and runs with it, in a conversation between her twin sisters, now old and making themselves young with makeup: "'It's every woman's tragedy,' said Nora, as we contemplated our painted masterpieces, 'that, after a certain age, she looks like a female impersonator.' Mind you, we've known some lovely female impersonators, in our time. 'What's every man's tragedy, then?' I wanted to know. 'That *he* doesn't, Oscar,' she said."[39]

Marge Garber recalls that when Gloria Steinem was given a 1973 award from Harvard's Hasty Pudding (a prize often given to cross-dressed actors and actresses, as Hasty Pudding specializes in drag shows), she remarked, "I don't mind drag—women have been female impersonators for some time."[40] And Garber comments: "The social critique performed by transvestite magazines for readers who are not themselves cross-dressers is to point out the degree to which *all* women cross-dress as women when they produce themselves as artifacts."[41]

It could be argued, and indeed has been argued, that every woman is, like Pandora, masquerading as herself. And although men may masquerade as *individual* men, the feminist claim is that women as a group have been forced to impersonate themselves. Over sixty-five years ago, in 1929, Joan Riviere published her article on "Womanliness as Masquerade." In our day, Elaine Showalter has argued that "the detour through transvestism finally makes clear that 'womanliness' is the putting on of veils, only masquerading in feminine guise."[42] In fact, among the women who dressed as men and were interviewed by Holly Devor,[43] "two women reported that when they wore dresses, makeup, and jewelry, people thought that they were transvestite men wearing women's clothing." For one, "there was a rumor going around . . . that she was a male-to-female transsexual. . . . She found these mistakes ironic and daunting, considering that in the past she had wanted very much to be a man and that at the time of these mistakes she had finally accepted that she was, and would remain, female." Another remarked, "I suppose I could wear dresses, but then I think I would just look like a man dressed in drag. . . . If I dress up and put on high heels, or makeup, or things like that, they will call me madame. But I'm not going to be a transvestite to myself."[44]

The longing for perfect feminine beauty is a mythological problem. As Yeats put it:

> If I make the lashes dark
> And the eyes more bright
> And the lips more scarlet
> Or ask if all be right
> From mirror to mirror,
> No vanity's displayed:
> I'm looking for the face I had
> Before the world was made.[45]

But this is not merely a feminist problem. Though in the West at present women construct themselves more artificially than men, men have their masquerades too (ties being the one quasi-phallic emblem that the conservative dressers have left); and in earlier periods in the West men's costumes were more elaborate than women's (think of the French court in the eighteenth century, and all those wigs), a situation that also pertains in many other parts of the world to this day. In East Africa, where men rather than women have the privilege of ostentatious costume, the response to the arrival of European women with their jewels and skirts was imitation, but cross-imitation: the men, rather than the women, started wearing skirts. Indeed, if anatomy is destiny, then we need only look to the animal kingdom to see that the male may not be deadlier than the female, but is usually a snappier dresser—think of the peacocks and the stags. But then, to the extent that anatomy is *not* destiny, that men and women are not (merely) peacocks and deer, we do construct ourselves, which is to say that we all masquerade not merely as our own multiple personalities, but in a broader sense as our own genders, and in some cases as other genders.

The mask frees the true self, lures it out of its repression, creates a safe-house for it to live in. Even outside the stage and the page, people masquerade as themselves. The sexual selves nest within one another like so many Russian dolls; one by one we peel them off, only to discover that the innermost doll is the same as the doll on the outside. Our masquerades are driven by the longing for the self who existed "before the world was made."

NOTES

1. Salman Rushdie, *The Wizard of Oz* (London: British Film Institute, 1992), p. 57.

2. Ibid.

3. Charles E. Passage and James H. Mantinband, trans., *Amphitryon: Three Plays in New Verse Translation (Plautus, Moliere, Kleist), Together with a Comprehensive Account of the Evolution of the Legend and Its Subsequent History on the Stage* (Chapel Hill, N.C.: University of North Carolina Press, 1974).

4. *Ramayana of Valmiki* (Baroda, 1960–75), 1.47–48, trans. Wendy Doniger O'Flaherty, *Hindu Myths* (Harmondsworth: Penguin Books, 1975), pp. 94–96.

5. Nathalie Zemon Davis, *The Return of Martin Guerre* (Cambridge, Mass: Harvard University Press, 1983), p. 85.

6. *Ramayana* 1.47.

7. *Mahabharata* (Poona: 1933–69), 3.52–54.

8. Sweating is the crucial criterion in a very different sort of text, the film *Total Recall*: when Arnold Schwarzenegger is told that he is merely a dream double of his true self, he sees through the illusion by noting a drop of sweat on the man making the argument (a man who claims to be, also, an illusion); evidently, illusory doubles, like gods, don't sweat.

9. Edward Washburn Hopkins, *Epic Mythology* (1915; reprint ed., Wiesbaden, 1968), p. 57.

10. *Ramayana* 1.30.37.

11. *Yogavasitha-maharamayana* 6.85–106 (Bombay, 1918). See my translation and discussion in Wendy Doniger O'Flaherty, *Dreams, Illusion, and Other Realities* (Chicago: University of Chicago Press, 1984), p. 281.

12. *Rg Veda* (London, 1890–92) 2.27.9 and 10.10.8–9. See Wendy Doniger O'Flaherty, *The Rig Veda* (Harmondsworth: Penguin Books, 1981), pp. 247-49.

13. Otto Rank, *The Double: A Psychoanalytic Study*, trans. and ed. Harry Tucker, Jr. (New York: New American Library, 1971), p. 48.

14. Charles Malamoud, "Les dieux n'ont pas d'ombre: Remarzues sur la langue secrète des dieux dans l'Inde ancienne" in *Cuire le monde: rite et pensée dans l'inde ancienne* (Paris: éditions la Découverte, 1989), p. 242.

15. See Wendy Doniger O'Flaherty, *Siva: The Erotic Ascetic* (London and Oxford: Oxford University Press, 1973).

16. *Ramayana* 3.4.14.

17. Barbara F. Fass, *La Belle Dame sans Merci and the Aesthetics of Romanticism* (Detroit: Wayne State University Press, 1974), p. 35.

18. Angela Carter, "The Tiger's Bride," in *The Bloody Chamber and Other Stories* (London: Victor Gollancz, 1979; Harmondsworth: Penguin Books, 1981), p. 53.

19. A. C. Krujit, quoted in Sir James George Frazer, *The Belief in Immortality* (London, 1913), 1:74.

20. Hesiod, *Works and Days* and *Theogony*.

21. This evocative phrase was suggested by Robert J. Lifton, personal communication, July 27, 1993.

22. This lovely phrase was coined by the singer Phyllis Curtin, in her response to the first version of this paper as presented to the Boston University Institute for Philosophy and Religion on April 12, 1995.

23. See Wendy Doniger O'Flaherty, *The Origins of Evil in Hindu Mythology* (Berkeley: University of California Press, 1976), chaps. 7, "The Birth of Death," and 8, "Crowds in Heaven."

24. See Wendy Doniger O'Flaherty, *Women, Androgynes, and Other Mythical Beasts* (Chicago: University of Chicago Press, 1980).

25. See Paul Friedrich, *The Meaning of Aphrodite* (Chicago: University of Chicago Press, 1978).

26. See O'Flaherty, *Dreams, Illusion, and Other Realities*, chap. 4.

27. Lal Behari Day, *Folk Tales of Bengal* (London: Macmillan, 1885), p. 198.

28. See A. K. Ramanujan, "Towards a Counter-System: Women's Tales," in *Gender, Discourse, and Power in South Asia*, ed. A. Appadurai et al. (Philadelphia: University of Pennsylvania Press), pp. 33–35.

29. *Padma Purana*, Anandasrama Sanskrit Series no. 131 (Poona, 1893), 1.56.15–53.

30. Muhsin Mahdi, ed., and Husain Haddawy, trans., "The Two Viziers," in *The Arabian Nights* (New York: W. W. Norton, 1990), pp. 157–206.

31. Keigo Seki, "The Spool of Thread: A Subtype of the Japanese Serpent-Bridegroom Tale," in *Studies in Japanese Folklore*, ed. Richard M. Dorson (Bloomington, Ind.: Indiana University Press, 1963), p. 284.

32. Barbara Fass Leavy, *In Search of the Swan Maiden: A Narrative on Folklore and Gender* (New York and London: New York University Press, 1994), p. 103.

33. Richard M. Dorson, *Folktales Told Around the World* (Chicago: University of Chicago Press, 1975), p. 266.

34. Wendy Doniger, "The Criteria of Identity in a Telugu Myth of Sexual Masquerade," in *Festschrift for V. Narayana Rao*, ed. David Shulman (New York: Oxford University Press, 1995).

35. Gittin tract p. 77.

36. See Wendy Doniger O'Flaherty, *Other Peoples' Myths: The Cave of Echoes* (New York: Macmillan, 1988; Chicago: University of Chicago Press, 1995).

37. *Ahalyasankrandanmu* 3, p. 129, cited by David Shulman, with Velcheru Narayana Rao and Sanjay Subrahmanyam, *Symbols of Substance: Court and State in Nayaka Period Tamil Nadu* (Delhi: Oxford University Press, 1992), p. 157.

38. Shulman, *Symbols of Substance*, p. 157.

39. Angela Carter, *Wise Children* (New York: Farrar Straus Giroux, 1991), p. 192.

40. Marjorie Garber, *Vested Interests: Cross-Dressing and Cultural Anxiety* (New York and London: Routledge, 1992), p. 65.

41. Ibid., p. 49.

42. Elaine Showalter, *Sexual Anarchy: Gender and Culture at the Fin de Siècle* (New York: Penguin Books, 1990), p. 168.

43. Holly Devor, *Gender Blending: Confronting the Limits of Duality* (Bloomington, Ind.: Indiana University Press, 1989), p. 119.

44. Ibid., p. 129.

45. William Butler Yeats, "Before the World Was Made."

Home and Zakhor—Remember![1]

ALFRED I. TAUBER

WHEN I WAS NO OLDER *than five, my father took me to a Yom Kippur service. We went to a small synagogue, actually a converted store front, which was crowded with men either sitting uncomfortably on wooden folding chairs or standing cramped together. There was no room for a little boy to explore. I stood next to my father, pinned between him and towering figures looming all around us. It was hot and humid, and the air was rank. But the room was brightly lit and there was an extraordinary energy expressed by the chanting. As the service was drawing to a close, night having fallen, the intensity seemed to grow. Some men began shouting, imploring with gestures, others quietly moaned, and some were simply silent. A few were softly crying and one was sobbing. Although I could not understand their prayers, I knew each was asking God's forgiveness. I also knew they were afraid. I could feel the immediacy of their fears. My father was lost in his private thoughts and would not speak to me. He only squeezed my hand tightly. Although there was nowhere to go, I would not have dared to move. I too was frightened, but more, I was awed.*

Since then, in over forty years of wandering, I have often recalled that closeness, the sense of the community enveloping me. More, I reflect on an innocence and intensity of feeling, which seems long lost, but nevertheless remains with me. Although of another place and time, it is in many respects more real than my present.

I wish to explore this Memory as the true Home of Jewish experience, expressed in a biblical context. Although I believe that this is a universal message, I will not explore that possibility here. The second caveat is that I make no pretense at being philosophical in seeking to *analyze* Memory or Home. I will be satisfied with a metaphorical description of Home as I know it. I am well aware that I am, in a profound

148

sense, both enveloped by and estranged from the biblical experience within which I attempt to describe my Memory. In this regard, I identify closely with the tension plaguing the Bible translation project of Martin Buber and Franz Rosenzweig. They were preoccupied with the poetic and philological demands of this work, but "translation" was more than rendering the Hebrew into German. They recognized that their work was an attempt to infuse spirituality back into the lives of their secularized brethren, who had forgotten not only the Hebrew, but the Bible's religious meaning. This was a consequence of *religion* becoming only one of our academic disciplines or our Departments of Life. As Buber wrote, religion

> is not a life-encompassing whole, and cannot on the basis of its present status become one; it cannot lead us to unity, because it has itself fallen into disunity, has accommodated itself to this dichotomy [sacred and profane] of our existence. Religion would itself have to return to reality before it could have a real effect on people today. But religion has always been reality only when it has been fearless—when it has taken upon itself the whole concreteness of reality, has signed nothing away as belonging by right to some other agent. . . .[2]

Despite this insight, they persisted, knowing that they might only approximate the Word, for those who might *read* still could not *hear*. Gershom Scholem correctly observed that their translation was "utopian" because in stretching the limits of language, they sought one language for one world.[3] I suspect they recognized that in reaching for that ideal they would fail, but their project was a deeply personal and religious authentication, of which one aspect is close to my own theme. Enlightened Jews, I dare profess, universally suffer a profound existential crisis concerning not only their place in the Diaspora, but, more profoundly, their place in history.[4] Here are the roots of my essay: I wish to explore how memory and history assume a distinctive Jewish character, and how home serves as a versatile and effective metaphor for that understanding. Further, I wish to indicate the limits of "translating" that experience either religiously or philosophically. Finally, in my own fashion, I wish to embrace Buber's project by recognizing that while we seek to translate our deepest spiritual experience into consciousness, this attempt to bridge an immense chasm leaves us groping for that which cannot be spoken.

I

> A wandering Aramean was my father, and he went down into
> Egypt, and sojourned there, few in number; and he became there
> a nation, great, mighty, and populous. And the Egyptians dealt ill
> with us, and afflicted us, and laid upon us hard bondage. And we
> cried unto the Lord, the God of our fathers, and the Lord heard
> our voice, and saw our affliction, and our toil, and our oppression.
> And the Lord brought us forth out of Egypt with a mighty hand,
> and with an outstretched arm, and with great terribleness, and
> with signs and with wonders. And He has brought us into this
> place, and given us this land, a land flowing with milk and honey.
> (Deut. 26:5–9)

This text, read at the Passover seder, concisely and with great
clarity summarizes biblical Jewish experience. But it is as spiritual
Memory, and not as secular, scientific history, that these words attain
their power and truth. The distinction lies at several levels of interpretation, but the most salient is that history as the objective repository
of the past is a different species from Memory, which is personal and
profoundly subjective. Arising from this fundamental subjectivity,
Memory assumes a spiritual dimension that is lacking in scientific history. Thus, Memory and Home are intimately intertwined, connected
at the deepest wellsprings of our psyche. Home in this formulation also
becomes a spiritual metaphor, and the vehicle of my Memory.

So Memory as invoked here is spiritual memory, and thus ex-
cludes the memory of everyday experience, the legal testament, the
political, social, economic history of a culture as usually construed, the
psychoanalytic reconstruction, the cognitive and neurophysiological investigations that attempt to account for recollection and its narratives,
to name the most obvious. In this sense, I am even eschewing the autobiographical. This focused account of Memory, namely, *to remember*,
seeks our deepest spiritual identities, fashioned in time. To remember
is to ask who we are, ultimately. Home is a metaphor for that identity.

We begin with the Jewish admonition, *Zakhor*—"Remember!"[5]
The fundamental relation of the Jew to the past, specifically to the original Covenant and to the Exodus from Egypt, dramatically illustrates
the primacy of historical memory for Jewish spirituality. Whether there
are unique elements to Jewish tradition in this regard, as some have
argued,[6] is not my concern here. I am simply stating an existential reli-

gious fact: integral to Jewish religious experience is the centrality of memory as the key component in defining one's relation to God, and in the process, defining oneself spiritually.

The essential point of course is that, being Jewish, I identify with the spiritual wasteland of the Wanderer. From the Jewish perspective, the current exile, the one that has lasted almost two millennia, is the result of the Roman destruction of the Jerusalem Temple in 70 C.E. The resulting Diaspora led the Jews to scatter into foreign lands and long for their redemption in the return. The exile reiterated the recurrent crisis decried by each of the prophets since Moses, namely, that the Jews were undeserving of God's bounty precisely because they had forgotten (or ignored) the Covenant. Beyond the human suffering endured by the exiled Jew, there is a spiritual aspect that must be explained, namely, that of God's own exile. This is a second and even more calamitous consequence of Jewish erring. With the destruction of the Temple, not only were the Jews enslaved and dispersed, but God lost his Dwelling Place.

Jewish lore ascribes the *Shekinah*, or Divine Presence, as the numinous immanence of God in the world. In some sense, this is the personification of the Divine in a worldly context, although the term is used only figuratively, as, for example, "After the Lord your God shall ye walk . . ." (Deut. 13:5), or " . . . the earth did shine with his Glory" (Ezek. 43:2) in reference to the Shekinah as light. The term *Shekinah*, derived from the Hebrew "the act of dwelling," does not appear in the Bible, yet the concept of a female attribute to God's maleness has a rich development in the Talmudic period and constitutes an important element in kabbalistic descriptions of the Divine as dwelling with us. For example, the notion of the Jewish people in spiritual union with the Shekinah was a popular interpretation of the Song of Songs. The Jew's exile is thus paralleled by the wandering of the nation's soulmate, the Shekinah, so that the lost homeland is only the worldly manifestation of a spiritual crisis. In other words, what is most obviously depicted as the disarray of Jewish nationalistic aspirations is fundamentally a religious disaster. We are left to live in a world bereft of divine presence and guidance.[7] The Shekinah is a profound image, articulating that lost peace we recall when God resided with us and representing the aspired-to resolution of our spiritual dysfunction.

In Jewish tradition, the lost Home, the destroyed Jerusalem, was to be restored upon the return of God to his Dwelling as the messianic mission of a reinstated King. This eventual return was viewed as a religious certainty, and codification of current and future legal doctrine accounted for this eventuality. For instance, the twelfth-century Jewish philosopher Moses ben Maimon (Maimonides) predicted as a tenet of faith that

> King Messiah will arise and restore the kingdom of David to its former state and original sovereignty. He will rebuild the sanctuary and gather the dispersed of Israel. All the ancient laws will be reinstated in his days. . . .[8]

It is important to understand that the codification of Jewish law pronounced by Maimonides did not make one set of precepts for the present era and another for the future messianic period. Each was part of an organic whole, representing only different phases of Jewish history.[9] This view naturally arises from a spiritual sense of history, which, in contrast to our modern notions, "is a chronicle about religion . . . not the record of terrestrial events. Periodization of history is constructed according to the evolution of faith, not political independence or loss of sovereignty."[10] Despite the assurance of divine restoration, the Jew in exile remains forlorn. Yehudah Halevi, writing in the same period as Maimonides, accurately captured this sentiment, still felt by observant Jews today, when he wrote:

> The Jewish People today is like a body without either head or heart. It is more correct to say that Jewry today is not even a body, because in reality we are only scattered limbs, such as the "dry bones" which Ezekiel saw in his vision (Ezek. 37).[11]

> Ever since our heart, the Holy Temple, was destroyed, we have been lost. When it is restored we too will be restored, regardless of the size or strength of our population, or the character of our political leadership.[12]

These messianic yearnings of course date from that catastrophic destruction, and are expressed in all current liturgies composed from the time of the earliest dispersion until our very day. For instance, the daily central prayer includes, "Raise the banner to gather our exiles and speedily gather us together from the four corners of the earth to our Land" to again receive God in Jerusalem. "Your city, may You return in compassion, and may You rest within it, as You have spoken. May You rebuild it soon in our days as an eternal structure." This is not the expression of only the devotedly religious, for the centrality of this theme was transformed by their nineteenth-century secular Zionist brethren, who chose to dispense with the religious observance altogether and build on Jewish nationhood alone. In each case, the metaphor of returning to a lost home was dominant.

I learned of the spiritual dimension of delayed messianism only as a adult, and I doubt that my vehemently anti-Hasidic parents even knew the rudiments of kabbalistic lore related to it. But the essential lesson of our nation's fate was transmitted directly in our family history, and as a child, I appreciated the emotional dimension profoundly. As a first-generation American, I learned at an early age of the seemingly endless migration of my family: with vague origins in the Spanish Inquisition of 1492, my mother's ancestors sought refuge in Central Europe. Her father, having left his Hungarian farm village in 1905, made his fortune in Berlin, and returned to Budapest with the ascendence of Hitler. There he felt safe, citing the four-hundred-year history of his ancestors amongst the Magyars, only to be rounded up in the Budapest ghetto of 1944 to die a broken man. On my father's side, direct lineage is traced to the eighteenth century, where Aaron Tauber, a well-known rabbi, scion of "ten generations of sages," sought elusive tolerance in Moravia, Germany, and Hungary. Wandering from one shtetl to another, he eventually spent his last years in Dunaszerdahely, where we have records that he and my maternal great-great-great-grandfather studied Jewish mystical texts together.[13] Eventually their distant progeny married and moved to the cosmopolitan metropolis to seek their fortune and to pursue emancipation from the confines of religious orthodoxy. And their children in turn, completing the secularization so commonplace in that culture, hardly recalled their origins as they attended the university and became cultured. The great irony of course was in the realization that there was no escape, some dying in the camps, others in the final days of the war in the ghetto. The lesson was well taught: there is no Home, no land of security. We are in exile.

II

Let there be no confusion concerning the uniqueness of the Jew's journey. It is no Odyssey. To be sure, leaving home to wander in the world, to encounter the alien and the dangerous, and finally to return is a renewal cycle that reaches into the wellspring of human existence. As Joseph Campbell describes it in *The Hero with a Thousand Faces*, the Ulysses of diverse cultures embarks on a quest in a universal psychological expedition of maturation, and by reaching into the world, breaks the juvenile bonds of home.[14] The power of the narrative—and Campbell found this myth in all cultures—resides in the evocation that allows identification with the hero, for each of us not only has experienced that adventure, but is powerless to resist it. To traverse the divide between home and the world is in large measure to define ourselves. No wonder that the diverse psychoanalytic theories of Freud, Jung, Erich Neumann, Melanie Klein, and others explicitly formulated hypotheses of individuation based on such myths. Although this view of home, as repository of our childhood, a place we must leave, serves a crucial function in our personal maturation, it is not the same metaphor constructed for the Dwelling Place of the Shekinah. In this latter view, Home is the object of the Jews' spiritual quest, their reunion with God.

Another distinction must be made from the Christian image of the Wandering Jew, which has different origins and a different moral lesson, one of punishment for a different kind of transgression. It begins with the tale of the Jerusalemite, who, when Jesus was carrying the cross, drove him away from resting at his doorstep: "Walk faster!" and Jesus replied, "I go, but you will walk until I come again!"[15] The key elements of the legend are encapsulated here: there will be an indefinite exile that knows no rest, a just punishment for a supreme insult, namely, the indignity of denying the legitimacy of the Savior. Henceforth, the Jew, like Cain, will be marked. There were of course many variations. In a thirteenth-century account of Bolognese origin, the Jew, repentant of his deed, converts to Christianity and leads an ascetic life while enduring his punishment. In the seventeenth century a chapbook was printed in Germany which accentuated the anti-Jewish implications of the legend: Ahasuerus (a cant name for Jew) appears in 1542 at a church in Hamburg and recites his historical fate of wandering. He laments, as the personification of the Jewish people, the guilt of the crucifixion, the condemnation to eternal suffering until Jesus' second coming, and the bearing of witness to the truth of Christianity. The legend had a vivid literary history in the nineteenth century and remains a poignant image in recent depictions.[16]

Interestingly, the universal ethical transgression of inhumane treatment of one's neighbor is also invoked by the rabbis to explain the destruction of the Temple. This same insensitivity apparently marked Jerusalem's conduct in that period and engendered divine wrath, resulting in the same outcome, to wander endlessly. But the Jewish orientation derives from the relationship between God and Jews, centered on the issue of maintaining the Covenant. For the Christian, the theme, richly developed during medieval and modern times, pertains to Jewish denial of Christian messianism, and thus emanates from the strained relation of Jew and Christian. The power of the resultant image, which may be only a caricature, nevertheless captures the desperation and forlorn state of the Jew ripped away from his home. Cast out among strangers, to roam seemingly without end, the Wandering Jew assumes different connotations from Jewish and Christian perspectives. Vilified and persecuted, the retributive aspects of punishment are emphasized in the latter case. In the Jewish context, the more important issue is the contrite condition of being in exile from divine favor, and perhaps more profoundly, sharing in God's loss. The parallel wandering of the Shekinah dramatically depicts God's own yearning for spiritual unity with his creation and his people.[17] It is from this latter perspective that Home achieves its spiritual locus.

III

For me to identify with the Wandering Jew is to place myself in spiritual history, in the unveiling of God's project. God is recognized through the faculty of Memory. For the rabbinic sages, the Bible not only was a repository of past history, but served as a guide to God's purpose.[18] And God is known only insofar as he reveals himself "historically." But this "faith history" or *heilsgeschichte* (Bultmann) is on a deeper spiritual level than scientific, secular *historie*. The Bible is concerned with the way historical events in Jewish life become part of this "faith history." For instance, when God declares himself in the First Commandment, he does so as the divine presence in history: "I am the Lord thy God, who brought you out of the land of Egypt, out of the house of bondage" (Exod. 20:2). Moses addresses the Hebrew slaves not in the name of the Creator of Heaven and Earth, but as the God of the fathers, the God of history:

> Go and assemble the elders of Israel and say to them: the Lord
> the God of your fathers, the God of Abraham, Isaac, and Jacob
> has appeared to me and said: I have surely remembered you. . . .
> (Exod. 3:16)

And after the Hebrews had received God's commandments and wandered in the desert for forty years, Moses again admonished them on
the dawn of their conquest of Canaan:

> I make this covenant, with its sanctions, not with you alone, but
> both with those who are standing here with us this day before
> the Lord our God, and also with those who are not with us here
> this day. (Deut. 29:13–14)

In other words, with me. These passages emphasize the two cardinal
tenets of Zakhor—reciprocal remembrance between God and human
beings, and biblical history continuing into the present, as the covenant
is renewed with each individual.

Perhaps the richest liturgical source for this reciprocal function
of Jewish remembrance is found in the Rosh Hashana service. This
Day of Judgment, observed at the New Year, is punctuated by the
command to remember, not only to recall one's personal transgres-
sions and to ask forgiveness, but to celebrate divine creation. The
Babylon Talmud invokes the following prescription:

> The Holy One, Blessed is He, said ". . . on Rosh Hashana recite
> before Me [verses that speak of God's] Sovereignty, Remem-
> brance [of all events], and Shofar blasts: . . . Sovereignty so that
> you should make Me your King; Remembrance so that your re-
> membrance should rise up before Me for [your] benefit." (*Rosh
> Hashana* 16a, 34b)

Thus, Jews plead for God to remember them, for it is in this recall of
the original Covenant that Jews appeal to God's mercy. In the service
itself, a repeated refrain asserts the primacy of remembrance:

> Our God and the God of our forefathers, may there arise . . . the
> remembrance and consideration of ourselves; the remembrance
> of our forefathers; the remembrance of the Messiah . . . the re-
> membrance of Jerusalem . . . the remembrance of your entire
> people, the Family of Israel . . . on the Day of Remembrance.[19]

And later, because of divine mastery of Memory, namely the original
covenant, God will display his everlasting mercy:

You remember the deeds done in the universe and You recall
the creatures fashioned since earliest times. Before You all
hidden things are revealed . . . for there is no forgetfulness
before Your Throne of Glory. . . . You remember everything
ever done. . . . You bring about a decreed time of remembrance
for every spirit and soul to be recalled, for abundant deeds and
a multitude of creatures without limit to be remembered. . . .
And through your servants, the Prophets, the following is written: Go and proclaim in the ears of Jerusalem, saying: "So said
God: I remember for your sake the kindness of your youth, the
love of your bridal days, how you followed Me in the Wilderness
in an unknown land." And it is said: "But I will remember My
covenant with you of the days of your youth, and I will establish
for you an everlasting covenant."[20]

Thus, to remember is a religious act, encompassing a central
tenet of Jewish belief. To recall the Covenant and the Exodus is to
recognize the special relationship of Jews to their God, and it is by
remembering that Jews renew that relationship. When Tevya, in *Fiddler on the Roof,* sings "Tradition," he evokes not only the centuries of
religious observance and social contract; he reaches into the depths
of Jewish experience to elicit the fundamental character of his being.
It is a matter not so much of cultural behavior as of spiritual identity.

I have already alluded to the critical distinction between *history* as developed in Greek and later Western thought, and the Jewish
sense of history and Memory. Some critics have argued, I believe
persuasively, that as Jewish historiography has developed in the post-
Enlightenment, the very character of the Jew as defined by Zakhor is
threatened.[21] The various reform challenges to religious orthodoxy
questioned the authenticity of a history defined exclusively by religious
traditions and mandates. The broadening of Jewish history to include
a complex cultural orientation, a new kind of religious rationalization
based on an Enlightenment scientific ethos, presented a very different
account of religious development. In the process, Jewish identity was
revolutionized:

The Halakist [interpreter of Jewish law] disappeared or lost his
hold on the community but the theologists were slow to assume
the roles that had been allotted them. . . . Instead, Judaism fell
into the hands of historians who described the events of the past
and reinterpreted them historically. Then along came the phi-

losophers with their interpretation of Judaism as a system of beliefs, a *weltanschauung*. Historians and philosophers alike were
however unable to offer a direct guide as to what was obligatory
observance or essential beliefs.[22]

This secularization of Jewish history (the historiography championed
by the *Wissenschaft des Judentums* movement of the nineteenth century) spawned a new kind of ethnic identity, one firmly embedded in
the Western tradition. Zakhor thus became confused with scientific,
secular history.

But I am less concerned with further accounting for this evolution of a secularized identity now found in most of the Jewish community than I am in an attempt to discern the profound lesson to be
learned from Zakhor, which should not simply be dismissed as dis-
credited history. This view of the past is not scientific history, for
Zakhor did not develop from modern aspirations of an "objective"
account of events. Zakhor arises from another realm altogether. And
as an explicit spiritual project, the events are "true" in a sense best
articulated by Franz Rosenzweig:

> The Jewish people does not count years according to a system
> of its own. For neither the memory of its history nor the years
> of office of its law-givers can become a measure of time. That is
> because the memory of its history does not form a point fixed
> in the past, a point which, year after year, becomes increasingly
> past. It is a memory which is really not past at all, but eternally
> present. Every single member of this community is bound to
> regard the exodus from Egypt as if he himself had been one of
> those to go. . . . And so the chronology of this people cannot be a
> reckoning of its own time, for the people is timeless; it has no
> time of its own. I must count years according to the years the
> world exists. And so . . . this people is denied a life in time for the
> sake of life in eternity.[23]

Heretofore, I have emphasized how Zakhor focuses on the
past, and now we must complete outlining its deepest constructions as
an ethical mandate pointing toward the future. By enunciating and
repeatedly declaring the human relation to God found in Jewish history, the Jew fulfills the essential moral nature of Zakhor. To remember *now*, which is basically an ethical mandate, we answer the original

covenant with its messianic promise.[24] So Rosenzweig illuminates a profound paradox: In Judaism, time has no normal reckoning, no past as normally understood; the Jew has traded finite time for eternity, by accepting the moral imperative of Zakhor.

Remembering the past as the present fulfills God's mandates, whose reward is a future messianic age. In the process, as the neo-Kantian Hermann Cohen observed, temporality assumes a novel character:

> Time becomes future and only future. Past and present submerge in this time of the future. This return to time is the purest idealization. . . . The Greeks never had this thought of a history that has the future as its content.[25]

And furthermore, Cohen regarded this Jewish construction of history as having a "future" (with its moral imperative) as Judaism's crucial gift to humanity:

> The concept of history is a creation of the prophetic idea. . . . What the Greek intellect could not achieve, monotheism succeeded in carrying out. History is in the Greek consciousness identical with knowledge simply. Thus, history for the Greek is and remains directed only toward the past. In opposition, the prophet is the seer, not the scholar. To see, however, is to gaze. . . . The prophets are the idealists of history. Their vision begot the concept of history as the being of the future.[26]

For Cohen, time has become a Neoplatonic ideal form, where only the future holds the full realization of humanity. More to the point, time has become a moral category, and thus history is personalized.

For the Jew, Zakhor explicitly delineates the singular relation with God, demanding that the spiritual be constructed from one's most personal being, both as part of the collective community, and also in the domain of personal identity. We are cast from our past, and we can escape neither its effects and consequences nor its lingering determinism. The past shapes us, and in turn we reconstruct the past to fashion ourselves in the present.[27] And we do so with a particular moral imperative. It is in this complex dialectic that we *become*. We cannot simply *be* in the present and ignore past events, as sometimes recalled or laxly referred-to neutral influences on our lives. Zakhor demands that we recognize the presence of the past, not only for particular moral demands, but for the crucial functions it commands in articulating our deepest character.[28] This particular sense of remembrance commands special attention. Memory, as I am describing it, is fundamentally personal. It is not subject to rational or scientific scrutiny without distorting it into something else. That is why the uses of memory in each of its everyday connotations leave us with a linguistic snarl. There is Zakhor, and then there is memory in all of its other guises. But I will further suggest that there is a deep philosophical conundrum facing us in defining Memory and its experience. To that issue we will now briefly turn.

IV

Memory is creative; we do not recall Home as we might remember the particulars of a lecture heard last week, nor the sequence of events that led to a car accident, each of which is problematic in its own right. We know each of these common memories are reconstructed with varying degrees of extraneous, if not false, supplements to fill out the experience and give it coherence.[29] The Memory of Home is of a different kind altogether.

When Steven Spielberg's homely yet charming extraterrestrial creature points to the heavens and moans to his young interlocutor, "E.T., home," we immediately empathize. E.T. is poignantly humanized, and the director has achieved the cathartic moment of the movie. Each of us is immediately drawn into the universal drama of returning to our Home. There is home, where we live, hopefully content and comfortable, and then there is the other Home, the sense of another place from which we originate and where we fully belong. This is a spiritual locale. E.T. pointed to the heavens, and well he might, because that Home is distant and far, far away. For each of us it resides in a deep recess of our memory, unarticulated but deeply felt. As we wander in the world, we recognize that the original hearth, that source of unity, integration, completeness, is forever lost, but we continuously turn and reach into the vague past to find our true bearings in our current journey.

One need not view this quest strictly in formal religious terms or metaphors. In its broadest context, the journey upon which we embark is no less than the actualization of ourselves as Selves. Georgio Agamben refers to this individualization as possible only because we recognize its origin in prelinguistic, prerational experience of *infancy*. Because we human beings have an infancy, a state without semantic language and only "pure experience," we must discern the world by splitting that experience and thereby constitute ourselves as the subject of language. And it is here, at this discontinuity of self-reflection empowered by language, that history is born.

> It is infancy, it is the transcendental experience of the difference between language and speech, which first opens the space of history. Thus Babel—that is, the exit from the Eden of pure language and the entry into the babble of infancy—is the transcendental origin of history. In this sense, to experience necessarily means to reaccede to infancy as history's transcendental place of origin.[30]

Agamben is using different metaphors from those I have employed, but the notion of *infancy* points to the same domain as that occupied by the vaguely recalled spiritual unity of the Jew with the Shekinah. How might we further describe this ineffable locale, which is essentially intuitive and perhaps inexpressible?

I said at the outset that I make no pretense at being philosophical in seeking to analyze Memory or Home. I take some solace from Wittgenstein's comment at the end of the *Tractatus*: "There is indeed the inexpressible. This *shows* itself; it is the mystical."[31] And perhaps more to the point is the famous ending, "Whereof one cannot speak, thereof one must be silent."[32] For Wittgenstein, "the task of philosophy is not to explain deep mysteries, but to bring clarification and therefore light to our thinking,"[33] for "philosophy simply puts everything before us, and neither explains nor deduces anything."[34] The task of philosophy then is to *describe,* and not seek "explanation where we should see the facts as 'primary phenomena,'"[35] placing before us the structure of our thought and experience. Thus Wittgenstein leaves us with no recourse for *philosophical* discussion of the metaphysical, but nevertheless poetry, art, and prayer attempt to capture that domain, and mystical visions in their various manifestations rely on such vehicles. That is my project. I have maintained that Memory, too, functions in this locale and must be distinguished from any analytical history. Memory in its purest guise is mystical.

Memory draws from the deepest wellsprings of prerational consciousness. Agamben argues that our present human consciousness is split from a unified state of humanity in nature. On the other hand, humanity in this primal, original experience is undifferentiated. This domain of "pure" and "unified" experience, Agamben again refers to as "infancy."

> What Wittgenstein posits, at the end of the *Tractatus*, as the "mystical" limit of language is not a psychic reality located outside or beyond language in some nebulous so-called "mystical experience," it is the very transcendental origin of language, nothing other than infancy. *The ineffable is, in reality, infancy.* Experience is the *mysterion* which every individual intuits from the fact of having an infancy.[36]

In short, the true source of mystical experience in this view is antecedent to any of its particular expressions.[37] This is Wittgenstein's true assertion of mystical reality. We need to speak of it, but cannot speak of it without changing its character into something else. The problem is not to deny the "reality" of our mystical or religious experiences, but to recognize them while facing the impossibility of their full articulation.

V

How do we conclude? Must we speak in metaphors of myth, poetry, or art? One of my favorite expressions of this elusive attempt was offered by Alberto Giacometti, who observed the futility of his art to adequately capture its object:

> If one could ever reach an understanding of a thing in its totality, then perhaps one could render it back; but it is impossible, because both that thing and I are caught in the ceaseless mutability of life, which can never be made to stand still.[38]

This is of course a reiterated theme of Heraclitus, but I find a particularly interesting extension of this problem in Wittgenstein's notion of the "unsayable." The artist is denied capturing his or her object not necessarily by the limits of language, but by the restrictions imposed by time, by mutability, by the essentiality of change. With this sensibility, there is no pretense of defining the relation, of capturing the experience, of freezing the moment. The artist must struggle to so render the "thing"; but in the contingencies of time, the creation becomes a construction, its own object, not a representation of a past, or for that matter, even the present. Moreover, the sculpture or painting, seemingly frozen in time, in fact also assumes its own temporal dimension, for our relation to it constantly evolves. The power of the statement is in the recognition of how the art becomes a paradigm for ourselves.

Giacometti's *The City Square* (1948) consists of five figures waking toward a central focus; they are "solitary, but when placed together, no matter how, they are united by their solitude. . . . He has sculptured men crossing a public square without seeing each other; they pass, hopelessly alone and yet *together*."[39] I find this a fitting image with which to conclude. We have drawn the Wanderer, and Home has served as our metaphorical focus. But unlike Ulysses, we do not know the Home from which we came, nor the certainty of our return. We are not engaged in a heroic journey, for we are aimless wanderers in the world. Our only guidance is Memory, a sense of original belonging in a domain unbounded by the contingencies of profane life.[40] This is the dimension of our search for Being, the expression of the source of our deepest understanding of identity in the particular category of ourselves in time.

From this perspective, the circuit from Home is more than a narrative myth of psychological maturation, but rather accounts for time and our relation to it. Home is that time and Memory which constitutes the repository of our most inner self. Home is an emotional place, a mysterious notion of deep belonging. We may have nostalgic longing to return, but that is subordinate to how we are defined by that Home, how we relate to the Memory, or perhaps how the Memory constitutes our present experience. The importance of Home resides in its power as origin or source. It is from where we truly come that in some profound sense identifies who we are, linking us to a past that to varying degrees determines the present. Memory *of* home would rob us of Agamben's "experience," that is, memory *as* home. Home resides *in* Memory—not locked in the past, but always with us in the present—and thus profoundly characterizes us.

We have considered how in Memory we make our quest. I have assigned Memory to mystical time, where the past is never truly the *past*. The past only exists as it is reconstructed, remembered, and responded to. In other words, the past, ironically perhaps, exists in the present as we construct it in remembrance. On one level, we return to the past, but only to capture it in the present. Our purpose is to return Home, to our beginnings, to our very origins, to a state of paradise and spiritual unity. "Re-member"—to become a member—is to assert an integration, to form a new union. And this reunion is at the very foundation of our psyche. We seek wholeness. This mythical thirst for the "ontic"[41] demands that we delve into the reaches of an elusive world to seek our own completion. To eschew history, denying the record of time in the modern Western sense of defining the past "objectively," is simply to experience the "old" as an integral element of our present. This sense of time is the need to integrate our full experience. Home is the common metaphor of that unifying locale.

Home describes what is best approximated by myth or art or prayer, namely, the realm Wittgenstein advised us to refer to in silence. Yet we seek to bring our yearnings for Agamben's "infancy" into consciousness and thus struggle for better articulation of an intuitive or primary experience. Home points us in that direction. This is clearly a mystical realm, for this Memory resides in a nonrational, preconscious, and preliterate domain, where it remains largely amorphous and unformed. Wittgenstein would leave it there, undisturbed and unperturbed. But I persist in speaking of that dimension that resists philosophy and analysis. Certainly, the need to engage in metaphysics, despite Wittgenstein's warning, is deeply embedded in our thinking. It is integral to our experience, shaping, if not defining, our very selves.

VI

It was the Sabbath, Friday evening. I was sitting next to the Rebbe, whose table was crowded with Hasidic men in animated discussion. Dressed in their distinctive garb, I felt transported to another era. Retreating from the conversation, I looked up, and there hovering above the table, I saw my grandmother. She was dressed, as I always remembered her, in black without adornments. She looked at me, with a faint smile. I saw her simply suspended there watching me.

I turned to my host, "Rebbe, I see my grandmother."

Without looking up, between mouthfuls of the fish he was eating, he matter-of-factly responded, "Of course, she is happy you are home."

I looked up again. She lingered briefly, the smile seemingly sadder, and then she slowly disappeared. Although long ago in Jerusalem, I remember the moment as if it was yesterday.

NOTES

1. This paper was inspired by the provocative and insightful interpretation of Wittgenstein's oeuvre offered by Burton Dreben, to whom I dedicate this essay.

2. Martin Buber, "People Today and The Jewish Bible," in Martin Buber and Franz Rosenzweig, *Scripture and Translation*, trans. L. Rosenwald and E. Fox (1926; reprint ed., Bloomington, Ind.: Indiana University Press, 1994), pp. 4–21 (quote from pp. 5–6).

3. Gerschom Scholem, "At the Completion of Buber's Translation of the Bible," in *The Messianic Idea in Judaism* (New York: Schocken, 1971), p. 318; discussed by L. Rosenwald, "Buber and Rosenzweig's Challenge to Translation Theory," in *Scripture and Translation*, pp. liii–liv.

4. The translation was no less than a call to accept biblical revelation as both the true meaning of history, from which human relationships to God and the rest of humanity would be defined. Buber proclaimed that there was "Creation" and there was "Redemption" and in the middle, where we are in time, "Revelation."

5. The command to remember is found throughout the Bible, and Yosef Yerushalmi notes that "the verb *zakhar* appears in its various declensions . . . no less than one hundred and sixty-nine times, usually with either Israel or God as the subject, for memory is incumbent upon both" (Yosef Yerushalmi, *Zakhor: Jewish History and Jewish Memory* [New York: Schocken Books, 1989], p. 5).

6. Ibid.; Ismar Schorsch, *From Text to Context: The Turn to History in Modern Judaism* (Hanover, N.H.: University Press of New England, 1994). For a superb short overview, see Paul Mendes-Flohr, "History," in *Contemporary Jewish Religious Thought*, ed. Arthur A. Cohen and Paul Mendes-Flohr (New York: Free Press, 1987), pp. 371–87.

7. The rich metaphorical guises of the Shekinah and her role in Jewish mystical tradition are detailed by Gershom Scholem, *Major Trends in Jewish Mysticism* (New York: Schocken, 1961); *Kabbala* (New York: New American Library, 1974); and *The Messianic Idea in Judaism* (New York: Schocken, 1971). More recent scholarship (and a challenge to Scholem's dominance) may be found in Moshe Idel, *Kabbalah: New Perspectives* (New Haven, Conn.: Yale University Press, 1988). A less detailed account of the Jewish mystical tradition is given by Edward Hoffman, *The Way of Splendor: Jewish Mysticism and Modern Psychology* (Boulder, Colo.: Shambhala, 1981).

8. Maimonides, *A Maimondides Reader*, ed. Isadore Twersky (New York: Behrman House, 1972), p. 222 (*Mishnah Torah*, bk. 14, chap. 11).

9. "The references to King Messiah are inconspicuously incorporated in various rulings and seem to appear casually, as a natural, ordinary matter. . . . We are dealing with a halakhic [legal] reality rather than a remote eschatology" (Isadore Twersky, "Maimonides and Eretz Yisrael: Halakhic, Philosophic and Historical Perspectives," in *Perspective on Maimonides: Philosophical and Historical Studies*, ed. J. L. Kraemer [New York: Oxford University Press, 1991], p. 279).

10. Ibid., p. 282. Raphael Patai, in *The Messiah Texts* (New York: Avon Books, 1979), has assembled a diverse anthology of Jewish messianic writings from biblical to modern times, which amply illustrate the divergent views of this matter. Obviously, I have chosen a particular orientation that can hardly be called "representative" of any consensus. None exists.

11. Yehudah Halevi, *The Kuzari*, trans. A. Davis (New York: Metsudah Publications, 1986), p. 81.

12. Ibid., p. 79. Note that Halevi and Maimonides differ in their respective views concerning the role of Jewish Exile. The former regards the Diaspora as serving some broad political or religious purpose, namely, that the Jewish people might lead other nations as an ethical beacon during their wandering. Maimonides regards this mission as essentially reserved for messianic times (Twersky, "Maimonides and Eretz Yisrael," p. 284).

13. Dunaszerdahely, in northeastern Hungary close to the present-day borders of Austria and Slovakia, was a center of Jewish education in the nineteenth century. Many of the stories narrated by my father about his parents' birthplace are not so different from those of the village in the highly romanticized *Fiddler on the Roof* and described by Mark Aborowski and Elizabeth Herzog in *Life is with People: The Culture of the Shtetl* (New York: Schocken Books, 1952).

14. Joseph Campbell, *The Hero with a Thousand Faces* (Princeton, N.J.: Princeton University Press, 1949).

15. George K. Anderson, *The Legend of the Wandering Jew* (Hanover, N.H.: University Press of New England, 1965, 1991), p. 11.

16. Ibid., pp. 355–96.

17. In Jewish mystical tradition, the issue of reunification does not restrict itself to God and his People, but is also a problem for God himself.

18. "[The Bible was the] revealed pattern of the whole of history. . . . They knew that history has a purpose, the establishment of the kingdom of God on earth, and that the Jewish people has a central role to play in the process. . . . [T]hey had learned from the Bible that the true pulse of history often beat beneath its manifest surfaces, an invisible history that was more real than what the world, deceived by the more strident outward rhythms of power, could recognize" (Yerushalmi, *Zakhor*, p. 21).

19. N. Scherman, trans., *The Art Scroll Machzor, Rosh Hashana* (New York: Mesorah Publications, 1986), p. 89.

20. Ibid., pp. 507–11.

21. For brief overviews, see Mendes-Flohr, "History"; Harold Bloom, "Foreword" in Yerushalmi, *Zakhor*, pp. xiii–xxv; and E. Luz, "Buber's Hermeneutics: The Road to the Revival of the Collective Memory and Religious Faith," *Modern Judaism* 15 (1995): 69–93.

22. Jacob Katz, *Out of the Ghetto: The Social Background of Jewish Emancipation, 1770–1870* (New York: Schocken Books, 1978), p. 212. See also Schorsch, *From Text to Context.*

23. Franz Rosenzweig, *The Star of Redemption* (1930; 2nd ed., trans. W. W. Hallo [Boston: Beacon Press, 1972]), p. 304. He goes on to make a stunning admission concerning the Jew's existential state of wandering relative to time and history: "It [the Jewish people] cannot experience the history of the nations creatively and fully. Its position is always somewhere between the temporal and the holy. . . . And so, in the final analysis, it is not alive in the sense the nations are alive: in a national life manifest on this earth. . . . It is alive only in that which guarantees it will endure beyond time . . ."(ibid.).

24. Recall that each Jew is responsible for hastening the Messiah's arrival, and moreover that arrival is imminent. As Walther Benjamin observed, "The future was not some homogenous, empty time. For every second of time was the strait gate through which the Messiah might enter" (Walther Benjamin, "Theses on the Philosophy of History" in *Illuminations*, trans. H. Zohn [New York: Schocken Books, 1968], p. 264).

25. Hermann Cohen, *Religion of Reason* (1918; trans. Simon Kaplan [New York: Frederick Unger Pub. Co., 1972], pp. 249–50.

26. Ibid., p. 261, quoted in Mendes-Flohr, "History," p. 375.

27. I have avoided placing the individual in the sociological context, but quite obviously history, both that of the individual and the culture, resides in group memory, specifically in a common spiritual experience.

28. Perhaps the most influential Jewish philosopher who has explored this theme is Martin Buber. Buber, in his famous dialogical explorations, regarded this immediate sense of history as instrumental to the Jewish encounter with God.

29. I have eschewed even alluding to psychoanalytic theory in this discussion, but I cannot refrain from noting that I find it strangely correct that the Nazis referred to psychoanalytic theory as a "Jewish science." That Freud, the Jew, captured memory as the focus of his investigations is quite consistent with my thesis, but despite much recent scholarship concerning the Jewish roots of Freud's enterprise, none have identified that Memory, as a religious category, analogous to a Kantian *a priori*, resides at the foundation of his thinking. Even in those studies devoted to the religious roots of Freud's think-

ing, this question is not explicitly posed. The most sensitive readings of Freud's intellectual and psychological indebtedness to Judaism are given by Emmanuel Rice, *Freud and Moses: The Long Journey Home* (Albany: State University of New York Press, 1990); Yosef Yerushalmi, *Freud's Moses: Judaism Terminable and Interminable* (New Haven: Yale University Press, 1991); and Moshe Gresser, *Dual Allegiance: Freud as a Modern Jew* (Albany: State University of New York Press, 1994).

30. Georgio Agamben, *Infancy and History: Essays on the Destruction of Experience*, trans. L. Heron (London: Verso, 1993), pp. 52–53.

31. Ludwig Wittgenstein, *Tractatus Logico-Philosophicus*, trans. C. K. Ogden (London: Routledge, 1922, 1933), p. 187.

32. Ibid., p. 189. We need not consider Wittgenstein's later development of meaning in language, where he dismantled the firm distinctions between "sayable" facts and "transcendental" values, to appreciate the common thread of his thought that religious experience is not subject to *analysis*.

33. Norman Malcolm, *Wittgenstein: A Religious Point of View?* (Ithaca, N.Y.: Cornell University Press, 1994), p. 78.

34. Ludwig Wittgenstein, *Philosophical Investigations*, 3rd ed., trans. G. E. M. Anscombe (New York: Macmillan, 1968), p. 50e, #126.

35. Ibid., p. 167e, #654.

36. Agamben, *Infancy and History*, p. 51.

37. The question arises as to whether such manifestations are the translation of a more primary experience, or are they the thing-in-itself? In short, how do we arrive at an epistemology of the mystical? There are those, most recently and notably, Steven Katz, who argue that "there are *no* pure (i.e., unmediated) experiences. Neither mystical experience nor more ordinary forms of experience can give any indication, or any grounds for believing that they are unmediated" (Steven Katz, "Language, Epistemology, and Mysticism," in *Mysticism and Philosophical Analysis,* ed. Steven Katz [Oxford: Oxford University Press, 1978], p. 26).

38. Alberto Giacometti, quoted in an exhibit of his work at the Peggy Guggenheim Museum, Venice, Italy, 1995.

39. Jean-Paul Sartre, "The Quest for the Absolute," in *Essays in Existentialism*, ed. Wade Baskin (Secaucus, N.J.: Citadel Press, 1965), p. 405.

40. In the context of discussing the foundations of mythical experience, Mircea Eliade observes, "The desire felt by the man of traditional societies to refuse history, and to confine himself to an indefinite repetition of archetypes, testifies to his thirst for the real and his terror of 'losing' himself by letting himself be overwhelmed by the meaninglessness of profane existence. . . . [T]his behavior is governed by belief in an absolute reality opposed to the profane world of 'unrealities,' in the last analysis, the latter does not constitute a 'world,' properly speaking; it is the 'unreal' *par excellence*, the

uncreated, the non-existent: the void. . . . [I]n fact this behavior corresponds to a desperate effort not to lose contact with *being*" (Mircea Eliade, *The Myth of the Eternal Return* [Princeton, N.J.: Princeton University Press, 1954], pp. 91–92).

41. One way of articulating the ontic realm is through myths. Eliade portrays the essential structure of cosmological regenerance as a keen window into how a mythic consciousness enunciates this vague, yet profoundly felt effect of our sense of time: "This eternal return reveals an ontology uncontaminated by time and becoming. . . . Everything begins over again at its commencement every instant. The past is but a prefiguration of the future. No event is irreversible and no transformation is final. . . . [T]ime is suspended, or at least its virulence is diminished . . ." (ibid., pp. 89–90).

Shekinah:
The Home of the Homeless God

JÜRGEN MOLTMANN

HOME; HOUSE; HOME COUNTRY; these are words that have a profound emotional value for all of us: "Home, sweet home." But can this value be transferred to God? Does God look for a home in this world? Where is God at home—in heaven, in the temple, or in his kingdom?

Let us first try to discover phenomenologically what people mean by home and why we are always longing to "come home," even though we are everywhere "on the move." When John Steinbeck set off on his *Travels with Charley,* he saw something in the eyes of his neighbor which he found everywhere in the rest of the nation too: "A burning desire to go, to move, to get under way, any place, away from any Here. They spoke quietly of how they wanted to go someday, to move about, free and unanchored, not toward something, but away from something."[1] That isn't just true of Americans. It is true of Germans too. And it applies to roaming-around women just as much as to roaming-around men. But this restless footlooseness is of course simply the other side of the much deplored rootlessness of our lost souls.

We shall then go on to look at Jewish Shekinah theology. When in 587 B.C.E. Jerusalem was destroyed, and God's temple with it, and the people of Israel were driven into Babylonian exile, what happened to God's special descent and indwelling in the temple? Did God withdraw it into heaven, or did it go into exile with the people, so that the people's homelessness became the homelessness of God's Shekinah too? And if God's indwelling goes with the people into the foreign country, accompanying them through exiles and persecutions, when does it come home again, and where? We shall find the Jewish Shekinah theology again among twentieth-century Jewish thinkers, and shall look at it in Ernst Bloch and Franz Rosenzweig.

"The Word became flesh and dwelt among us," says John 1:14. So there is a Christian Shekinah theology too. And if we look into the eschatology of the book of Revelation, we find at the end the great promise: "Behold, the dwelling of God is with men. He will dwell with them, and they shall be his people" (21:3). What can this mean for Christians and Jews, and for heaven and earth? At the end will God live in the world, or will the world live in God? I shall close with some ideas about the God who is both on the move and at rest, making that *our* orientation in our own human footlooseness and rootlessness, in order to find with God "what gleams forth to everyone in childhood and where no one as yet ever was: home." It is with these words—the last words of his book—that Ernst Bloch describes the place to which "the Principle of Hope" leads us.[2]

I. WHAT ARE WE LOOKING FOR, WHEN WE WANT "TO COME HOME"?

Modern philosophical anthropology maintains that human beings are "beings open to the world," because, unlike animals, they do not possess any environment specific to their species.[3] But at the same time, human beings cannot live in an open world or a completely unrestricted space. Wherever they are, they always create their own environment. They hollow out their caves, peg out their boundaries, build their houses. It is only in a restricted and surveyable environment that human beings can find peace, and relax, and feel "at home." In this sense all human civilizations are places for human beings to live in. These living places can be expanded and rebuilt, but we cannot live without them, or outside the spaces they provide. We human beings define our dwelling places and our living space through boundaries. In German, an enclosure of this kind can be called an *Umfriedung* or an *Einfriedung*; and in both these words *Frieden*, "peace," is an element. Or we can use the word *Einhegung*, a place that has been enclosed so that it can be cultivated. Inside is our home; outside is "foreign country." Within our boundaries there is domestic peace; outside, life can be dangerous and hostile. Inside, it is homely and "right"; outside it is sinister. In the place where we live we feel comfortable. Outside it is "comfortless." Today these words have merely emotional connotations, but they are really very old ways of defining the line drawn round the environment which we need for living.[4] "Good fences make good neighbors."[5]

The space which earthly life requires, whether it be animal life or human life, is a limited space. It is as much a part of life as the physical extensions of the body. Our minds live in their bodies, and the physical organism is organized by the mind. When we are seriously ill, our bed is our living space. So no one paying a pastoral visit should ever sit on the sick person's bed. This gesture won't be felt as an act of friendly intimacy; it will be experienced as an intrusion into the living space the sick person needs for his or her protection. The boundaries of a person's living space protect life, and ward off attacks from outside.

But that is only half the truth about the boundary. On the other hand boundaries offer a chance to communicate with "neighbors" and *their* living spaces too. Boundaries also constitute neighborhoods and communities, in villages and city boroughs and apartment blocks. It is on the boundaries that the configurations of different life acquire contours. That is why the boundaries of human living spaces must be as nonexclusive as the environments of other living things. The boundaries of life are living, moving, and open frontiers. Once they are closed, exclusive and self-isolating communities grow up. And for all living things, and hence for human beings too, self-isolation is the beginning of death. Whether we have our frontiers watched, so that no stranger can come in, or whether we are watched at our own frontiers, so that we cannot get out, comes to the same thing in the end. At the conclusion of the Second World War, Karl Popper made the politically necessary points about this in his famous book *The Open Society and Its Enemies.*[6] The possession of one's own living space, and community with other living things in a shared living space, are not mutually exclusive; they condition one another mutually. We cannot live in the kind of socialism in which we have everything in common, and can never be on our own; but we cannot, either, live in the kind of capitalism that merely protects private property, and in which everyone is his own—or her own—best neighbor. We can only live in a "communitarianism" which creates an equitable adjustment between our own interests and the interests of the whole.

And yet "home" and the yearning "to come home" have deeper roots still, and it is child psychology that can best lay these bare. Once upon a time we were completely "at home" and in entirely "safe keeping"; that was the time when we were growing in our mother's womb. Then we were completely and wholly "in someone else" and were surrounded and nourished by our mother. That is why Heidegger calls living *In-sein*—"being-in"—and in the language of German piety, to have faith is called "being safe in God."[7] Birth is our first expulsion from paradise. The child becomes free, but it becomes solitary too. In its earliest years it then discovers that "Mummy" is not always there, and that it has to rely on itself. "Mummy" was the child's total presence; now she becomes a counterpart instead, an opposite number, someone who can be present but can be absent too. As it grows up, every child has the natural wish to be free and to act independently, and to live its own life; and yet buried in that same child is the yearning for the "paradise lost" of its mother. It is with a cry for their mothers that many soldiers have died.

Later on comes the step into adult life. A man "leaves his father and mother and cleaves to his wife" (Gen. 2:24), as the Bible says. In other words, we have to leave the superego of father or mother in order to develop our own ego, and to arrive at our own selves. That is the next step to freedom—and it is a step that some people never manage to take. The all-determining patriarch and the all-providing mother remain. Only both these figures are now projected into heaven, so that God or Christ takes over the role of the superego. If the step to independent, adult life succeeds, it leads to the same double experience: the experience of liberty and the experience of homelessness. Without the dissolution of the personal roots of life in the mother and the family, liberty is impossible. But the experience of freedom is probably always accompanied to some extent by the desert wind of an experience of exile.

Let me close this sociological and psychological account of our ambivalent relation to home with an epistemological comment. We discover what home really is only when we are away from it. It is only after we have been driven out of paradise that we know what that paradise was. Stay-at-home people don't know these things, because they never acquire the necessary detachment. If Adam and Eve had never sinned, they would never have known what the paradise where they lived together with God really was. That kind of knowledge requires detachment and difference; for like is not known by like; it is only the unlike who know each other.[8]

II. JEWISH SHEKINAH THEOLOGY

The destruction of Jerusalem and the Babylonian exile of 587 B.C.E. put their stamp on Israel's consciousness far beyond that year itself. For with it began the life of the people in exile, the *galuth*, and a Jewish exilic religion of its own special kind. The monarchy had been snuffed out, the city of God destroyed, the temple razed to the ground. And the religious damage was even greater than the physical devastation, because the destruction touched the power of Israel's God as well. Why did God allow his temple to be destroyed? Where was God in the defeat of his chosen people?

> O God, why dost thou cast us off for ever?
> Why does thy anger smoke against the sheep of thy pasture?
> Remember thy congregation, which thou hast gotten of old,
> Remember Mount Zion, where thou hast dwelt! (Ps. 74:1–2)

In the Jewish writings of the exilic period, a new theology of the Shekinah came into being. Shekinah means the descent and special indwelling of God in the midst of Israel and in his temple on Zion. The concept of the Shekinah links the infinite God, whom even the countless heavens cannot contain, with a historical people and an earthly, limited space. This special divine presence issues from God's self-committing bond with the people of his covenant, and from his gracious descent to the innermost part of the temple on Zion. This special presence is not just one part of the general presence of the Creator in his creation; it has its foundation in the particular act of God's election of the people of Israel: "I will be your God and you shall be my people" (Ezek. 37:23).

Later rabbinic theology conceived this presence as a contraction and self-restriction on God's part: "God forsakes the high assembly of his council and restricts (or contracts) his Shekinah within the sanctuary." It was also possible to talk about God's self-humiliation, as Arnold Goldberg and Peter Kuhn have shown.[9] The result of the "descent" of God is God's indwelling, God's Shekinah. This idea has its roots in Israel's early days, in the Exodus from Egypt and the covenant on Sinai, in God's presence in the Ark of the Covenant which the Israelites carried with them, and among the wandering people. So it is probably not an invention of exilic religion; exilic religion is rather a prolongation or development of Israel's primal experiences of God.

After the destruction of the temple and the loss of the Shekinah in the temple, two different traditions about "God's dwelling" grew up. The one tradition says that God lives and is enthroned in heaven, not in the temple on Zion. Deuteronomy belongs to this tradition. It isn't God himself who dwells in the temple; it is God's name, as guarantor of his will. God himself lives and is enthroned in the heavens that overarch the whole earth; so he is omnipresent. The other tradition says that, after the destruction of the temple, God's indwelling presence in the temple went into exile with the people. That is understandable, because God dwelt in the midst of his people before his indwelling in Solomon's temple. The people are carried into captivity, and the Shekinah goes with them. The people suffer exile and persecution, and the Shekinah suffers with them. The Shekinah suffers exile and ignominy, and the people suffer with the Shekinah. Later rabbinic literature describes this sympathy, this cosuffering of God's, in profoundly moving images. God is like Israel's twin brother. The two are so much one heart and one soul that every hurt Israel suffers becomes God's hurt too. "In all their affliction He was afflicted" (Isa. 63:9), for God says: "I am with him in trouble" (Ps. 91:15). These are the two texts which the rabbis drew on, to support the concept of "the God who suffers with us."[10]

In his Shekinah, God himself suffers the exile of his people. So this is God's exile too. God's Shekinah has become homeless, and wanders restlessly through the dust of this world's streets. This leads on to the idea that God and his people are waiting in shared suffering for their redemption, or deliverance. Israel knows that it will be delivered when God himself is delivered, and his Shekinah returns home. This doesn't have to lead to the notion of God's "self-deliverance," but it does mean that the event of deliverance, or redemption, becomes a mutual happening between God's Shekinah and God's people. In what way? Exilic religion put two important things in the foreground: one of them is the *sabbath*, and the other is the sanctification of God's name, the *kiddush ha-shem.*

The theology of the sabbath transfers God's Shekinah from the limited space of the temple into the rhythms of time. God is now no longer present on ruined Zion; he is present on every seventh day, in every seventh year, and in every forty-ninth year. Abraham Heschel called the sabbath "the Jewish cathedral," declaring that Judaism in exile was "the religion of time."[11] On the sabbath, eternity and time touch. God dwells in the sabbath day. This means that sacred spaces are replaced by a certain sanctification of time. We go beyond Heschel when we point not only to the *historical* link between the sabbath and the Shekinah but to the *eschatological* bond between the two as well: the weekly and yearly sabbath is God's homeless Shekinah in the period of the exile, in the estrangement from Jerusalem. That is why the sabbath points beyond itself, and its own time, to the deliverance of God and his people in the final homecoming, which will be the cosmic indwelling of God in the temple of the new creation. So we might say that the sabbath is God's Shekinah in time, and the Shekinah is God's sabbath in space. The inward unity of sabbath and Shekinah is to be found in the *menucha* of God: God comes to his home country, and God comes to his rest.

The sanctification of God's name takes the place of the priesthood and the sacrificial cults of the Jerusalem temple. God's name can be sanctified ("hallowed," as the English Lord's prayer says) everywhere and by everyone, not just in the temple and not just by priests. Consequently, for Judaism in exile the sanctification of the name came to take first place among God's commandments. Through the election of the people, God bound his name to the name of that people; so he also put his honor in their hands. That means on the one hand divine protection for his people: anyone who touches them touches God's name. On the other hand it means that God puts himself into his people's hands, waiting for the sanctification of his name by men and women. Through the sanctification of his name, people give God's name back to God, as it were, and return to God the honor which he has surrendered into their hands. It is only when his name is sanctified in his whole creation that God finds rest, and his creation becomes the home in which he can live.

I note that there are two interpretations of the *kiddush ha-shem* by Jewish philosophers in Germany.

Ernst Bloch counts as an atheistic philosopher nowadays. Yet as far as I know he is the only philosopher—I will pass over in silence the theologians of the modern world—who closed a philosophical work with a prayer. *Der Geist der Utopie* ("The Spirit of Utopia") ends: "For only the wicked exist through their God; but the just— there God exists through them, and the sanctification of the Name is in their hands; to them the naming of God himself is given, the One who moves in us and drives us forward, surmised gateway, darkest question, rapturous Within: given into the hands of our God-invoking philosophy, and truth as prayer."[12] Here Bloch links the Jewish (and Christian) sanctification of God's name in the world with "the naming of God as God." Whether the world becomes God's home depends on the act of human beings. In 1963 Bloch commented on these early thoughts of his, saying: "The world is not true, but through human beings and the truth it strives to arrive at its homecoming." How can human beings acquire this power, this energy, for God? Isn't this sanctification of the Name superhuman? For Bloch the sanctification of God's name proceeds from the God "who moves in us and drives us forward . . . rapturous Within."[13] That is the hidden divine quality in us, from which we live, every moment. That is the divine Shekinah at the roots of our existence. It is only when it emerges from us, and we are no longer hidden to ourselves but live with unveiled faces, that we can be at home in the space which Bloch in true Jewish-messianic fashion calls "the home of identity."

Almost at the same time, in 1921, Franz Rosenzweig presented a Shekinah theology with Hegelian concepts. He called it *Der Stern der Erlösung* ("The Star of Redemption").[14] He writes: "With the doctrine of the Shekinah, mysticism builds its bridge between 'the God of our Fathers' and 'the remnant of Israel.' The Shekinah, the descent of God to human beings and his dwelling among them, is conceived of as a division which takes place in God himself. God cuts himself off from himself, he gives himself away to his people, going with them into the misery of the foreign land, wandering with them in their wanderings."[15] In "God's self-surrender to Israel" Rosenzweig sees a divine suffering. God makes himself in need of deliverance, and Israel seeks a dwelling for "the exiled God." What does this deliverance of God look like? According to Jewish mysticism, the sanctification of God's name and the doing of God's will always means "uniting the holy God with his Shekinah."[16] The countless sparks which are struck off from God's glory and scattered throughout the world will be gathered together out of their dispersion and brought home to God's glory once more. Every sanctification of God's name and every doing of God's commandment completes a fragment of the Becoming of this divine unity. "To confess God's unity—the Jew calls it: uniting God. For this unity *is* in that it becomes—it is a Becoming Unity. And this Becoming is laid upon the souls of human beings, and in their hands."[17] So the redemption or deliverance is a process which embraces God, the world, and human beings.

This Jewish Shekinah theology leaves unanswered the eschatological question: if God has put his ability to find a home in the world in the hands of human beings, will God ever arrive at his rest? Doesn't this demand too much of human beings? Could it not be that in this mysterious fellowship and mutual dependence the deliverance comes from God's side? This is what every messianic hope is waiting for, and it is this for which every prayer calls upon the coming God.

III. CHRISTIAN INCARNATION THEOLOGY

In the basic ideas of exilic and rabbinic Shekinah theology, it is not difficult to discover the premises and patterns of Christian teachings about the incarnation of the divine Logos, and the indwelling of the Holy Spirit. They go back to the same traditions, and the Christian ideas have developed in the spiritual neighborhood of the Jewish ones. We shall try to see the similarities and the differences without asserting that the one is better than the other. The two ideas exist side by side, in different religious communities, and can provide a mutual stimulus for one another. Both point beyond themselves to the future of the coming God, who will make his creation his cosmic home and the world his temple.

John 1:14 declares that Christ is the descent and indwelling of God: "The Word became flesh and *dwelt* among us, and we beheld his glory"; while according to the letter to the Colossians, "in him the whole fullness of deity *dwells* bodily" (2:9). Here *Christ* doesn't mean the private historical person, Jesus of Nazareth; it means this person Jesus as the Christ of God—that is to say, as the messianic representative of God and Israel for the Gentile peoples. That is why the Gospels give Jesus' biography the form of a collective biography of Israel: the flight into Egypt, the return home from Egypt, the forty days' temptation in the wilderness, and so on. So the Israelite statement that "God dwells in the midst of his people" (Ezek. 37:27) can be transferred to Jesus the Christ: "The fullness of deity dwells in him" (Col. 2:9). Since God's people had already been called the firstborn son, it is not surprising that Christ should be called the Son of God.

In Christian terms, the descent of God is explained as the self-distinction of God, an idea which led on to the later doctrine of the Trinity. When the doctrine of the Trinity talks about three divine Persons in one divine substance (Tertullian's formulation), this formulation is of course using the terminology of Greek philosophy. But as the New Testament shows, in actual fact it goes back to the Israelite theology of the Shekinah. The God who lives in heaven and among the wretched of his people reveals a double presence—what Abraham Heschel in his interpretation of the prophets calls a "bipolarity."[18]

We also find Shekinah theology in Christian experience of the Holy Spirit and talk about the Spirit's descent and indwelling. According to the Pentecost story, the Spirit is "poured out on all flesh." It is "poured into our hearts" (Rom. 5:5). Our bodies become "temples of the Holy Spirit" (1 Cor. 6:19). What once happened in Solomon's temple, when God's Shekinah entered it, resting and dwelling there, now happens in the bodies of believers. The living, physical community becomes the temple of the divine, lifegiving Spirit. "Where two or three are gathered together in my name, there am I in their midst" (Matt. 18:20), say the Jewish Shekinah and the Christian Jesus in the same words. This experience also leads to a new expectation, for the experience of the creative and awakening divine Spirit is no more than a foretaste of the coming glory, which will fill the whole world.

The difference between Shekinah theology and Christian incarnation theology is probably that—even though God's Shekinah can certainly assume human characteristics of sympathy and solidarity (especially in the view of the rabbis)—the Shekinah does not actually "become flesh" and does not "dwell among us" in person. According to Israelite expectation this can be said only of the Messiah. To him the Shekinah in the people no doubt points, but the people itself is not the Messiah, since in exile it is still in need of the Deliverer. That is why there is never any talk about the death and resurrection of the Shekinah.

The difference is also that "the self-division in God"—which, as Franz Rosenzweig says, precedes the descent of the Shekinah—is gathered up and ended in "the Shekinah's homecoming," so that the

One God will then at last be the All-One God.[19] But according to Christian interpretation, the distinction between God the Father and God the Son endures, so that at the end the Son will give the consummated kingdom over to the Father, perfecting his obedience, so that "God will be all in all" (1 Cor. 15:28). The triune God is a unity in that the Father, by virtue of his love, is wholly in the beloved Son, and the Son by virtue of his love is wholly in the beloved Father, and the Spirit by virtue of his love is wholly in the Father and the Son. "I am in the Father and the Father is in me," says Christ according to the Gospel of John (14:10, 11). They are one by virtue of their mutual indwellings.

This leads us, finally, to the Christian sanctification of God's name and the Christian doing of his will. The Lord's prayer is a Jewish prayer through and through. It puts the sanctification, or "hallowing," of the Name before all other petitions. It circumscribes or encompasses the coming of the kingdom by the sanctification of the Name on the one side, and by the doing of God's will on the other. The kingdom in which God "dwells" with all his glory will not come without the sanctification of God's name, or without the doing of God's will. These first three petitions all relate to God and ask something for God. But where will these petitions be fulfilled, and through whom? If they have to be fulfilled through us human beings, then God's future is still open and uncertain. According to Christian belief they are fulfilled through Christ. The Christian response to the Our Father prayer is:

> Our Father who art in Christ,
> In his self-surrender your name is sanctified,
> In his obedience unto death on the cross your will is done,
> In Christ your eternal kingdom has come to us in person.

The sanctification of God's name and the doing of his will both come about *in the discipleship of Christ*. To follow Christ means participating in his messianic mission and bringing God's kingdom to the poor. To follow Christ means fulfilling the Messianic Torah, which is the Sermon on the Mount. To follow Christ, finally, means taking his cross on oneself and fighting against the demons of violence. If we sum all this up with the New Testament writings, it means *life in love*. In the love lived, and in the joy of being loved, God is "at home": "He who abides in love abides in God and God in him" (1 John 4:16). People who love, live in God, and God lives in those who love.

IV. THE NEW JERUSALEM

"We do not know whether God is the space of his world, or whether the world is his space," says a Jewish midrash, which Max Jammer quotes in his book *Concepts of Space*.[20] The Jewish answer was: the Lord is the living space of his world, but his world is not his living space. Yet that can only be *one* Jewish answer. Jewish Shekinah theology sees it differently.

The prophet Ezekiel (chaps. 40–48) turned the remembrance of the destruction of God's city and of the temple on Zion into hope for the coming God: God in his glory will enter the new eternal temple of the future, in order "to dwell in the midst of the people of Israel for ever." The promise "for ever" makes hope for God's coming Shekinah an eschatological hope. The link between Shekinah and *kabod* ("glory") emphasizes the unity between God's coming indwelling and his revelation. When God is revealed in his full glory, the Shekinah will finally return, and will no longer be threatened by anything at all. The prophet describes the new temple in images of overflowing rapture, images that are not only a remembrance of the temple that was, but cast back to paradise itself: from the temple the water of life will flow (chap. 47). The temple's dimensions are unearthly too; and when God's glory enters this new temple, the whole earth will shine (43:2ff.). Again we are face to face with the same paradox: God's glory, which heaven and earth cannot contain, enters into a temple and dwells there enduringly. So this new temple is undoubtedly the Lord's "living space." It is even the Lord's final and indestructible living space.

The new Jerusalem, which John on Patmos said would come down to earth from heaven, is nothing other than the cosmic temple of the new, eternal creation of heaven and earth (Revelation 21–22). This new Jerusalem isn't just a fairytale.[21] It is the realistic counterpart and counterimage to Babylon and Rome, the two capital cities in whose name the earthly Jerusalem had been destroyed in 587 B.C.E. and 70 C.E. When the book of Revelation talks about Babylon this is always a code word for Rome. Rome is the godless city, the city of the tyrant, with a tyrant's contempt for human beings. It was Rome that crucified Christ and it was Rome that persecuted the Christians. The goddess Roma is "the Great Whore," while the new Jerusalem is "the Lamb's bride." In Rome, blasphemy reigns; in the new Jerusalem, the true worship of God. There wealth is dominant; here God's glory.

There people get drunk with wine; here they enjoy the water of life. And so on.

As "the city of God," the new Jerusalem is the holy city, both a cosmic temple and paradise itself. It will become the center of the new world. It stands on "a great, high mountain" (21:10). The throne of God and of Christ will be in it (22:3). God's glory will radiate from it, lighting up heaven and earth, for it is built of transparent jewels and crystal (21:11). The new Jerusalem no longer has any temple, and yet it is not a "secular city," for the city itself is the cosmic temple. This new Jerusalem is the model for the true city: it is the city of gold, the city of light, the garden city. John has picked up Ezekiel's visions and expanded them even more into cosmic and eschatological dimensions.

Here God will "dwell among human beings" for ever (21:3). They will be "his peoples." The English and German translations always quote the ancient Israelite covenant formula here, rendering the phrase: ". . . and they will be his people." But the text actually uses the plural form of *laos*, the Greek word always used for the people of the covenant. The covenant with God will be expanded to take in everyone. All the nations will enjoy the privileges and promises of the people of the covenant. And what will happen to the faithful Jews, and the Christians who have resisted? Revelation 7 already added to the "hundred and forty-four thousand sealed out of the twelve tribes of Israel" "a great multitude which no one could number" from all peoples and tongues, who had resisted persecutions and temptations. So in the new Jerusalem the twelve tribes of Israel are present in the twelve gates of the city, and Christ's twelve apostles in the foundations of her walls. Whereas these gates and walls are quite small, the city itself is a huge cube—12 kilometers long, 12 kilometers broad, and 12 kilometers high. This is in no way a city any more. It is nothing other than the Holy of Holies in Solomon's temple (1 Kings 6:17–20), expanded into cosmic dimensions: an immense rectangular crystal casket, binding together and illuminating both heaven and earth.

In this new cosmic temple God's glory dwells for ever, and interpenetrates heaven and earth. The indwelling of God in his creation is the really new thing about the new Jerusalem. From this city God's holiness and his glory radiate, making everything holy and glorious, good, whole, and beautiful. For all created things partake of the indwelling divine life, and reflect in protean abundance the radiant beauty of the indwelling Godhead. Here God's unresting and restless

Shekinah arrives at its rest and its eternal sabbath. Creation's destiny is to become this eternal living space for God.

So much for the eschatological revelation about the home of the homeless God. Let me close with a few remarks about our own, human homecoming:

1. The initial result of Jewish and Christian experiences of the divine Shekinah is an inward *unrest*, and the perception of this world as a *history* open to the future. The God of history is a restless God of promise and of hope. The God of the Exodus and of the raising of the crucified Christ is a God who controverts oppression and death, a God of liberation and of pursuing new experiences. All other peoples and religions make themselves at home in this world. Only Jews and Christians declare: "Here we have no lasting city, but we seek the city which is to come" (Heb. 13:14). Is it this experience of God which won't let us come to rest but keeps us continually on the move? Does it make us "foreigners" wherever we are, "strangers in the night"?

2. The second result of this experience of the Shekinah is deep inward *rest*, and the perception of this world as God's home. If God comes down to us and lives among us, then we are at home already. Where does this happen? According to the Jewish idea, on the sabbath. That is God's dwelling in *time*. Christians ought to associate their *Sunday* with the *sabbath* again, so as to find rest. That would make many meditation gurus superfluous, and many psychiatrists too. But according to the Christian idea, God dwells in our lives where we live love—*ubi caritas et amor gaudet, ibi est Deus* ("where love rejoices, there God dwells").

3. To be on the move and to come to rest; to arrive home and to go out: we have to fulfill the claims of both these dimensions of our lives. Repose and movement aren't opposites. We have to preserve repose in movement, and remain capable of movement in repose. In the rhythm of the two our life is alive and in harmony with the God who journeys with us, and who dwells among us.

NOTES

1. John Steinbeck, *Travels with Charley: In Search of America* (1962; reprint ed., New York: Penguin Books, 1980), p. 10.

2. Ernst Bloch, *Das Prinzip Hoffnung* (Frankfurt, 1959), p. 1628.

3. M. Scheler, *Die Stellung des Menschen im Kosmos* (1927; reprint ed., Munich, 1947), 41: "Menschwerdung ist Erhebung zur Weltoffenheit kraft des Geistes."

4. Jürgen Moltmann, *God in Creation: A New Theology of Creation and the Spirit of God* (San Francisco: Harper & Row, 1985), pp. 142 ff.

5. Robert Frost, "Mending Wall," line 27.

6. Karl R. Popper, *The Open Society and Its Enemies* (Princeton, N.J.: Princeton University Press, 1950).

7. Martin Heidegger, *Sein und Zeit* (1927; reprint ed., Tübingen 1957), pp. 104 ff.

8. Jürgen Moltmann, "Knowing and Community," in *On Community*, ed. Leroy S. Rouner, vol. 12 in Boston University Studies in Philosophy and Religion (Notre Dame, Ind.: University of Notre Dame Press, 1991), pp. 162–76.

9. Arnold M. Goldberg, *Untersuchungen über die Vorstellung von der Schekhinah in der frühen rabbinischen Literatur*, Studia Judaica, vol. 5 (Berlin, 1969); Peter Kuhn, *Gottes Selbsterniedrigung in der Theologie der Rabbinen* (Munich, 1968).

10. Elie Wiesel's books are deeply influenced by Shekinah theology. See Elie Wiesel, "Der Mitleidende," in *Die hundret Namen Gottes: Tore zum letzten Geheimnis*, ed. R. Walter (Freiburg, 1985), pp. 70–76.

11. Abraham Heschel, *The Sabbath: Its Meaning for Modern Man* (New York: Farrar, Straus & Young, 1951).

12. Ernst Bloch, *Der Geist der Utopie* (Berlin, 1923), p. 365.

13. Ernst Bloch, *Tübinger Einleitung in die Philosophie* (Tübingen, 1963), p. 254.

14. Franz Rosenzweig, *Der Stern der Erlösung* (1921; reprint ed., Heidelberg, 1954). Translation: *The Star of Redemption* (Notre Dame, Ind.: University of Notre Dame Press, 1985).

15. Ibid., sec. 3, bk. 3, pp. 192 ff: "Die Irrfahrt der Schechina."

16. Ibid., p. 194.

17. Ibid.

18. Abraham Heschel, *The Prophets* (New York: Harper & Row, 1962), pp. 221 ff: "The Theology of Pathos."

19. Rosenzweig, *Der Stern der Erlösung*, pp. 195–96.

20. Max Jammer, *Concepts of Space* (Cambridge, Mass.: Harvard University Press, 1954), p. 28.

21. Elisabeth Schüssler Fiorenza, *Revelation: Vision of a Just World* (Minneapolis: Augsburg Fortress, 1992); Richard Bauckham, *The Theology of the Book of Revelation* (Cambridge: At the University Press, 1993).

PART III

Nostalgia and Hope in a Homeless Age

Dwellers, Migrants, Nomads: Home in the Age of the Refugee

EDITH WYSCHOGROD

WHAT IS HOME IN A TIME of enforced exile, the age of the refugee? What can the expression *to dwell* mean in the era of homelessness? How is home to be construed when the circumambient world of life-giving elements—elements in the ancient pre-Socratic sense: earth, air, fire, water—have become sources of pollution or death, in this age of environmental collapse and apocalyptic weaponry?

These questions cut through the images of home that were until recently the staples of American popular imagination. The home from which one came was depicted as rural or small town, a preserve that shut out the pressures of industrialization with their attendant moral decay. The home that one would build in the future was portrayed as shielding a new generation from the same evils. These images displayed a double temporal structure, past and future, but neither home could exist in the present.

Even when relatively unchallenged, these notions of home presented difficulties. One's past home remained elusive not only because home was an idyllic *post hoc* reconstruction, but because only the fact that one would never again possess that home could produce the bittersweet pathos of memory. Consider the yearning for candlelight gleaming through the sycamore trees, for the scent of new-mown hay wafting through the fields expressed in the popular song that ends with the familiar lines: "When I dream about the moonlight on the Wabash / Then I long for my Indiana home."

Similarly, the hope for a future utopia captured in the lyrics of another old hit tune—"We'll build a little home for two or three or four or more in Loveland for me and my gal"—was not only a displacement of the dystopic conditions of the present but a kind of

Kantian regulative ideal towards which one might ceaselessly strive, a home that would shelter romantic love in perpetuity. I shall designate this view of home as territorial, as referring to a bounded space in which activities and emotions that accord with generally accepted values can be actualized.

American culture has remained the guardian of still another and quite different motif, that of the frontier. The French philosopher Gilles Deleuze and coauthor psychoanalyst Felix Guattari assert:

> There is the . . . West, with its Indians without ancestry [i.e., lacking European roots], its ever receding limit, its shifting and displaced frontiers. There is a whole American map in the West. . . . America reversed directions. It put its Orient [i.e., a place where there is always more to explore] in the West.[1]

The sense of moving on as expressing life's transitoriness, of settled life as a point of departure rather than a locus of stability, the feeling of inexhaustible space, creates a new nomadic conception of home. I shall refer to this flight from fixity, this movement of escape from sedentary existence into an unbounded milieu, as deterritorialization. Depicting the sensibility of the frontier, American philosopher Josiah Royce writes in 1898:

> The Californian, like the Westerner in general, is likely to be somewhat abrupt in speech, and his recent coming to the land has made him on the whole indifferent to family tradition. . . . [E]very man . . . was precisely what God and himself had made him. . . . This type of individuality . . . seems to me due not merely to the newness of the community . . . but to the relation with nature. It is a free . . . an emotionally exciting . . . , an engrossing and intimate relation.[2]

Far from dodging the idea of home, the frontier creates a new sense of it, home as the flight from enclosure, as freedom from sedentary life. The present-day mobile home, touted as "your home on wheels," is not in the American context an oxymoron: home is as much an uprooting as an emplanting. Shelter in the context of the frontier can also be construed as a way station that, like a ledge of rock, both protects against and continues the surrounding terrain. Lest I, a northeasterner now living in Houston, Texas, forget the sentiment that home is "where the deer and the antelope play," I am reminded of it every afternoon of the long hot summer when, like vespers, the melody of "Home on the Range" wafts from the local ice cream vendor's truck.

Is there any connection between the questions raised earlier about the refugee, homelessness, and ecological disaster, and the ideals of home that have aroused American popular imagination? I shall argue that the images of home as settled existence and as deterritorialized wandering or nomadism can offset each other to useful effect. Settled existence, when supported by claims about tribe, ethnicity, and religious exclusivity, can engender territorial wars on a grand scale. In less volatile regions home as a house may become a commodity in a network of properties that circulate as real estate. Home as fluid and mobile, as the "other" of settled life, can be seen as a counter force to the excesses engendered by proprietary claims. Still, if home as something stationary gives way to a notion of home as roving, none of the beguiling nomads of past cultures—not the knight errant, not the cowboy, not the Comanche, not the forest wanderer of Vedic tradition nor the desert fathers of early Christianity—is likely to come to the fore in this postmodern age, but rather the drifter or the itinerant member of an international crime gang.

SOME GENEALOGICAL GLEANINGS

Before pursuing this inquiry further, it may be useful to see what can be learned about the meaning of *home* from a brief etymological survey. The stem *kei* from which home derives has several senses worth pondering: first, bed, couch, or night's lodging; second, beloved or dear; third, members of a household; finally, covering.[3] The first meaning, home as bed or lodging, suggests that home is a milieu of safety, that at home one can drop one's wariness, allow oneself to fall asleep. Here the sense of security is primary and determines what is homelike, rather than the fact that home is a specifiable space or locale. On this interpretation of home, the child asleep in his bed who is killed in a drive-by shooting is in a building, a habitation, an architectural artifact, but not in a home. The idea of home as a safe enclave has been used to shore up the notion that women belong in the home so that, in return for the protection that home provides, they are to act as its custodians by performing the requisite labors in its upkeep. The social, cultural, and economic fallout of this relationship as it has affected women demands and is receiving separate study in numerous quarters but such study lies outside the scope of my essay.

The second meaning, home as dear or beloved, opens up new layers of complexity in that no geographical locale or place appears to be implied, a fact that does not mean that home thus understood lacks a topography. To be sure, these terms refer to the affective dimension of home, less a place than a plane of intensity, a locus of emotional energy, an idea still reflected in sentimentalized fashion in the cliché, "Home is where the heart is." Yet the experience evoked by home as beloved or dear is also spatially configured as that which is near or close. But what is one's ownmost, inseparable, most proximate place, if not the body? As home, as the space of intimacy, the body remains a "where" that cannot dissolve into a pure stream of affects. The body also experiences itself as extending beyond the enclosure of the skin, linked to what is exterior to it so that the body and its "outside" result in a new assemblage or aggregate of meaningful objects. Such an assemblage, for example, infant and cradle, is so organized that it is felt as an uninterrupted flowing from one to the other. One's most intimate possessions can constitute such an assemblage, but the dazed Hutu woman with her portable belongings or the bag lady in her cardboard lean-to are instances of flawed composites of the same type. Here the flow of body and possession is broken by the threats to life to which both are subject.

The third meaning of home, the members of a household, suggests home's social dimension: home is a community in which there is a common habitation united through some tie such as the consanguine relations of family or tribe, a common language, interest, or shared task. Lest household as community be too narrowly construed as denoting the occupants of a single edifice or architectural complex, consider the expression "I'm going home," when uttered by the traveler. "Going home" does not principally express the intention to return to the building in which she lives but to the country she inhabits, her community of law, language, and custom. Similarly, the camper or naturalist who says "Nature is my home" refers to a community of living things that interacts with an environment unaltered by human intervention, and that, at its widest, constitutes a cosmic assemblage. The ancient Stoic philosopher who claims his home is the cosmos extends the boundaries of home in this way by bringing together the meaning of home as the body in affective connection with what is outside it so that they form a single assemblage, and home as community. This melding of meanings manifests itself in the Stoic Marcus Aurelius's meditation: "All things are implicated with one another, and the bond is holy; and there is hardly anything unconnected with any other thing. . . . For there is one universe made up of all things";[4] and even more powerfully, "That which has died falls out of the universe. If it stays here, it also changes here, and is dissolved into its proper parts, which are elements of the universe and of thyself."[5]

Home as community may be threatened when two or more groups, each with exclusionary internal bonds based on lineage, tribe, religion, or language, enter into conflict over a single territory. Rather than repatterning old territorial claims into new assemblages, the claimants invoke various modes of communal connection such as ethnicity and religion to reinforce them. For example, Serbs speak of ethnic cleansing in relation to Croats, thus investing what is in fact a religious difference with an aura of racial hatred.

The fourth meaning of home, home as covering, is bound up with the idea of a physical structure that we inhabit, but, unlike the related idea of home as lodging where the notion of secure shelter is primary, home as covering is related to disclosure and concealment. How the items to be hidden or revealed are parceled out varies considerably with time and place. In Western societies, home is the place where food is eaten in full view of those who share it but sexual encounters are hidden from the larger community. There have been and are of course numerous exceptions to this rule. The flow of disclosure and concealment can slip into confrontational patterns when the home as covering becomes the site for violent and abusive behavior, for physical and verbal wounding inflicted in secret and camouflaged as love. The man who batters the woman with whom he cohabits, the parents who beat their children, hide the violence that has hardened within the organizing form of these homes.

SETTLED EXISTENCE AND ITS UNDOING

To grasp the meaning of settled existence, it is important to consider more closely the significance of home as lodging. In sorting out several meanings attributable to lodging, I shall refer to a distinction developed in Heidegger's philosophy, the difference between entities as measurable physical objects, as *res extensa*, and things as useful, as gear or tools which answer to one's concerns in one's purposive dealings with the world. In order to bring out the instrumental notion of home, I am importing these distinctions from a context that is foreign to Heidegger's own interpretation of dwelling and building as developed in his later works.[6]

Home can be thought of as an edifice, a house, and, as such, an object that occupies space, that has length, breadth, and depth.[7] This is the meaning of home, for example, that underlies the house depicted in architectural drawings that specify site measurements and room dimensions for the use of the builder. It is also the connotation of such ordinary expressions as "John is inside the house," in that inside and outside are characteristics that belong to objects extended in space. This perspective focuses on a house's thing-like aspect: things are objects that can be laid out side by side with other things in conjunctures in which both form and content are determined by contiguity and distance. In this context, lodging is an enclosure of stipulable geometrical shape and measurable dimensions and the door or threshold marks the boundary between home and world.

But if lodging can be viewed as a house with specifiable physical properties, it can also be seen as a safe haven where the watchfulness exercised in the outside world can be abandoned. The home is still, to be sure, a building, but it is organized by a system of ends. Just as the wrench enables me to tighten a bolt in my car's motor so that I can reach my destination, or the printer generates the text I have composed so that I can dispatch my letter, the house too is organized by a wider and often tacit complex of ends. Thus the house, in providing protection against weather, implicates me in a wider nexus of relationships with equipment, objects of use that surround me. In preventing unwanted incursions by others it involves me in a social world. In providing a locale for food preparation and sleep, it brings to the fore the biorhythms of everyday life. Seen in this light, the house is not a material object but an instrument, something that refers beyond itself to a nexus of ends. Heidegger writes of equipment:

> To the Being of any equipment there always belongs the totality of equipment, in which it can be this equipment that it is. Equipment is essentially "something in order to. . . ." [There are] various ways of in-order-to, such as serviceability, conduciveness, usability, manipulability.[8]

When some piece of equipment malfunctions, the latent meaning of these overall purposes emerges so that, for example, if a fuse blows or my lock fails to protect me against forced entry, the larger pattern of ends (light, safety, and the like) becomes all the more prominent.

But if the failure of equipment calls attention to the precariousness of settled life, it does not undo it. To see how such an unmaking or deterritorialization comes about, it is useful to reconsider the question of the home's inside and outside. I have already suggested several interpretations of this relationship. Inside and outside can be understood as a connection between physical objects. On that view we may think of a structure's interior as the part away from the edge on one side, its exterior as the part away from the edge on the other side. Inside and outside are spaces—homogeneous, measurable, and only arbitrarily marked off from one another. As I suggested earlier, a house's inside is a complex of functions governed by rules of utility, such as its deployment in protecting dwellers against the elements or against hostile persons. When lodging is viewed in terms of utility, there are functional distinctions between inside and outside, but the inside is linked to the outside in widening networks of purposes. From the perspectives of the house both as material object and as a nexus of functions, inside and outside are homogeneous spaces, and in that sense an inside that is outside and an outside that is inside.

It is possible, however, to imagine a condition in which there is no inside and, because they are correlative terms, no outside, but only a formless unbounded environment in which one loses oneself. This milieu cannot be reduced to a system of ends, to a space for the actualization of projects. French philosopher Emmanuel Levinas calls such an environment "the elemental" and describes it thus:

> [The element] lies escheat, a common fund or terrain, . . . non-possessable, "nobody's": earth, sea, light, city. The element has no forms containing it; it is content without form. . . . It has [only] a side: the surface of the sea and of the field, the edge of the wind. . . . It unfolds in its own dimension: depth which is inconvertible into the breadth and length in which the side of the element extend. The depth of the element prolongs it until it is lost in earth [or sky].[9]

The elemental is pure quality without support. One cannot think it, make it the object of a concept, but only, says Levinas, bathe in it.

One "enjoys [it] without utility, in pure loss, gratuitously, without referring to anything else."[10]

If the metaphors seem florid and the notion far-fetched, imagine the elemental in the context of sport, as an encounter between surfer and wave. Thus surfer Phil Edwards writes: "That big hollow motherless wave comes crashing down behind you and it vibrates the whole ocean. . . . For a few seconds you are spinning around in a world that is neither land nor sea nor air."[11] The wave can be enjoyed but not domesticated, not turned into a home. Might it not be argued that the body itself is home in the milieu of sea and surf? Although there is always a residuum of the fixed and stationary about the body, when immersed in the elemental the body can never be constituted as protection, as an organized functional whole. Rather in the elemental it is pure sensibility; it "lives" the qualities of the element in which it is submerged. The body becomes the wetness of the wave, the whiteness of snow. So radical is this experiential shift that it can no longer be described in terms of an aesthetics of qualities but rather as a metamorphosis, a becoming-wetness or a becoming-whiteness.[12] In the elemental, the body is pure unshieldedness or, to use Deleuze and Guattari's tropes, deterritorializes itself, becomes a body without organs, a body whose spatiality melts, as it were, into a sequence of shifting intensities. In the elemental, the stationary or the sedentary has come undone.

The process can also be looked upon in reverse. Starting with the elemental as a place of enjoyment, it can be felt as a locus of insecurity: the elemental is chameleon, changeable. Although the surfer's dream of paradise may be the perfect wave, he cannot stay in it forever, for neither it nor he will remain the same. Bodily needs, the urgencies of everyday life, reassert themselves. In sum, one must be able to withdraw from the elemental into an enclosure from which one can think about the world, conceptualize it, work on it. As earlier etymological inquiry showed, home is a place of covering, of privacy, and, as Levinas remarks, home "has a 'street front' but also its secrecy."[13]

On the face of it, home as the space of retreat from the elemental would seem to be more primordial than home as material object or as implement. This would be the case if the elemental in its basic structure were tantamount to a state of nature, a putative prehistorical condition. Home could then be depicted as the locus of the first primitive severing of human life from its milieu. Quite apart from difficulties associated with the state of nature as an explanatory concept in the context of social contract theories where it is generally invoked, existence in the elemental as I have described it is not life in the state of nature but the process of becoming immersed in a milieu, a possibility that perpetually rearises. Home as emergence from the elemental is the place that stands fast for me, the site in which I am grounded, and in which I can "get a take" on the world, re-present it to myself. For all the hedonic potential of existence in the elemental, life would collapse without such groundedness. For all the praise that Deleuze and Guattari lavish upon the undoing of the sedentary, they remain constrained by these caveats: "Staying stratified—organized, signified, subjected— is not the worst that can happen; the worst is . . . if you throw the strata into demented or suicidal collapse. Lodge yourself on a stratum, experiment [from there].[14] The Hutu refugee whose only abode is an unroofed encampment where tens of thousands of people are herded without basic facilities and who is surrounded by the dead and dying represents this extreme point of ungroundedness.

Separation from the elemental as groundedness should not be thought of as a foundation upon which other conceptions of home are built. Each notion of home—as measurable space, as implement, as dear or beloved, as community, as covering—can be interpreted as an aspect of settled existence, as a stratum upon which one can station oneself. From the surface of each stratum, varying lines of flight or deterritorialization are possible from which new assemblages may emerge.

NOMADS AND MIGRANTS

Granting the necessity for a certain groundedness, for remaining planted on a site, how does a sense of home that is linear, wandering, errant—in sum, nomadic—undo sedentary existence? How does life in the elemental reshape itself in new contexts: the desert, the ocean, outer space, the American West? How do individuals[15] and communities become nomadic? How is the contrast experienced? Larry McMurtry's description of an aging Texas Ranger's eros for the frontier in his novel, *Lonesome Dove*, through its very romanticization highlights the affective character of the process:

> It struck [Gus] that he had forgotten emptiness such as existed in the country around him. For years he had lived within the sound of the piano in the Dry Bean [inn], the sound of the church bell in the little Lonesome Dove church. . . . But here there was no sound, not any. The coyotes were silent, the crickets, the locusts, the owls. There was only the sound of his lone horse grazing. From him to the stars in all directions there was only silence and emptiness. Not the talk of men over their cards, nothing. Though he had ridden hard he felt strangely rested, just from the silence.[16]

Here the frontier as a community of silence, of nature that has been stilled and is without language, is contrasted with home as a community of talk, of cowhands, gamblers, lawmen, prostitutes, and small farmers as they go about their business. Gus, lawman and cowhand, is America's nomad, object of its love affair with the frontier.

Nomads like Gus are distinguished from settlers by their creation of zones of freedom. This assertion can be misunderstood if it is taken to mean that wandering is a state of being from which social and political constraints are absent, whereas settled life is an abiding within the boundaries of a state so that to be settled is to be a citizen subject to positive law. But wandering and errancy is not a static condition, an inert state of being; rather it is descriptive of a style. Nomadic life is not a being free, but a manner of becoming free. Because home can never altogether lose its spatio-geographic aspect, the nomad remains territorial but the relation to space reverses that of sedentary life. Like the settler, the nomad must traverse space from point to point, but the point is not a landing place, a site on which to establish herself. Rather, the point is a place to leave behind. Thus Deleuze and Guattari maintain:

> [E]very point is a relay and exists only as a relay. A path is always between two points, but the in-between . . . enjoys both an autonomy and direction of its own. The life of the nomad is the intermezzo. Even the elements of his dwelling are conceived in terms of the trajectory that is forever mobilizing them.[17]

In McMurtry's novel the trail followed by the cattle drivers from the town of Lonesome Dove in southern Texas to Little Rock, Arkansas, moves through an open expanse, indefinite and noncommunicating. By contrast a present-day road between the same points marks off a terrain of parceled out spaces. Not only is the nomad's movement a shifting from place to place, but the motion itself is an investment of intensity. The nomad may be coiled so as to spring up at any point.

But nomadic and settled existence do not exhaust the meanings of home. Neither sedentary nor nomadic, the migrant represents another alternative. She moves from one destination to another in response to political persecution, poverty, or threat of genocide—but always in the hope of finding a temporary or permanent dwelling. Thus, for example, the migrancy of Solzhenitsyn and other Russian writers differs from that of the Haitian boat person or the victim of famine in Somalia. Enforced migrancy may lead to the creation of new aggregates in which nomads and migrants may figure. If migrancy continues over centuries, it may evolve into nomadism, often with socially marginalizing outcomes. Consider the metamorphosis of the biblical image of the Jew in exile by the waters of Babylon into the wandering Jew of medieval myth. A poignant and recent example of itineracy and social ostracism as reported in the *New York Times* of July 21, 1994, can be found in the Tinkers of Ireland, a nomadic group whose caravans traveled the Irish roads for the last three hundred years. Devoutly Roman Catholic and having their own language, a patois of Gaelic and English, Tinkers are now largely illiterate, show high unemployment rates, and are disparaged by many Irish as "bad-smelling, lazy, drunken, too fertile, and inclined to crime."[18] Like the bedouin of the sub-Sahara or the gypsies of Europe, they embody the tension between the need for a territorial foothold and the need for maintaining something of their itineracy.

If nomadism, the romance of wandering and exile, has thus far been sympathetically depicted, this should not be taken as a recommendation to "go nomadic" such as that expressed by Foucault in his endorsement of Deleuze and Guattari: "Prefer what is positive over what is multiple, difference over uniformity, flows over unities, mobile arrangements over systems. Believe that what is productive is not sedentary but nomadic."[19] Contemporary existence often offers little to choose between nomadism and sedentary existence when each implodes upon itself. Consider, for example, the way in which territoriality and sedentariness, versus deterritorialization and nomadism, are parceled out in gang life. The functional distinction between them is maintained but brutality and bloodshed are endemic to both types. In an article on Asian gangs in Texas, the *Houston Press* of July 14-20, 1994, reports:

> [A]sian gangs are not territorial. Although black and Hispanic gangs may fight over a tract of real property, only rarely is the concept of turf a factor in the actions of Asian youths. . . . One of [their] most distinctive characteristics is their fluidity. Local groups have members who . . . move in from somewhere and move out to somewhere else. The groups themselves, and not just the individual members can be extremely migratory. Commonly they move with the same ease across state lines.[20]

Even if media accounts are taken *cum granum salis*, they serve to highlight the extremes of territoriality and deterritorialization. While endorsing many social experiments that encourage the nomadic, even Deleuze and Guattari concede with rhetorical flair: "Marginals have always inspired fear in us. . . . It is a disaster when they slip into a black hole from which they no longer utter anything but the micro-fascist speech of their dependency"; and, in the same vein, "the luminous and clearly dissected city now shelters only nocturnal troglodytes, each embedded in his own black hole."[21]

INNER EXILE: SAINTS AND HACKERS

While it is easy to grasp nomadism as a kind of movement, as the itineracy of the cowboy or the Tinker, or in its "nocturnal form" of nomadic gang life, Deleuze and Guattari stress that nomadic movement should be seen in terms of intensity, that the speed of movement does not concern the time it takes to traverse a given distance but rather is bound up with "filling space in the manner of a vortex."[22] This description is surely counterintuitive and not especially helpful in understanding the movements of peoples. However, if nomadism is envisaged as a return to the elemental, the metaphor of the vortex is valuable. What is more important, the vortex opens the way for an entirely new conception of wandering, that of the spiritual journey that is effected without the traversal of space but rather by remaining in a single place.[23] Insofar as interior itineracy is without relative movement it can be thought of as lodging, but because it is also a transformation in intensity, it is nomadic. Consider Saint Teresa's journey into the soul, her interior castle from which the objects of the world are absent, an inner retreat that is emptied so that God may enter. The castle is the place from which God may speak, commune with the soul. Saint Teresa declares, "It is that we consider our soul to be like a castle made entirely out of a diamond or of very clear crystal, in which there are many rooms, just as in heaven there are many dwelling places."[24] The soul is both stationary abode and nomadic terrain. It is also Saint Teresa's zone of freedom, the place in which she can stroll without institutional authorization. Even if she can enter its precincts only when led there by God, it is neither her confessor nor the prioress who is doorkeeper. Praising the delights of the castle to the sisters of her order, Saint Teresa exults:

> Considering the strict enclosure and the few things you have for your entertainment, my Sisters, and that your buildings are not always as large as would be fitting for your monasteries, I think it will be consolation for you to delight in this interior castle since without permission from the prioress you can enter and take a walk through it at any time.[25]

Unlike the convent, the interior castle is one's own, not in the sense of private property but rather in the sense of inseparability from it. Thus even if entry to the castle is barred, so to speak, one cannot divest oneself of it just as one cannot jettison one's body. It is both interior macrocosmic space, home as an infinitely expanded inner universe, and home as one's ownmost secret haven.

There is yet another macroscopic space, an escape route or line of flight from sedentary existence as encumbered by enclosure, that is especially compelling today. Cyberspace is that nonplace or dimension in which electronic signals are transformed into information, and in which this information circulates, and in which the computer user either becomes bodiless or acquires a new nonphysical body.[26] Like the infinite spaces of Saint Teresa's interior castle, cyberspace can become a private domain in which computer-generated actual and possible worlds can be experienced. Or it can become (in its own lingo) a communication superhighway traveled by multiple users, a community. Systems that mimic or invent worlds, virtual reality systems, replicate physical space by substituting computer-generated data for normal sensation, generally in the interest of hedonic experience, so that the user, if I may put it thus, bathes in an ersatz elemental.

Mark C. Taylor and Esa Saarinen contend that "along the channels of the fiber optic network, disembodied minds travel at the speed of light. As speed increases, distance decreases. Space seems to collapse into a presence that knows no absence and time . . . into a present undisturbed by past or future."[27] Is this not space that is filled in the manner of a vortex as Deleuze and Guattari describe it?

HOME AGAIN

I argued earlier that, for all its experiential pleasures, nomadism can self-destruct into black holes of incoherence. Sedentary existence too can self-implode, but I have not yet discussed how settled existence collapses nor how this bears upon the problem of homelessness with which this inquiry began.

Consider once again home as lodging, this time in the context of the one who is protected, grounded, covered, by a house: myself, I. At the same time that I become aware of myself as grounded, as inhabiting an abode, I establish a proprietary relation with this space. The house I inhabit, even if it is the property of the bank or mortgage company, belongs to me in usufruct. Just as I experience my self and my home as an indissoluble aggregate, I am aware of others who are like me by virtue of interests we hold in common, perhaps job or political orientation, who form similar aggregates. I envisage them as potential sources of support for my proprietary concerns. My actual relations with such others can have satisfactory pragmatic outcomes. The residents of a neighborhood may transcend an interest in enhancing real estate values and unite to form a new community to create aesthetically satisfying public spaces. In considering common interests, the other is one who, in specifiable respects, shares my concerns. The realization of communal purposes depends upon joint ventures based upon such cooperation.

However, the other may not only share my goals but may be seen by me as another myself. Perceived consanguinity, common religion, or common culture may be used to support such identification. The commonality of shared interests becomes ontological identity—I am she and all the others who are extensions of myself and they are me. This engorged self, this I who is all the others, may in addition be linked to property interests. The aggregate of dwellings becomes a territory, a larger more unified whole, an enclosure inhabited by a homogeneous multitude that has dissolved into a single subject. In its romantic versions these proprietary relations to home and land are aestheticized, thereby reinforcing the affective bonds to both. Deleuze and Guattari reject the notion that such an aggregate is a mere appearance, insisting that when it takes shape as a nation it is "a passional and living form" based on "collective subjectification" and "qualitative homogeneity," one that may brutally subjugate those who lie outside this higher unity.[28] It would be absurd to suggest that territorial conflicts and clashes between ethnic groups can be explained without considering such matters as economic and political forces, but, by focusing on home, some significant affective dimensions of these conflicts can be brought to the fore.

Despite the deformations of home I have sketched, home as groundedness, as shelter, as covering, is indispensable. Without housing bodily existence breaks down, a dissolution that is occurring in vast areas of the world. To be sure, I can station myself upon some plateau of pleasure, some stratum of hedonic existence, so as to ignore the exposedness, the homelessness of the other—the Thai prostitute with AIDS driven first from her village, then from her cage to the streets, or the Yanamamo expelled from the Brazilian jungle. Yet even if the real and the imaginary are fast becoming indistinguishable in this age of images, the very images of their displacement and unshieldedness shatter my sheltered existence and my nomadic pleasures.

NOTES

1. Gilles Deleuze and Felix Guattari, A Thousand Plateaus: Capitalism and Schizophrenia, trans. Brian Massumi (Minneapolis: University of Minnesota Press, 1987), p. 19. In what follows I often station myself within the analytic framework of this work without subscribing to the desiderata it endorses.

2. Josiah Royce, Basic Writings, ed. John J. McDermott (Chicago: University of Chicago Press, 1969), p. 197.

3. American Heritage Dictionary of the English Language, 1981 ed., s. v. "home."

4. Marcus Aurelius, Meditations, trans. G. Long, in The Stoic and Epicurean Philosophers, ed. Whitney J. Oates (New York: Random House, 1957), 7.9, p. 536.

5. Ibid., 8.18, p. 546.

6. See Martin Heidegger, "Building, Dwelling, Thinking," and ". . . Poetically Man Dwells . . ." in *Poetry, Language, Thought,* trans. Albert Hofstadter (New York: Harper and Row, 1971), pp. 143–62, 211–29.

7. Martin Heidegger, *Being and Time,* trans. John Macquarrie and Edward Robinson (New York: Harper and Row, 1962), p. 123.

8. Ibid., p. 97.

9. Emmanuel Levinas, *Totality and Infinity,* trans. Alphonso Lingis (Pittsburgh: Duquesne University Press, 1969), p. 131.

10. Ibid., p. 133.

11. Phil Edwards with Bob Ottum, *You Should Have Been Here an Hour Ago* (New York: Harper and Row, 1967), p. 14.

12. Although there are significant resemblances between Levinas's and Deleuze and Guattari's understanding of qualities, their interpretations serve quite different ends. Levinas's phenomenology of the elemental as a field of enjoyment, nonutilitarian and infracognitive, is developed to contrast with Heidegger's analysis of the purposeful structure of equipment. Deleuze and Guattari are interested in integrating their account of qualities into a radically processive philosophy of becoming. In *A Thousand Plateaus* they write:

> We are not at all arguing for an aesthetics of qualities. . . . [They] still seem to us to be punctual systems: They are reminiscences, . . . either transcendent or floating memories of seeds of phantasy. . . . The quality must be considered from the standpoint of the becoming that grasps it. . . . For example, whiteness . . . is gripped in a becoming-animal of Captain Ahab [his becoming Moby Dick]. (p. 306)

13. Levinas, *Totality and Infinity,* p. 156.

14. Deleuze and Guattari, *A Thousand Plateaus,* p. 161.

15. Rather than defining individuals as substances having qualities, Deleuze and Guattari, like Charles Sanders Peirce before them, develop a relational view of individuality by adapting the medieval notion of haecceity. In *A Thousand Plateaus* they write:

> A season, a summer, an hour, a date have a perfect individuality lacking nothing even though this individuality is different from that of a thing or a subject. . . . They are haecceties in that they consist of relations of movement and rest between molecules or particles, capacities to affect or be affected. (p. 261)

16. Larry McMurtry, *Lonesome Dove* (New York: Simon and Schuster, 1985), pp. 466f.

17. Deleuze and Guattari, *A Thousand Plateaus,* p. 380.

18. *New York Times* (international ed.), 21 July 1994, p. A4.

19. Michel Foucault, Preface to Gilles Deleuze and Felix Guattari's *Anti-Oedipus: Capitalism and Schizophrenia*, trans. Robert Hurley, Mark Seem, and Helen R. Lane (New York: Viking Press, 1972), p. xiii.

20. Ken Englade, "The Gangs among Us," *Houston Press*, 14–20 July 1994, p. 10.

21. Gilles Deleuze and Claire Parnet, *Dialogues*, trans. Hugh Tomlinson and Barbara Habberjam (New York: Columbia University Press, 1987), p. 139.

22. Deleuze and Guattari, *A Thousand Plateaus*, p. 381.

23. Ibid.

24. Saint Teresa of Avila, *The Interior Castle*, trans. Kieran Kavanaugh, O.C.D. (New York: Paulist Press, 1979), p. 35.

25. Ibid., p. 195.

26. Michael Heim, *The Metaphysics of Virtual Reality* (New York: Oxford University Press, 1993), pp. 78–81, 160.

27. Mark C. Taylor and Esa Saarinen, *Imagologies* (New York: Routledge, 1994). This work does not use page numbers. The citation can be found on the page headed "speed 4."

28. Deleuze and Guattari, *A Thousand Plateaus*, p. 456.

Hospitality: Home as the Integration of Privacy and Community

ROSEMARY L. HAUGHTON

I WANT TO PROPOSE THE NOTION of hospitality as a way to break open the dualism of thought, policy, and practice that is, I think, responsible for the terrible dead end into which we have wedged ourselves as a society. In doing this, perhaps not surprisingly, I find myself redefining, or rather rediscovering, the idea of home as the place of encounter between the private and the public, and as a kind of solvent of the dualistic division which imprisons us—often literally.

The Enlightenment categories of thought and living which have shaped Western society are so thoroughly constitutive of how we perceive our condition as a society that any alternative view is closed to us as thoroughly as if we had driven into a cul-de-sac of high stone walls and found the reverse gear didn't work. The only way out is the dismantling of the enclosing walls, which sounds like an impossible task, since these walls represent not only their own height and weight but the existence of the huge structures of which they are part. But I shall suggest that, in one sense, dismantling them may be in fact very easy. All that is required is the recognition that the walls have no reality except what we give to them, and melt when we become aware of alternative ways of perceiving the reality of our lives. On the other hand, however, the dismantling is in practice very difficult. We are so conditioned to regard these enclosing walls as insurmountable—as actually the structures of our very selves—that the personal and philosophical and spiritual revolution involved in questioning their reality is so great as to seem suicidal.

What we are dealing with are the basic descriptions of reality which we learned as soon as we learned anything, and which are encoded in our legal systems, our political systems, our scientific systems, our religious systems, our economic systems, and our view of history.

In all these areas we have learned to think in terms of *separations*, of spheres of interest or influence that do not interact though they may indirectly affect one another. We recognize a public sphere and a private one, a sphere of work and a domestic sphere; we base our politics and law on the distinction between the rights of the individual and the demands of the public good; we separate the secular and the religious and frequently identify those also as respectively public and private. Scientifically we separate the observer from the observed, the object from the subject. We posit truth as something to be perceived from a point of detached judgment, uninvolved with the process of actual living. We separate teacher from taught, employer from employed, and when there is conflict we set up elaborate machinery to reestablish contact between these alienated functions. We separate the human from the nonhuman, and the human inhabitants of the earth from the earth they inhabit.

Some of the results of all this are such things as the definition of prosperity as the level of profit, regardless of the quality of life either of the people who produce goods (or lose the opportunity to do so) or of those who buy them. It is taken for granted that the market is to be stimulated to create more and more demand for goods, apparently regardless of the effect on social structures—real lives—through the reshaping of expectations and the encouragement of debt. We measure the costs of production and development in ways that leave out the invisible costs of destruction of lives, environments, and the future of entire nations and ecosystems. We measure individual productivity solely in terms of output of goods or services paid for by earnings. It is significant that, for instance, a woman is only described as "working" if she earns a wage or salary; the hours of hard and skilled labor that go into rearing children, making a home, or doing many kinds of volunteer work are not measured in the GNP of any nation. In Africa, where in many areas women have been the farmers and gardeners, their labor has not been measured as "productive" in modern economic calculations. But when their men are persuaded to produce for a cash economy, for the benefit of distant markets, rather than the nourishment of their village and family, then that is measured as bona fide production. And, very significantly, we shape what we call history to make normative the situation created by a dualistic pattern of thought and decision. Such a "history" proposes greatness as a matter of individual achievement without social or cultural context, and measures progress in terms of productivity and productivity in terms of profit. When such "history" is challenged, and a few people propose to teach the stories of the marginal or of popular movements, stories about how real people live and change, the resulting outcry of anger reflects the way in which many perceive this alternative reading of history as a threat to their basic self-image as Americans.

All of this, and a great deal more which is very familiar to you, is the result of those separations in thought and practice, a dualism so deeply embedded that we don't even notice it—it is our language, our way of thinking—until the results become so appalling that we are forced to wonder what has gone wrong. And even when we do notice we are very restrictive in the options we perceive in trying to deal with the problems, because we are still stuck in that dead end, with no room to turn and no view beyond the walls.

There are encouraging signs, however, that more and more people are recognizing the situation on such terms as I have suggested. It is becoming commonplace for scientists, for instance, to say that detached observation is not possible; the observer is part of what is observed and helps to create this situation which is being researched. It is more and more recognized that the way science—or business or politics—poses its questions conditions the possible answers. Some can admit that there is no such thing as objectivity, and even wonder whether it is desirable—a heresy that most professionals still find hard to admit, for it undermines their authority as dispensers of knowledge.

Paulo Freire has challenged what he called "banking" education, the putting in and recovering of information as if it were chunks of some valuable commodity—and many educators have heard and acted on that challenge. Organic farmers have rejected the thinking that treats the earth as a vast factory floor with chemical inputs going in at one end and marketable units of food coming out at the other, regardless of the effect on the health of the soil or the worker or the consumer. Doctors and patients have come together to break down the expectation of expert decisions makers on the one hand and passive recipients of care on the other. Philosophers have very importantly and significantly exposed the roots of the problem and tried to break down the apparently solid clumps of language which restrict imagination and the possibility of breaking out of the impasse. Perhaps most exciting of all, physicists have, through study of quantum mechanics and chaos theory, enabled us to perceive reality in new ways.

Meanwhile, however, in spite of such exciting eruptions of changed thought, the machine so expertly constructed on the dualist model continues to rule the lives of virtually all of humankind. Although it is a Western construct it dominates the globe, and even Himalayan villagers and Amazonian tribal people are drastically, sometimes lethally, affected by it.

The disaster is already so vast, and the very plausible forecasts of the further results of the system are so much more horrible and huge, that it is easy to feel paralyzed. Most of us are not experts, not scientists or environmentalists or historians or influential in politics; and we perceive that many of those who do have the power are likely to be and are being coopted by the system—or, if they won't play the game, suppressed by it. But one of the dualisms we have to break down is the separation between the experts—the ones who have knowledge and hand out bits of it at their discretion—and the ordinary people who gratefully accept their small ration. A first step is for each of us to identify that area of experience that can be our own gateway into an area of sharing, of dialogue, which is about real and essential change. Each of us has knowledge which, when shared, becomes a different kind of knowledge expressed in a different kind of language, a language that is aware of itself as a conversation, constantly changing and developing and revealing new insights and making possible new perspectives. Each one's own modest contribution to the conversation is made by entering through the gateway of things we have experienced; our knowledge meets other kinds of knowledge and, in conversation, begins to dismantle structures of our oppression.

In my own case, I am not a philosopher or a scientist, but I am a gardener and a homemaker as well as a writer. My experiences of gardening taught me, long before I had the language to pose adequate questions, to feel unease about the received wisdom of dualist thought and practice and its effect on the land and its fruits. In time, my own knowledge met and grew with the thought of people who were questioning dualist concepts like cost-benefit analysis, reductionist forms of biology and medicine, or the assumption that small mixed farms were inefficient and large specialized ones progressive. As a homemaker my knowledge became part of the conversation that included architects who believed that homes are not just "machines for living," in Le Corbusier's famous phrase, and that the people who live, or plan to live, in a place should be partners in designing it. I found my thought meeting the thought of those who challenged deserts created by so-called urban renewal and so-called slum clearance, who recognized the meaning of neighborhood and community. I gave thanks for the creation of untidy chaotic "adventure playgrounds" and the decline of bleak concrete expanses with their rows of rusty metal swings. I marveled at the beauty of community gardens blooming in abandoned city lots and the courage and joy of the people who cared for them. My knowledge engaged the knowledge of people creating Community Land Trusts, in cities and rural areas, taking responsibility for building community and common responsibility as they built or rebuilt homes that were affordable.

It was out of such experiences, direct and indirect, that I began to perceive the idea of *home* as a paradigm and *hospitality* as how *home* functions. I began to see *home* both as an aid in understanding the causes of the damage done to human lives and to the earth by our inherited dualistic language and structures, and also as a sign by which we might recognize alternative ways, ways to dismantle the walls that imprison us and to imagine, and realize, a solution.

I use the word *hospitality* in a wide sense that expresses the willingness to make common, at least temporarily, what is in some sense private, which is how we think of home. But hospitality, even in its most restricted sense, is about breaking down barriers. To invite another person into the space I regard as my own is, at least temporarily, to give up a measure of privacy. It is already to make a breach in the division between the public and the private to create the common— and it happens in the space called home. Ancient rituals and symbols govern the practice of hospitality. The guest is sacred, because the guest represents the "other," that which cannot be entirely controlled once the door is opened, and is therefore in some sense the God. Indeed, the stories of divine requests for hospitality, either in disguise or in the person of another, are common in many traditions, from the touching story of Philemon and Baucis, through Abraham's mysterious visitors, to Elijah the prophet's coming to the widow's house, to the saying of Jesus that the one who receives the homeless receives him. In all cases the way the guest is received is the measure of the moral and spiritual status of the host.

Hospitality can be dangerous, in the very literal sense that makes people put double locks and spy holes on their doors and in the more profound sense that the breaching of barriers is also a breaking of categories and therefore a harbinger of revolution. That's why our culture normally protects the home space by restricting hospitality to chosen friends and relatives and setting limits of time and space: visitors are to be kept in the living room for a few hours; others more intimate may stay longer and penetrate the bedroom; while still others are to be entertained appropriately only in impressive public spaces. But however we try to control it, hospitality is of its essence a surrender of total control. The private sphere, the domestic sphere, home as we think of it, is in some sense redefined. It is no longer entirely private; it has become common.

For the occasion and the ritual, whether it be a formal dinner, a children's birthday party, a casual sharing of coffee and doughnuts, a family Thanksgiving, a charitable meal-program dinner for the indigent, or a presidential banquet, the guests as well as the hosts have it in their power to disrupt the occasion or to make it enjoyable by all. There is therefore a real partnership, a necessary if unspoken contract, a temporary community in which all have responsibility in some degree for the well-being of all the rest.

Hospitality can be much more than a social function or a gesture of temporary generosity. Under oppressive regimes, or in times of war, to provide hospitality to those whose lives are threatened by the powers in control means that hosts risk death, or at least prosecution. Those church communities which offered hospitality to refugees from El Salvador fleeing the death squads risked legal penalties and often, for the organizers, imprisonment, loss of a job, and a place in the files of the CIA. In the Second World War in Europe households that sheltered resistance fighters, escaped prisoners of war, or Jewish people incurred terrible risks not only for themselves but for their families. This kind of hospitality is undertaken out of moral conviction of a very profound kind. It implies that those the space is inhabited by, those who pay the rent or the mortgage, those for whom it is home, are *required* by a moral imperative to invite into it people in need of shelter. There is here no question of whether such hospitality is pleasant; it may prove rewarding in the long run but in the immediate present it is difficult and dangerous. It is undertaken because of a conviction overriding all private convenience or safety that this space is, in *fact*, common. The guest in need has a right to be accepted, if human life is to make moral sense.

In the village of Le Chambon in the mountains of southwest France, the people of the Lutheran parish, led by their pastor and his wife, made the sheltering of Jewish people, especially children, a full-time mission during the Nazi occupation of France. They did it with thoroughness, with ingenuity, and with practical good sense, and they did it for years. They consciously thought of themselves on the model of the cities of refuge required by the Book of Deuteronomy, places where those in danger because they were accused of a crime could take refuge and be safe from arbitrary vengeance. When some of the villagers were asked, later, how they could take on such a perilous task and endanger their families and indeed the whole village, the reply, spoken with a shrug and certain surprise, was "What else could we do?" For as long as it was necessary their homes were common space, shared with people in danger of death.

Hospitality, then, is about breaking categories, because it does not merely make a temporary door between the public and private spheres; it actually brings into question this way of thinking in terms of separate spheres. Hospitality can be a moral requirement and it is, consciously or not, a perceived requirement for the affirming of bonds of family and friendship. The rituals of hospitality are statements about how we perceive ourselves in relationship. To refuse hospitality is to reject the household which is "at home."

However, on close examination, the effects of hospitality are more peculiar and complex than they might seem at first sight. Here is not merely a question of one party, the homeowner and host, making room for another party, the guest. There is an ambiguity which further tends to dismantle fixed dualistic categories, because the actual practice of hospitality clearly implies that the host can only be host, can only play that role, in the degree to which he or she exercises hospitality. There is a role to be played in the creation of community, and that is the role of host. But to play it the host depends on the cooperation of the guest for his or her identity as host, his or her justification for what we call "ownership," as an element in the creation of community.

We don't usually think of ownership as having much to do with community, except when we envisage some kind of communal ownership. Yet hospitality as a creator of communal space, of community experience, requires that there be ownership. That idea obliges us to look hard at the whole idea of what ownership means.

Hospitality and ownership are closely linked. If someone (or a group of someones) has the right, in common expectation, to take the initiative for hospitable community action, then that right is bestowed by the community; the need for such an initiative is built into the way the community functions. For instance, if some people in a small town want to create a youth center they will need permission and approval from whatever bodies are locally appointed to give them. The fact that it is possible for such an initiative to be undertaken at all means that there is a general expectation of some such thing. The project is in some sense a project of the community as a whole; thus, exercising hospitality to a particular group by a particular group is already perceived as appropriate and as an enhancement of the common life, at least in principle. Particular initiatives might not win approval, but the very fact that machinery exists for the legitimization of projects of hospitality indicates that the community regards such projects as perfectly normal.

And it is the community's "ownership" of that machinery for giving particular permission that makes the project possible and even conceivable. In the light of the exercise of hospitality, ownership—of a building, of land, of the means of providing for the wants of others— is seen to be simply a kind of legal or customary fiction to ensure that certain community functions are carried out, among them, the function of host. Continuity of control of whatever is needed to perform these functions is obviously necessary. At its simplest, I can't give a dinner party unless I can be sure that the means to cook it and the dishes to eat it off and the place where it is to be eaten are certain to be available to me. If I don't actually "own" them, then whoever does own them must make them available to me. Whether ownership be private or communal, the possibility of hospitality, and indeed the possibility of most human functions that are not totally individual, depends on the continuity of control and availability which we ensure under the heading of ownership.

But the very dangerous concept of ownership is also challenged, and in some sense regulated and protected from abuse, by the moral requirement of hospitality. The exercise of hospitality depends on ownership, but when what is owned is also, by common consent, committed to the exercise of hospitality, then it becomes hard to justify an interpretation of ownership which inherently *denies* hospitality— what we might call the Scrooge syndrome. Our whole Western culture, however, is based, in effect, on Scrooge principles. The way we have tried to be true to Scrooge while not openly rejecting hospitality (nobody really wants to do that publicly) is by privatizing it and making it a gesture of optional generosity, something morally creditable to the person or group that practices it. We can gain this moral credit by, for instance, giving money to charity, by giving lavish dinners, by volunteering in a soup kitchen, or by joining the Peace Corps, for these are all examples of being "host" in a moral sense. Even when we don't exercise it on our own turf we exercise hospitality when we make what we own—money, skills, space—available to others who don't own them. But all this can be regarded as "extra," none of it necessarily involving an acceptance of hospitality as a general moral and social imperative. This is true even when individuals actually do act out of a sense of personal moral obligation.

For instance, a person who has inherited wealth may decide that the personal ownership of such wealth is incompatible with sane political, social, and economic principles and so may decide to give it away or have it administered by a trust for the public good. He or she may regard this simply as a human religious duty and repudiate the notion that it is particularly meritorious. But the surrounding culture will regard such an act as heroically unselfish or possibly even as fiscally irresponsible, and in either case as exceptional—a matter of individual moral choice, not social principle.

We now have two very problematic metaphysical concepts in play: hospitality and ownership. Like hospitality, ownership paradoxically breaks down the division between private and public and creates a communal space. Ownership as a concept is only needed in order to define the division between that which is to be controlled by one individual or collective, and that which is to be controlled by another individual or collective. The place, as I have suggested, where these two concepts naturally encounter one another is in fact "at home," and that being so we need to look more closely at what *home* means.

Home as an experience can be both very personal and emotional in its identification and also very practical. It has a huge range of intensity of meaning. When I say, "I'm going home," I can mean merely that I am returning to the place where I currently put my furniture, raise my family, pay rent or mortgage—or even to a temporary lodging. In this context home involves things like boundary lines or mortgages or leases and who mends the roof. But I can also say "I'm going home" and mean that I am returning to the place of my ancestors, and that can be a place where I have no ownership in the legal sense at all. For Jewish people, for instance, Jerusalem is "home," in a deep and profoundly important sense. For people of Irish descent the land of Ireland can have a similar meaning. In colonial days, British people serving in India talked of "going home" even though they might spend many years in India, make a career there, and even prefer it to their homeland. Until fairly recently settlers in Australia, even in the second or third generation, talked of England as "home" though they had never seen it. Families can gather in the house of grandparents for vacations or celebrations and refer to this as "going home," and it has great significance in terms of family memories and relationships.

It is this emotional power in the idea and experience of home that makes hospitality so significant as a solvent of social and moral dualisms. The history of humankind is horribly also the history of the lengths to which groups of people will go to protect the bit of ground they call home, or to regain it if it has been conquered. Yet also history is about the settling of refugees in another land, about emigration and immigration, about how aliens become inhabitants, able to claim ownership and often, in their turn, to resist and denounce new immigrants. When nations, as well as individual homeowners, practice hospitality, they take great credit for it and also surround it with safeguards, as I have suggested, and they do this because home is about identity. Home is the place where I belong, and that belongs to me. It defines who I am. The image of home, the symbols and festivals and memories, assure me of who I am and give me a specific value. Even the travelers' wagons and the tents of nomads are home; they define the people and the culture—and are often perceived as a threat to the settled people who claim, or want to claim, ownership of the places where the wanderers travel. That is also why homelessness is so spiritually as well as economically traumatic, and why homeless people are often objects of fear and suspicion. They don't fit in and their "not belonging" is a threat to the sense of stability everyone wants. It could happen to us; perhaps if we can blame them and remove them we shall feel more secure.

Hospitality is difficult and dangerous because it threatens to weaken that sense of identity that home gives us—even the homeland where we only go occasionally or in thought. The spiritual integrity of home can be threatened as much, for instance, in the imagination of some American Jews, by the claims of Arabs to part of Jerusalem, as by someone breaking into my apartment. Yet it is just this dangerous thing, and only this dangerous thing, that can give to the experience of home the full moral and spiritual value that makes it more than merely the place to which I have legal or ethnic claim. The ability to welcome others into the home ensures that home does not become isolation. Hospitality means a letting go of certainty and control—and paradoxically it's only this letting go that allows the richness of growth and change that makes real and not pretended continuity possible.

I personally live in a home whose work, among other things, is to provide hospitality for homeless families. The house is an old one, built in the seventeenth century, and it has been an inn in its time, as well as home to many generations of the family that originally built it, and others later on. In the nineteenth and early twentieth centuries it housed three or four generations of a black family who were given freedom and a bit of land. The theme of hospitality is built into the house; first through the hospitality of the native American people who welcomed the settlers and helped them until they realized their hospitality was being abused; then through the use of the home as an inn "for the entertainment of man and beast," as its license defined it; and on to its present use as a place where families who have lost their homes—and with them their identity and self-respect in large measure—can begin to rebuild their lives.

The old house is a home, not an institution. It is a place where some people have chosen to live and to make their home available to others in need. Hospitality is the principle under which this home operates and it is the vision that makes sense of the daily life within it and out of it. That means letting go of a degree of privacy and control. It means a lot of heartache as well as a lot of satisfaction. But it also means that hundreds of other people have found there a symbol of something they need—that intersection of private and public, the creation of a common space which is given and received, in which hosts and guests together create something new.

The experience of hospitality is the experience of the creation of something new, something which does not fit the dualism of public and private because any attempt to draw a line between them quickly proves untrue to the experience. In the place of dualism we discover an experience of community which is not simple, which does not solve problems but rather redefines them. Home is not dissolved by hospitality but in the experience it does become quite different, and the difference needs work if it is not to become chaotic and destructive.

Taking the lock off the door or opening the borders of the country is not to be identified with hospitality because such actions can destroy the home that makes hospitality possible. But the impregnable home where the only comers are clones of the hosts becomes not a home but a fortress and a prison combined.

Thus we are in need of a social revolution which is also a linguistic revolution, because our dualistic language imprisons us as much as our fear of the stranger—or rather it creates that fear. Hospitality entails giving a meaning to *home* which is founded in common responsibility and relationship, not in individual rights, and in which people are protected by a common moral imperative that defines the goals of society in terms of those bonds of responsibility. In that case the exclusion of anyone from the reality of home, and what home implies of shelter and the possibility of growth and common work, would be seen as a violation of the very foundation of a viable society. Yet those who refuse the responsibility of the common task, by word and act, exclude themselves.

The concept of home can only acquire such a meaning when hospitality becomes the defining criterion. Hospitality then becomes, in a sense, a description of the body politic and of the relationships required between citizens in order for it to function. It can enable us to judge whether certain kinds of behavior might or might not be socially and legally acceptable, and that includes behavior on the part of the one who needs hospitality as well as on the part of the one whose responsibility it is—in any particular instance—to work at providing it.

I don't think I am talking about socialism, since that is about the abolition or centralization of ownership and so, in a sense, the abolition of the possibility of home as a defining experience for groups of people. Without ownership there cannot be hospitality; but ownership becomes something different—legally, emotionally, morally—when it is governed by a question: ownership for what? And the answer is itself hospitality, of space, of ideas, of creativity.

I began with the image of a society stuck in a dead end, and suggested that the imprisoning walls were, in fact, imaginary. The task of reimagining a situation, dismantling those strong walls, is colossal. On the other hand it does not leave us feeling helpless because each of us has the power to dismantle those walls for ourselves, as far as our own priorities and decisions are concerned. The chance is very small that the people in power will soon perceive that the walls they believe in are as illusory as the Emperor's new clothes. And as long as they are believed in, the walls continue to dictate perverse, inhuman—and ineffective—policies and decisions. But it is important that we not allow ourselves to be coerced into believing in the forced options of people who are imprisoned in their own false language and the greed it serves. We are free to make other choices, and above all to think other thoughts.

Hospitality is a thought and an experience. It is very practical and very simple and very complex. It is a way to dismantle the illusion of the dominant consumers and give ourselves new hope.

Ecofeminism and the Longing for Home

KAREN J. WARREN

WHAT IS A HOME?

WHAT IS A *home*? As I use the term, there are at least three distinct senses of *home* and one fourth, generic sense of *home* that are variously at play. In the first sense, what I will call "the house sense," a home is a house, a domicile or residence, a dwelling place. In this sense, homes can be human or nonhuman, as in "a home for orphans or veterans" and "the home of the seal or eucalyptus." Since ecology typically signifies the relationships among living organisms and their natural habitats, ecosystems are homes in this first sense, that is, habitats or dwellings for nonhuman beings.

In the second sense, what I call "the intentional community sense" of *home*, a home is a self-consciously, deliberately chosen, familiar or accepted, abiding place of one's affections, as in "home is where the heart is." These homes may or may not be nurturing, functional, good places to be, but they are where one's affections lie. Presumably it is here that E.T. wants to go, that makes Alabama "sweet home" for some, and that makes her native farm in Kansas more than just a dwelling place—a house—for Dorothy in *The Wizard of Oz*.

In a third sense of *home*, what I call "the bioregional sense," home is a "bioregion" or natural place (for example, a watershed) laced with local natural history and human lore. A home in the bioregional sense may, but does not necessarily, include either a house (the first sense of *home*) or an intentional community (the second sense of *home*). It is the sense of *home* in "this land is my home" or "the great plains of Minnesota are my home."

217

What does it mean, then, to "long for home"? Longing for home is at least *wanting or desiring something one presently lacks but holds valuable or worthwhile*. E.T. longs for home, as do so many soldiers during wartime. In the movie *Gone with the Wind*, Scarlett O'Hara longs to "see Tara again"; she longs for home—perhaps in all three senses. Sometimes this longing is a longing to "go home," to be in an intentional community, or to be "home on the range, where the deer and the antelope play." So one can long for home in any of the three senses of *home*.

Can one meaningfully be said to "long for home" when one already is "at home"? I think the answer is yes, and yes for an important reason: one can be at home, that is, in one's house, intentional community, or bioregion (in all three senses of *home*) *without* being in sustaining, nurturing, life-affirming surroundings or relationships. So, one can be "at home" while being quite lonely and unfulfilled. "Longing for home," then, is, minimally, a yearning or desire for what is (or is perceived to be) a safe, comfortable, satisfying, life-affirming, loving, self- and other-respectful place; one "finds home" or is truly peacefully "at home" when one is in such a place. So one can be in a house, intentional community, or bioregion and *not* be "at home" in yet a fourth sense of *home*.

This fourth sense of *home* provides one explanation why this "yes" answer is important: it provides what I call "the ecofeminist sense" of *home*, that is, a house, intentional community, *and* bioregion *where one's individual and community basic needs, life-affirming values, and sustaining relationships are met*. These are needs, values, and relationships that take into account both human and nonhuman environmental concerns, and are satisfied in respectful and ecologically sustainable ways. This is the sense of *home* in which one can say, with deepest respect and veracity, that the earth is our ultimate home: it is where we dwell, form intentional communities, and live in relationship with nonhuman nature. When we "commune with nature" in a personally and ecologically respectful way, we are treating "the earth as our home" (that is, as our *home* in the fourth, ecofeminist sense).

Some have even claimed that "the [human] body is an ecosystem."[1] If this is correct, then our *embodied selves* are also our *ecological self*, and our human homes *must* also be our bioregional homes. As a philosophical position, this means that at the most basic level, the human body—where we live—also ought to be our ecological home (in the fourth, ecofeminist sense).

Note that this notion of the human body as our home is not the notion of the Cartesian body, fractured from all that is mental and spiritual. Rather, it is the whole *embodied*, interactive, social, *relational self*. I assume that part of what is involved in "longing for home" is the yearning to be where one's relational, embodied self is genuinely safe, comfortable, and respected. As I will show, *homes in an ecofeminist sense* are nonpatriarchal and nonnaturist; they are free not only from such familiar yet unacceptable phenomena within patriarchy as sexual assault and verbal abuse, but also from impermissible pollution and toxins.

Where the homes and institutions which house them (for example, patriarchy) are "dysfunctional,"[2] the homes are, ultimately, unhealthy. They are neither life-affirming nor nurturing. They are disrespectful, that is, literally "not good for you." They are characterized by rigid roles, inflexible rules, a primary value on exaggerated rationality and control, where basic individual needs tend not to get met. These are homes (senses one, two, and three) in which millions of people presently find themselves—homes characterized by such social realities as domestic abuse, emotional neglect, sexual assault, disrespectful gender-role expectations, and divisions of labor. In contrast, "functional" homes and institutions are ones which are genuinely safe, where roles and expectations are clearly negotiated, and the basic needs and life-affirming values of its members are met—what I am calling ecofeminist homes. They are homes where domestic abuse, emotional neglect, sexual assault, gender subordination, and unjustified gendered division of labor do not occur.

Why call this fourth sense of *home* ecofeminist? After a brief discussion of ecofeminism, in what follows I show that there are at least six important insights into the nature of women and homes that ecofeminism can contribute to a cross-cultural, historically accurate understanding of both life-affirming homes and of a "longing for home." It is because of these contributions that I have chosen to identify homes in this fourth sense of *home* which are functional and worth yearning or longing for as "ecofeminist homes."

ECOFEMINISM

Just as there is not one feminism, there is not one ecofeminism.[3] Despite differences among ecofeminists, all ecofeminists agree that there are important connections—historical, empirical, conceptual, literary, linguistic, theoretical—between how one treats women (and other subdominant groups) and how one treats the nonhuman natural environment (or, simply, "nature"). As an *ecojustice* theory, ecofeminism uses sex-gender analysis to make *visible* the connections among all *"isms of domination"*—sexism, racism, classism, "naturism," etc. (Naturism refers to the unjustified domination and exploitation of nonhuman nature.) All ecofeminists claim that a failure to see these connections results in an inadequate feminism, environmentalism, and analysis of environmental problems. An ecofeminist analysis of *home* and *longing for home*, then, is one which sees both women and nature as integral to any adequate analysis of what a home is or ought to be.

Why must an ecofeminist *philosophical* perspective on homes also be a social justice perspective on homes? To answer that, consider the importance of *oppressive, especially patriarchal, conceptual frameworks*. As I have argued elsewhere,[4] a conceptual framework is a set of *basic* beliefs, values, attitudes, and assumptions about oneself and one's world, including one's home (senses one, two, and three). Oppressive conceptual frameworks are characterized by five features: (1) *Value-hierarchical ("Up-Down") thinking* which ranks as most valuable, prestigious, or high status that which is associated with whatever is "Up"; (2) *Value-dualistic ("either-or") thinking* which uses a spatial metaphor to describe things in oppositional (not complementary) and exclusive (not inclusive) pairs, where one member of the pair is more highly valued than the other; (3) *Power-over conceptions and relationships of power* which are exercised by the "Ups" over the "Downs"; (4) *Conceptions of privilege* which systematically advantage or give higher status to what is "Up"; and (5) *A logic of domination*, a moral premise which "justifies" the subordination of what is "Down" by what is "Up." It functions in an argumentative structure which presumes that *superiority justifies subordination* ("Upness" justifies "Downness").

In patriarchal, racist, classist, colonial oppressive frameworks, all five features are present. These features "justify" behaviors that subordinate the "Downs" by the "Ups": the subordination of women, people of color, the poor, and colonized peoples are "justified" by the same logic of domination (5). Since all feminists must oppose this logic of domination, all feminists must oppose oppressive conceptual frameworks and the behaviors they sanction. What an ecofeminist adds to the analysis is that in a "naturist" conceptual framework, the exploitation and degradation of nonhuman nature is justified by the same logic of domination: environmental degradation—degradation of *oikos* or home—involves a logic of domination (5), which functions to explain, maintain, and justify systems of domination.

SIX ECOFEMINIST INSIGHTS

Throughout this paper I assume that, in the ecofeminist sense, a home is a good thing; it is something worth longing for and cherishing. I now suggest six insights ecofeminist philosophy can provide for why one should conceive of homes under systems of domination as not fully functional or "dysfunctional"—not worth longing for—and why one *should* revision or reconceive homes as ones worth longing for in a liberating, functional, ecofeminist sense.

First, ecofeminism can describe and analyze why historically both the alleged private, domestic sphere of "the home" and the nonhuman, noncultural "natural" environment are devalued vis-à-vis the male-gender-identified public sphere or culture, at least in those cultures which are part of "historical civilization," typically associated with the rise of intensive agriculture about ten thousand years ago. How? Remember that ecofeminism is opposed to oppressive, especially patriarchal, conceptual frameworks and the sorts of behaviors they sanction, maintain, and justify. Women and what historically (in Western peasant, agricultural, and industrial cultures) has been female-gender-identified have included commonplace references to both the home and nature. Both homes (in at least the first and third senses of "house" and "bioregion") and nature historically have been feminized. Homes (during the last ten thousand years anyway) belong to the care and work of women. This is especially true of Western, industrialized society, where the so-called female-gender-identified "private" or "domestic" sphere typically is contrasted sharply with the so-called "public," male-gender-identified sphere of "culture," business, and government.

Furthermore, in American English, language feminizes nature in a sexually exploitative way. "Mother nature" or "mother earth" is "raped," "mastered," "conquered," "mined," "penetrated"; her "womb" is put into the service of "the man of science" (Sir Francis Bacon).

"Virgin timber" is "felled," "cut down." "Fertile soil" is "tilled" and land that lies "fallow" is "barren," "useless," like a childless woman.

Just as homes and nature have been *feminized*, both historically have been *naturalized*. In the case of nature, whatever is instinctive or animal-like is deemed inferior to whatever is rational, consciously chosen, willed. Behaviors of "mere brutes," in contrast to "rational animals" (Descartes), are devalued behaviors of automata. In the case of women, language once again both evidences and reinforces the *naturalization* of women and, as such, our inferiority: we are pets, cows, sows, foxes, chicks, serpents, beavers, bitches, bats, old hens, mother hens, pussycats, pussies, cats, cheetahs, bird-brains, hare-brains, and flea-brains. In a patriarchal culture, where women and nature are already deemed inferior or "Downs," relative to superior male-gender-identified reason and culture, a language which both *animalizes* and *naturalizes* women and feminizes nature simply rein-forces and authorizes the domination of both women and what women do, and nature. Thus, one way the exploitation of women, especially women's domestic or "house" work, and the exploitation of nature are justified is by naturalizing and feminizing both.

Thus, ecofeminism can show that the five sorts of characteristics that typify patriarchal oppressive conceptual frameworks are mani-fested linguistically and behaviorally in social reality; they affect how one perceives nature and women-identified homes—namely, as infe-rior, lower status or prestige, or important in a less valued sense than that in which the polis or culture is important. Ecofeminism thereby can show what is wrong not only with such patriarchal conceptual frameworks but also with the language and behaviors they sanction.

Second, ecofeminism can show that homes in all three senses— houses, intentional communities, and bioregions—must be recognized as historically either the special province of women or places where women's role is of supreme importance. It can thereby show why women ought to long for homes that are genuinely empowering— ecofeminist homes. This is because what homes as houses, intentional communities, and bioregions have in common is that historically they have been associated with women and so-called women's work.[5] For instance, in the so-called developing countries, women have gendered role responsibilities to collect firewood and water. In places where trees and water are scarce, this means it is *women* who must walk far-ther for firewood and water and often must carry the firewood and water back themselves. As the primary users of forest commodities in most of the Third World, women's day-to-day, hands-on involvement with forestry provides them with *epistemic privilege* (or "indigenous technical knowledge") that many men and outside, professional foresters lack. For example, in a Sierra Leone village, local women were able to identify thirty-one products from nearby trees and bushes while local men could only identify eight.[6] This means that local women know more about uses of trees than even local men. This knowledge grows out of and reflects their lived experiences as household, community, and bioregional managers of trees, tree products, and water, that is, as managers of homes, in all three specific senses of *home*.

As a third and related point, ecofeminism can show why women and their homes—in all three senses of home—are disproportionately harmed by environmental destruction, especially in the Third World.[7] Consider again trees. In the so-called Third World, women are more dependent than men on tree and forest products.[8] Trees provide five essential elements in household economies: food, fuel, fodder, products for the home, and often the only income-generating activities available to women. Where there are tree shortages, women are the primary sufferers of resource depletion. According to one estimate, women in New Delhi walk an average of ten kilometers every three or four days for an average of seven hours each time just to obtain firewood.[9] As men increasingly seek employment in towns and cities, women must carry out men's former jobs plus the laborious tasks of collecting and processing forest products on degraded soils.

Fourth, ecofeminism can show why environmental racism is a major factor in the exploitation both of the homes of communities of color (in all three senses of home) and of nature as our ultimate home. In 1987, the United Church of Christ Commission for Racial Justice published a study entitled *Toxic Waste and Race in the United States*. The study concluded that race is a major factor in the location of hazardous waste in the United States. Three out of every five African- and Hispanic-Americans, and over half of all Asian-Pacific Islanders and American Indians, live in communities with one or more uncontrolled toxic waste sites. Seventy-five percent of residents in the rural southwestern United States, mostly Hispanic-Americans, drink pesticide-contaminated water. Native American women face noteworthy health risks because of the presence of uranium mining on or near

Indian reservations. Reproductive organ cancer among Navajo teen-agers is seventeen times the national average.

Such environmental racism is a reality which ecofeminism can describe and analyze by reference to the oppressive conceptual frameworks and emanating behaviors that characterize patriarchy and racism: "Ups" with power and privilege over "Downs" exercise that power and privilege in ways which sanction and justify such racist behaviors.

Fifth, ecofeminism can show why poor women and women of color, along with more traditional white middle- and upper-class women, have become a new core of environmental activists motivated to save their homes from the insanities of intensive growth. As Cynthia Hamilton claims,

> Women often play a primary role in community action because it is about things they know best. They also tend to use organizing strategies and methods that are the antithesis of those of the tra-ditional environmental movement. Minority women . . . have found themselves part of a new radical core of environmental ac-tivists. . . . These individuals are responding not to "nature" in the abstract but to their *homes* and the health of their children. . . . Women are more likely to take on these issues than men pre-cisely because the *home* has been defined as a woman's domain.[10] (Italics added)

The Chipko movement, Mothers of East Los Angeles, and the Eco-feminist Greens are just a few of the hundreds of grassroots organi-zations begun by women and low-income minorities throughout the world to stop the destruction of their homes—houses, intentional com-munities, and bioregions.

Sixth and lastly, ecofeminism shows why earth-respectful spiritu-alities can, and often do, play an important role in healing the wounds of the deterioration of bioregional homes and the creation of eco-feminist homes. How does ecofeminism do this? It attacks patriarchal conceptual frameworks and the behaviors and rituals they sanction and perpetuate. Although I have argued for the philosophical signifi-cance of ecofeminist spiritualities elsewhere,[11] the main point here is that *within patriarchy* there may be no such thing as a totally healthy or "functional" home. The dysfunctionalities of patriarchy arise out of and are justified by a logic of domination based on androcentric values and beliefs. *This* is where earth-respectful ecofeminist spiritualities may fit in.

Earth-respectful ecofeminist spiritualities upset a patriarchal conceptual framework, and the behaviors and institutions it supports. They do so by *challenging patriarchy at its core*—its basic beliefs, values, attitudes, and assumptions. How do they do that? Quite simply, they replace patriarchal conceptual frameworks and behaviors with ones which are not.

Consider, for example, what makes these earth-based ecofeminist spiritualities *spiritual*. They are spiritual in that they are conceived and practiced as *life-affirming, loving, caring, nurturing, respectful, nondominating, nonpatriarchal, nonoppressive responses* to life *within* patriarchy which posit or assume some creative power greater than any one individual, rationally self-interested, "autonomous" ego-self. They presume, instead, that there is liberating, life-affirming power which people can individually and collectively tap to challenge, for instance, the beliefs that women are inferior and that humans have a God-given right to exploit the earth; and thereby they begin to make their homes ecofeminist homes. Ecofeminist spiritualities thus rely on nonpatriarchal conceptual frameworks and relationships with nature to challenge basic anthropocentric and androcentric domination.

Why are these spiritualities *feminist*? Because these earth-based spiritualities are opposed to patriarchy. According to ecofeminists, the dysfunctionality or unhealthiness of patriarchy is viewed as a socially constructed, historically molded, economically fashioned, politically nurtured, and socially engineered phenomenon. So understood, earth-respectful feminist spiritualities constitute a diversity of proactive, corrective responses to patriarchy *within* patriarchy. In effect, they serve as contemporary 1997 antidotes to the felt, lived experience and social reality of the twin dominations of women and nature. They name patriarchy as *dysfunctional* and consciously intend to replace patriarchal conceptual frameworks and behaviors with nonpatriarchal ones. These spiritualities represent important visions and strategies of recovery and change. They implore one to become a *recovering naturist, racist, sexist, classist* in the immediate patriarchal present. Ideally, they represent intentional personal and communal practices exercised at any particular time and place to challenge the "isms of domination" while, *at the same time*, replacing them with liberating, nondominating beliefs, values, attitudes, assumptions, behaviors, and institutions.

In short, they are offered as disruptive challenges to present forms of oppression which replace oppressive practices with ones that are not oppressive in the nonutopian, prefeminist present.

What makes these spiritualities *ecofeminist* is that they recognize that, under patriarchy, the domination of women and whatever is women-gender-identified is intimately connected to the domination of nature. They therefore could become practices which break that dysfunctional system of domination and instead honor, cherish, and respect the value of the earth as our home and our responsibility to preserve and protect it. Ecofeminist spiritualities undergird the notion of homes as life-affirming, respectful places—ecofeminist homes worth longing for.

CONCLUSION

In this essay I initially distinguished three senses of *home*: home as house, intentional community, and bioregion. I then argued that "longing for home" is a yearning, a searching, a remembering, a desiring for a place and set of practices that is life-affirming and where one's basic needs (physical, emotional, and spiritual) get met. For ecofeminists, "longing for home" is a yearning for healthy homes—for homes in the fourth, ecofeminist sense.

In dysfunctional patriarchal systems, it is extremely difficult, if not impossible, for homes to be fully life-sustaining, healthy, and respectful, *regardless* of the intentions of individuals who attempt to make them so. That is because the basic conceptual and institutional structures which constitute the theoretical core and practice of contemporary patriarchy interfere with what a healthy home requires. For ecofeminists, unless and until patriarchy is dismantled, and healthy, functioning ecofeminist homes are put in their place, we will continue to "long for home."

I suppose I unknowingly have been an ecofeminist "longing for home" since I first took a trip around much of the world when I was fourteen. For it was then that I first began to truly *see* systems of domination in practice and the role that nature played in determining whether or not humans and nonhumans survived. I now know that what I began to see then was the interconnected systems of domination among women, people of color, the underclass, children, indigenous peoples, and the earth. And I am still in process, trying to see more clearly those connections in order to help eliminate systems of domination which keep them intact. In this sense, I, too, am still profoundly "longing for home."

Sometimes this "longing for home" is a troubling, nagging, uncomfortable feeling about what I have. Sometimes it is a hopeful, empowering sense of what I can do to make my own home, intentional community, and ultimate dwelling place—earth—a better place. I know, because of the sense of shame and bewilderment I felt as a child traveling around the world, that this longing for home is a rejection of the conception of the earth as a "lifeboat" or "spaceship" manned by scientists who don't see the interconnected nature of human and nonhuman relationships. It also is a rejection of notions of the earth as a "frontier" to be conquered and controlled, or as simply a pristine "wilderness" to be preserved with no attention to urban ecological issues. I know my longing for home is a rejection of all these because they are too simplistic: they fail to see the complex and interconnected roles which the "isms of domination" play in the creation and maintenance of environmental problems.

Many ecofeminists have objected to a very popular poster of the earth as seen from outer space: it is the photo of a round, blue ball, accompanied by the caption, "Love Your Mother." Presumably, the popular power of that slogan is its challenge to patriarchal devaluing of mothers' work and roles, and its elevating of the earth to some level of sanctity of idealized motherhood.

Nonetheless, I share many of these ecofeminists' concerns. It is an unsettling poster for me because, for many of the earth's inhabitants, mothers and what they do have *not* had a very positive or valued status in historical, socioeconomic reality. Furthermore, many of us often have had very ambiguous, if not outright destructive, relationships with our own mothers. If the best we can do to preserve the planet in contemporary patriarchy is to love it as our mothers, we are in deep trouble.

What the image of the earth as seen from outer space *does* suggest is that we *are* all in this together—humans and nonhumans alike. It *does* suggest a sense of the earth as home to all of us, humans and nonhuman natural objects alike. Earth is a home which must be clean and well kept, nurtured and respected, protected from unwarranted exploitation and destruction.

So, I suggest that we recaption the poster featuring the earth as seen from outer space to read, simply, "Love the Planet—Your Home," in the ecofeminist sense of *home*. Perhaps then one would really *see* what I think ecofeminism is attempting to show, namely, that there are important connections between how one conceives and treats women and how one conceives and treats our ultimate home, the planet earth. According to ecofeminists, a failure to dismantle unhealthy homes and put in their place healthy homes—ecofeminist ones—will simply perpetuate the twin dominations of women and nature.

Why focus on the planet earth in an analysis of "longing for home?" Because it is *here, on planet earth* that we build our houses, establish intentional communities, and do so within specific, cross-culturally varied bioregions. Stated differently, it is on the planet earth that we build our earthly homes. The earth truly *is* our home.

In conclusion, I am reminded of an age-old wisdom: "If we don't take care of our bodies, where will we live?" To paraphrase that wisdom, if we don't take care of the planet earth, our ultimate home, where will any of us, human and nonhuman natural beings, live? Even if not realizable in 1997, still, in 1997, we all need and ought to long for a healthy, life-affirming planet as our ultimate, embodied home—that is, *home* in the ecofeminist sense of *home*.

NOTES

1. Graydon Royce, "The Body Is an Ecosystem," *Minneapolis Star Tribune*, 12 September 1994, p. 8A.

2. For a discussion of the notion of a dysfunctional system, and, in particular, patriarchy as a dysfunctional social system, see my essay "A Philosophical Perspective on Ecofeminist Spiritualities," in *Ecofeminism and the Sacred*, ed. Carol J. Adams (New York: Continuum/Crossroads Books, 1993), pp. 119–32.

3. See Karen J. Warren, "Feminism and Ecology: Making Connections," *Environmental Ethics* 9, no. 3 (1987): 3–20; and "The Power and the Promise of Ecological Feminism," *Environmental Ethics* 12, no. 2 (1990): 125–46.

4. See my essay "Towards an Ecofeminist Peace Politics," in *Ecological Feminism*, ed. Karen J. Warren (London: Routledge Press, 1994): pp. 179–99.

5. More will be said on the third, bioregional sense of *home* in the text, point three. For a more elaborate discussion of women-bioregion connections

see my essay "Taking Empirical Data Seriously: An Ecofeminist Philosophical Perspective," in *Ecofeminism: Women, Nature and Culture*, ed. Karen J. Warren (Bloomington, Ind.: Indiana University Press, 1995).

6. United Nations Food and Agricultural Organization, "Restoring the Balance: Women and Forest Resources," with assistance from the Swedish International Development Authority (Rome, 1987), p. 4.

7. I consider this issue in detail in my paper "Taking Empirical Data Seriously" (see note 5 above).

8. For a more complete discussion of the ways in which women are disproportionately harmed by environmental destruction, see my "Taking Empirical Data Seriously."

9. Marilyn Waring, *If Women Counted: A New Feminist Economics* (New York: Harper and Row, 1988), p. 263.

10. Cynthia Hamilton, "Women, Home, and Community," *Woman of Power: A Magazine of Feminism, Spirituality, and Politics*, no. 20 (Spring 1991), p. 43.

11. Warren, "A Philosophical Perspective on Ecofeminist Spiritualities" (see note 2 above).

The Indian Diaspora and Its Conception of Home

BHIKHU PAREKH

THE MODERN WORLD IS distinguished by several diasporas, such as the Jewish, the Chinese, the Irish, the Indian, the African, and the British. Each has a distinct history, has undergone unique cultural mutations, and has developed a distinct mode of conceptualizing itself and its relation to its land of origin. To call them all diasporas is to run the risk of overlooking these and other important differences between them and to invite misleading comparisons. For centuries the term *diaspora* referred to a group of people who had *no* homeland of their own and were scattered over different parts of the world. This is why the term was long confined to the Jews, and often spelled with a capital *D*. Toward the beginning of the twentieth century it was extended to cover the African diaspora, and has been of late used to refer to any community that is spread out over different parts of the world. For linguistic convenience we may accept this broad usage, but we should not allow it to obscure deep differences between the self-consciousness and self-confidence of those diasporic communities who have no home of their own (for example, the Jews, until recently), those who do not think in terms of a home (for example, the Gypsies), those who do have a home (for example, the Indians, the Irish, and the Chinese), and those who have a continental but not an identifiable national home (for example, the Africans). In this paper I shall concentrate on the origins and dynamics of the Indian diaspora and analyze its distinct mode of being at home in the world.

I

Indians have a long history of traveling, trading, and establishing settlements abroad. Buddhist pilgrims and missionaries penetrated most of central and eastern Asia. Several Hindu dynasties ruled over parts of Indonesia and Southeast Asia, and Hindu businessmen established themselves in Afghanistan and parts of central Asia. Indian contacts with East Africa were among the oldest and the closest. According to one Arab tradition, Aristotle advised Alexander the Great to establish a Greek colony on the island of Sokotra off northeastern Africa. The enthusiastic Greeks "subdued the Indians who were established there, took possession of Sokotra, and removed a colossal idol to which Indians paid homage."[1] As the famous *Periplus of the Erythraean Sea* makes clear, Indian traders continued to visit trading centers along the East African coast well into the first century C.E. Chinese blue-and-white porcelain that found its way to East Africa during the medieval period owed its origin largely to Gujarati ships. Indian, mainly Gujarati, commercial establishments existed in Africa from the thirteenth century onward, and Gujarati businessmen, many of them Muslims, acted as bankers and money lenders. Their business acumen endeared them to the Arabs, who had acquired a hold over the coastal areas of East Africa and who offered them protection and commercial immunity in return for finance and successful economic management.[2] Indian merchants, mainly Muslim, also financed some of the Arab slave traders. By 1860 they are said to have controlled almost the whole of Zanzibari trade. Indian traders married or had liaisons with African women, and their offspring were to be found not only on the East African coast, where they were called *chotara*, but also in the coastal regions of Gujarat, where their racially mixed features earned them the name of *habsis* (meaning "blacks" or "Negroes").[3]

Although Indians have traveled abroad for centuries as traders, pilgrims, and missionaries, they (especially the Hindus) were antipathetic to migration. The Hindu way of life is marked by notions of purity and pollution, and feels threatened by migration. It is closely bound up with the Indian soil in terms of its holy places, gods, goddesses, diet, dress, life cycle rituals, modes of worship, and so on, and feels disoriented and rootless outside India. Hindus have also traditionally regarded their civilization as the oldest, uniquely spiritual, and superior to most others. For these and related reasons they regarded migration as an act of disloyalty, desertion, and even betrayal, and strongly disapproved of it.[4]

The practice of migrating abroad for work began in the 1830s. When Britain abolished slavery in 1833, sugar, tea, and rubber plantations in different parts of its empire badly needed labor. The emancipated slaves were unwilling to work on plantations. The Chinese, Portuguese, and other workers were tried out, but for one reason or another they proved unsatisfactory. In Fiji Polynesian labor proved inefficient and expensive, and the Japanese suffered so severely from beri-beri and other diseases that the survivors had to be repatriated. Colonial governments in the British empire turned to India. When the French abolished slavery in 1848, they too began to recruit labor— initially from their Indian colonies and later from British India. The Dutch banned slavery in 1863 and began recruiting Indian labor ten years later. Requests for what Lord Salisbury called "these intelligent and industrious people" began to come between 1870 and 1914 from places as far apart as Peru, Cuba, and West Africa (to do agricultural labor in the Niger Delta), but the British government in India declined to comply with them.

Indian labor took two forms, contract labor and indentured labor. The former, resembling the ordinary form of wage labor with the two-way passage paid, was limited to Burma, Malaysia, and Sri Lanka. It was mainly recruited from the Tamils and Telugus in South India, and continued between 1832 and 1937. Indentured labor, a wholly novel form of labor invented by the British and bearing the imprint of slavery which it had just replaced, was far more common. Under it the workers indentured or "contracted" themselves to work for an employer for a fixed period, usually for five years. They lived on the plantation and were forbidden to leave without a pass, worked unlimited hours, were barred from taking any other employment, and were in case of misconduct subjected to financial penalty and physical punishment. In return they received a basic pay, free accommodation, food rations, and a fully or partially paid return passage to India. At the end of the contracted period, indentured laborers could return home (which about a third of them did), or reindenture on the promise of a free plot of land (which most of them did), or work elsewhere (which was rare), or buy a piece of land in the colony (which only a few of them could afford). Most Indians reindentured either because of the promise of land, or because they needed more money to buy land or set up shops as artisans and craftsmen. Indentured laborers included women and children as well, and their working conditions were just as harsh. The number of women was restricted to the ratio of between one and four women to ten men.[5] This led to prostitution and trading in women, deeply corrupted the relations between husband and wife, and virtually destroyed the institution of the family among the indentured Indians.

In addition to the contract and indentured laborers, several other classes of Indians also migrated abroad. Some were recruited as clerks, administrators, craftsmen, and technicians, whereas others, such as traders and professionals, went on their own. This last group, called "passenger Indians," came mainly from Gujarat and the Punjab, and included a large number of Hindus, a sizable number of Muslims and Sikhs, and a small number of Christians. Unlike the Hindus and Muslims, the Sikhs were mainly concentrated in East Africa and parts of Southeast Asia. Muslim traders were generally more enterprising than the Hindus. As we saw, they, especially those from Gujarat, had a long tradition of trading overseas, mainly along the East African coast. The more prosperous among them went to South and East Africa, taking Hindu accountants, lawyers, and managers with them. Over time the latter set up their own businesses and were joined by other Hindu traders and professionals. In no country save East Africa did the number of "passenger Indians" exceed that of the laborers. Since they had a more balanced sex ratio, their number increased considerably, but in no country save East Africa do their descendants exceed those of the contract and indentured laborers.

Indians began to go to Canada in significant numbers around 1875, mainly to help build the Canadian Pacific Railway. According to the Canadian census of 1881, they numbered 25,661 in the province of British Columbia. Many of them went back on completion of their contract. A few years later a small number of Indians, mainly Sikhs from the Punjab, sailed to the west coast of Canada. Turned away once, they returned a few months later and were (after much negotiation) allowed into British Columbia. Initially they worked in the lumber industry and over time became traders and professionals. Some of them moved south and settled in California, where they initially worked on the Western Pacific Railroad and on the land, and later set up small businesses. A few of them also went to Mexico and some parts of Latin America. The Indian presence in North America has been more or less continuous ever since. According to the 1991 census the Indian population in Canada was 324,840, of which over half were concentrated in Ontario and a quarter in British Columbia.

The second major Indian migration occurred after the Second World War, at first to Britain, then to the United States, and a little later to Australia and the continent of Europe. The labor-hungry British industries recruited Indians mainly from the Punjab and Gujarat, the peak period of migration being between 1956 and 1965. Professionals, mainly doctors, came a little later, joined in the late 1960s by the British passport-holding Indians from Kenya, and in 1971 by those expelled by Idi Amin of Uganda. The Indian population in Britain today is around one million, of which just over a third are Hindus, about 40 percent are Sikhs, around 16 per cent are Muslims, and the rest are Christians, Parsis, and Buddhists. In the United States the migratory trend was quite different, in the sense that very few Indians went there as laborers. Of the total Indian-American population of just under one million, 48 percent are professionals, engineers, or in managerial positions, and include as many as 35,000 doctors.[6] The Indian population in Australia, numbering just over 100,000, consists of professionals, traders, clerical staff, and workers, and is barely twenty years old. Many of them went directly from India, some were migrants from Fiji, and a few were East African Indians who, having initially settled in Britain, decided to move on to Australia in the late eighties. Some of these people have migrated twice or even thrice in their lifetime, and have apparently settled down with relative ease at each stage in their fascinating journey.

The third wave of Indian migration occurred in the 1970s, mainly to the Gulf countries in response to their demand for labor. From a small Indian presence in the 1960s, the number of Indians grew to several hundred thousand in 1975 and to over a million in 1990, when the Gulf crisis precipitated their return to India in large numbers. Most of the Indians were single laborers, mainly from Kerala, but they also included professionals, artisans, technicians, builders, nurses, and small and large traders. The Gulf Indians are not really a migrant community, because they neither intended nor were allowed by the laws of the countries concerned to stay beyond their contracted period. They do not even enjoy some of the rights and liberties of the German *Gastarbeiter* and may be expelled at will.

Thanks to the three phases of migration from 1829 onward, the oldest Indian overseas settlement is 168 years old and the youngest barely 15. And thanks to their patterns of migration, the nearly eleven-million-strong Indian diaspora is unevenly distributed in over 40 countries, in 15 of which they constitute between just under 2 and just over 70 percent of the population.

II

Since Indians left India with a broadly shared cultural capital, underwent a common migratory experience, and encountered common problems, their modes of settlement had many common features. Since, however, they came from different parts of India, had different traditions, went to different countries, and had to fit into different colonial structures, their modes of settlement showed variations. Not surprisingly, different Indian communities, and within them different social groups, developed along different lines and evolved distinct identities that marked them off both from each other and from their counterparts in India. Over time little and large "Indias," each with a distinct history, social structure, and mode of self-conception, sprang up in different parts of the world.

The Indian diaspora then contains multiple identities, all sharing some common features but relating them differently and additionally having distinct features of their own. They are like a group of people sharing in common a basic grammar and vocabulary, but possessing distinct idioms of their own and using their complex conceptualized resources to say different things. Fijian Indians, for example, have different social practices, sense of humor, cuisine, fears, anxieties, and ways of relating to each other from those of their counterparts in other countries as well as in India. However they also share enough in common to understand and cooperate with one another.

Although overseas Indian communities evolved differently and related to India in their own different ways, they all took an affectionate interest in it and regarded it as their cultural and spiritual home. Over time the ties weakened, but they were never severed. The ties were weaker in the case of Muslims than in other Indian communities. Muslim holy places are located largely outside India, and that reduced Muslims' visits to the country. Besides, unlike the Hindus, whose choices of spouses are largely restricted to their castes and linguistic groups, Muslims had no objection to marrying the natives, and hence they did not need to visit India regularly in search of spouses or to sustain their social ties. By contrast, overseas Hindus made regular pilgrimages to holy places in India, invited Hindu priests, and imported spouses, vernacular literature, and above all Hindi films—which only a few of them understood but whose stories and music had a seminal influence in sustaining their Indian identity. The Indian struggle for independence caught the imagination of them all, both because it promised a brighter day for India and because of its anticipated implications for the rest of the British colonies including their own. Indeed, as many of them have remarked, they used to feel ashamed of being Indians until the Indian struggle for independence restored their pride and dignity. Of all the Indian leaders, Mahatma Gandhi meant most to them, because he was himself an overseas Indian, having spent nearly two decades in South Africa, and he acted as an eloquent bridge between them and India. After India's independence, overseas Indians' contacts with India increased. They sought India's help in their struggles for independence, and later for the better protection of their rights.

For many overseas Indians, increased contacts with India meant picking up the thread of history after nearly a century and a half. During that period both they and India had undergone profound changes, and the reunion was not always happy. No overseas Indian feels completely at home in India, but none is wholly ill at ease either. How comfortable they feel depends on such factors as the extent of their past contacts, their knowledge of one of its languages, the kind of India they retain and cherish, and the distance between the reality and their nostalgic illusions about it. The older generation of Indians from East Africa, Malaysia, Singapore, and South Africa who have retained their ties with India tend to feel at home there, whereas those from the West Indies, whose contacts are minimal, feel least at home. This is also broadly how the Indians in India feel toward them. They have their own ways of grading their diasporic cousins on an intuitive scale of intelligibility and social acceptability.

Although overseas Indians took considerable interest in India, they neither wrote about it nor developed a tradition of discourse comparable to those developed by the Jewish, English, Irish, and other diasporas about their respective homelands. Indeed, hardly any overseas Indian has produced a major study of Indian civilization or social structure or of Hinduism from their unique vantage point. Several factors seem to be responsible for this. Overseas Indians' interest in India was largely nostalgic, sentimental, patchy, and without a focus. The level of education of most of them was also low. The more talented among them went into the professions and had little interest in cultural self-exploration, with the result that such interest as they took in India found little literary articulation. Many of them were busy trying to survive or prosper, and had little energy left to look beyond their daily routine. The poorest among them found history a burden and a liability which they would rather not remember, and the rich had no obvious reason to trace their roots or to reflect critically on their social and cultural background. It is striking that overseas Indians took little literary interest in their countries of settlement either.

V. S. Naipaul, a descendant of the late-nineteenth-century Brahmin migrants to Trinidad, was one of the first to feel the urge to understand India in order to make some sense of the wretched moral, cultural, and social life of his people in Trinidad. *An Area of Darkness* was a product of his lonely voyage of self-discovery, and showed all the signs of a pioneering diasporic work. It was infused with a sense of rage at the civilization that had given so little cultural and moral capital to its people. It was powerful, perceptive, and passionate, but also unbalanced and one-sided in viewing India almost exclusively from the perspective of its most unfortunate overseas children. Indians in India, who had no previous experience of being written about from the diasporic point of view, did not know how to read Naipaul's book, and were disturbed not so much by its content, though that was painful enough, as by its tone of indignation and superiority. Since they had generally taken a low view of overseas Indians, they were angered by Naipaul's lecturing them on their deeply flawed civilization and invoking the tired strictures of Western orientalists. However, they also felt that his criticisms were informed by concern, compassion, sorrow, and a sense of solidarity, all of which suggested his deep identification with India. This insider-outsider perspective of his book confused Indians even more. Naipaul learned from his experience and has written much on India since, in each case not only revising his earlier views on the country but, what is far more important, exploring a more satisfactory way of conducting a diasporic discourse on it. His lead has been followed by others, and a rich tradition is now beginning to develop.

While the diasporic discourse on India is acquiring a clear and coherent character, the same cannot be said about the Indian discourse on the diaspora.[7] India took little interest in overseas Indians. Initially it was concerned about the plight of the indentured laborers and protested against their terms of employment. But it more or less washed its hands of them after they decided to settle down in their new countries. Gandhi was one of the first to stimulate Indian interest in them while he was in South Africa and also on his return home.

After independence successive Indian governments adopted an attitude of studied indifference to overseas Indians, lest they should appear to be interfering in the internal affairs of another country. They were also anxious not to appear as their protector, nor to encourage their return to India, nor to expose them to the suspicion of divided loyalty. In 1948, a year after Indian independence, several Trinidadian Indians threatened to commit mass suicide unless their government agreed to facilitate their return to India. In spite of the Indian prime minister's advice to the contrary, they went to India, but most came back. In 1947 hundreds of Indians in Jamaica organized "back to India" demonstrations, but nothing came of these. Nehru, the Indian prime minister at the time, was right to panic and to avoid close contacts with overseas Indians.

The Indian lack of interest in overseas Indians also had its roots in its patronizing attitude to them. As we saw, Indians, especially Hindus, disapproved of emigration and thought rather lowly of overseas Indians. For the high-caste Hindus the latter had lost or compromised their religion and values, and were culturally inauthentic. For the politically minded Indians, including Nehru and the socialists, overseas Indians were either poor and illiterate and thus a liability, or rich men who had exploited the native people and were a moral embarrassment. Many Indians also felt that overseas Indians had gotten into the habit of clinging to India, and had as a result neither integrated with the natives nor evolved an autonomous life of their own. It was now time to wean them away from mother India.

In recent years the Indian attitude to overseas Indians has undergone important changes for two main reasons. First, as more and more Indians came into contact with their diasporic cousins, they realized that their stereotypes were deeply mistaken. Not all overseas Indians had come from low castes, and many of them were reluctant migrants. The rich among them had often made money by hard work and entrepreneurial skills, often in the teeth of much local gratuitous harassment. And while adjusting to their new environment, all of them had endeavored to retain their culture and affection for India. A greater understanding of overseas Indians generated pride in their struggles and achievements, a desire to reciprocate their affection, and a sense of guilt at having neglected them for so long.

Secondly, India's self-interest has also played an important part in the reassessment of its attitude. Since the late 1970s it had been badly short of foreign exchange. Now that Indians had begun to settle in the West and were reasonably prosperous, they were in a position to help their country not only by their remittances but also by their technological, scientific, managerial, and other skills. Overseas Indians now became extremely important and were called nonresident Indians, a remarkably aggressive expression that reclaims them wholly for India and reduces their diasporic existence to a matter of mere residence.

India's current interest in overseas Indians then has two sources. Its interest in the older diaspora is largely cultural, patchy, and patronizing. Its interest in the recent migrants to the West is largely economic and political, intended to attract their capital and skills and to mobilize their political influence. It would seem that India expects them to behave toward it in broadly the same way as the Jewish diaspora behaves toward Israel or the Irish diaspora towards Ireland, and gives them considerable prominence and privileges. This has had several unfortunate consequences. Since recent Indian migrants to the West do not have the same moral and emotional relation to India as the Jews have to Israel, they are unable to meet the demands made on them, with the result that there is much disappointment and frustration on both sides. The prominence given to them also arouses considerable resentment and envy among both the Indians in India and the older diaspora, who feel that mother India is only interested in their money and power and discriminates against those possessing neither. Unless the three sides put their relations on a healthy and mutually beneficial basis, there is a grave danger that the long-awaited reunion of the globally extended Indian family could break up in mutual recrimination. As Indians should know, the joint family can turn into a veritable hell if the patterns of interaction between its members are not clearly defined and charitably interpreted.

Thanks to several interrelated factors, there is a far greater intradiasporic movement among Indians than within any other diasporic community. In the aftermath of their painful experiences of racist harassment and expulsion in several parts of the world, insecure Indians have gotten into the habit of spreading out their investments and members of their families in different countries. The expulsion of prosperous and talented Indians from East Africa led to their scattering over half a dozen countries. Their harassment in Guyana, Surinam, and Fiji led some of them to leave these countries and resettle elsewhere. Furthermore, as overseas Indians resumed their ties with India after its independence, they discovered not only India but also their long-forgotten overseas cousins, leading to an unexpected reunion of the globally extended Indian family. As a result of all this, overseas Indians are beginning to build up social, economic, cultural, and other ties with India and with their counterparts elsewhere. If one of them goes bankrupt or runs into difficulties, he moves to India or to another country where he can count on the help of a friend or a relation to reestablish himself. And if she can't get her children into a school of her choice in her own country, she sends them to India or to friends or relations overseas.

All this has rendered the diasporic Indians' conception of home extremely complex. They do, of course, regard their countries of settlement as their home. After all, they have lived there for years or decades, intend to continue doing so for the foreseeable future, and are reasonably well versed in the cultural languages of these countries. However, they retain and often cherish their religion, culture, values, social practices, and so on, all of which link them to India. Not surprisingly, a large number of diasporic Indians regard India as their cultural and spiritual home. It is a land of their holy places, especially for the Hindus and Sikhs. It is also a place of their historical origin, and many of their unconscious collective memories are associated with it. For understandable reasons, Indians of the older diaspora had suppressed these memories for decades. As they have become politically more self-confident and culturally more self-conscious, these memories are being dusted up and revived, albeit often in crude forms, and India has once again begun to dominate their consciousness. Since ethnicity is increasingly becoming a form of group self-definition in parts of the world where Indians have settled, and raises the spectre of ethnic cleansing, that too is leading them to reidentify with India and to think of it as their ethnic homeland. What is more, since the diasporic Hindus and Sikhs have failed to develop autonomous forms of their religions in the light of their experiences, they continue to depend on religious movements in India for their spiritual and religious inspiration. However, although India remains a spiritual home to a large number of overseas Indians, they know that they can never be fully at home in it. Contemporary India is vastly different from the India of their folk memory. And for their part they too have undergone profound changes, partly as a result of their diasporic experiences, and partly because of the inescapably deep impact of the societies in which they are settled. If home means a place which satisfies one's deepest yearnings and where one feels fully at home, most diasporic Indians have none, for part of their innermost being belongs to India and part of it to their countries of settlement. If home means a place where one has struck deep roots and which commands one's total affection and loyalty, again, most diasporic Indians have none, both because they have affection for India as well as their countries of settlement and because some of their siblings and close relations live in other countries. If home means a place where one's children live, many of them have none because children cannot give vicarious roots and are sometimes scattered in several countries.

This does not mean that diasporic Indians are homeless or rootless; rather that like the banyan tree, the traditional symbol of the Indian way of life, they spread roots in several soils, drawing different kinds of nourishment from them and relying on one when the rest dry up. This is why overseas Indians are among the greatest travelers. Traveling, which to them is not going *away* from home but rather going from one home to another, is the only way they can stay in touch with their multiple homes. Thanks to their historical experiences and their way of life, most of them do not have and do not even wish to have a single home where they can be fully at home. Instead they have several homes, some no doubt more important than others but none to the exclusion of the others, and that is the only way most of them know how to feel at home in the world. The diasporic Indians' divided being, multiple belonging, and scattered roots are not unique to them. They characterize the other great diasporas as well, albeit in different forms and degrees; and they even perhaps symbolize the predicament of postmodern humanity in the increasingly globalized and multicultural world.[8]

NOTES

1. Colin Clarke, Cari Peach, and Steven Vertovec, eds., *South Asians Overseas: Migration and Ethnicity* (Cambridge: Cambridge University Press, 1990), p. 152.

2. Hatim Amiji, "The Bohras of East Africa," *Journal of Religion in Africa* 7 (1975).

3. Joseph E. Harris, *The African Presence in Asia* (Evanston, Ill.: Northwestern University Press, 1971).

4. This is true of many communities, so much so that some of them do not have an equivalent term for the neutral English word *migration*. Its two Irish equivalents (*deorai* and *dithreabhach*) respectively mean "exile" and "being homeless." See Kerby A. Miller, *Emigrants and Exiles: Ireland and the Irish Exodus to North America* (New York: Oxford University Press, 1985), pp. 102 ff.

5. Not surprisingly the subsequent restoration of the Indian family involved considerable domestic and state violence.

6. According to the U.S. Census Bureau's report, there were 450,406 Indian citizens and 293,196 Indian noncitizens in the United States in 1991. This was seen as an undercount and there have been additions since the figures were collected.

7. In contrast to both, the intradiasporic discourse, that is, the self-reflective diasporic discourse on itself, has gained considerable currency.

8. For a more detailed discussion of the development and cultural dynamics of the Indian diaspora, see Bhikhu Parekh, "Some Reflections of the Hindu Diaspora," *New Community* (July 1994); and Bhikhu Parekh, "Patterns of Cultural Adjustment in the Indian Diaspora," in *India's Search for Identity*, ed. Fred R. Dallmayr (New York: Oxford University Press, forthcoming).

The Terror of Land Loss, the Dream of Finding Home

MARTIN E. MARTY

I. LAND AS NATURE AND HISTORY, PLACE AND POLITICS

A. The Instance of Jeremiah and Israel

Biblical scholar Walter Brueggemann in *The Land: Place as Gift, Promise, and Challenge in Biblical Faith*[1] conveniently summarized the place of place in Hebrew scriptures. All the predictable motifs are there, familiar to those who study the Bible and reflect on the meanings of land and place. Brueggemann treats "Land as Promise and as Problem," and, indeed, even "Land as a Prism for Biblical Faith." Then, to the point of our topic, Brueggemann treats both "Israel as God's Homeless People" and "Israel as God's Landed People."

Brueggemann dedicated his book, as millions of others of various descendants could have, "To my father and mother who lived from the land [and] who taught us promises they never doubted." His book opens with a contemporary reference that is relevant to the theme of this volume:

> The sense of being lost, displaced, and homeless is pervasive in contemporary culture. The yearning to belong somewhere, to have a home, to be in a safe place, is a deep and moving pursuit. Loss of place and yearning for place are dominant images. They may be understood in terms of sociological displacement, as Americans have become a *"nation of strangers,"* highly mobile and rootless, as our entire social fabric becomes an artifact designed for obsolescence, and the design includes even us consumers! They may be understood in terms of psychological dislocation, as increasing numbers of persons are disoriented,

243

characterized as possessors of "the homeless mind." The despair
and yearning are expressed in the pathos of the "top forty" songs
among the young, in the fear among the old that they are forgotten, in the helplessness of the poor in the face of "urban progress." Remarkably the same sense of loss and the same yearning
for place are much in evidence among those whom the world perceives as being well rooted and belonging, the white middle class
at the peak of success and productivity. Those whom we imagine
to be secure and invested with "turf" in our time experience profound dislocation, and we are, young and old, rich and poor, black
and white, "as having everything, and yet possessing nothing"
(cf. 2 Cor. 6:10).

Brueggemann hastens to add that his own interpretation will
deal less with *actual earthly turf* than with land "in a *symbolic* sense,
as the Bible itself uses it," because, note well, "land is a central, if not
the central theme of biblical faith." The senior Brueggemanns on their
farm told the stories associated with this scriptural theme to little
Walter, as did rabbis in *shul* on New York's Lower East Side, nuns in
parochial school, and Baptists and Methodists, African-American or
other, in their Sunday Schools. It is a relatively consistent theme in
the public school textbooks down toward the middle of our century.

For all that, argued Brueggemann, land by itself is not sufficient:
"it is now clear that *a sense of place* is a human hunger which the
urban promise has not met." That is why Brueggemann engaged in a
reality check by reference to the Hebrew scriptural pre-scripting of
America, as he connects land in nature with land of history. He deals,
then, not with "space" but with "place":

> Place is space which has historic meanings, where some things
> have happened which are now remembered and which pro-
> vide continuity and identity across generations. Place is space in
> which important words have been spoken which have estab-
> lished identity, defined vocation, and envisioned destiny. . . .
> Place . . . is a declaration that our humanness cannot be found
> in escape, detachment, absence of commitment, and undefined
> freedom.

Soon I must stop quoting Brueggemann, who might well have
been on the Institute program; the fact that there is a temptation to

continue doing so helps substantiate the *point that Americans tend to look at their storied land, a "space turned place" because of events, as being somehow sacral.* As such it represents a dream, a promise, as much as an environment for practical and quotidian existence. The prospect of loss of that land as such, not the loss of one's home on another continent, one's land in Dust Bowl Oklahoma, the sod house in Nebraska, or the trailer in the path of the hurricane, induces the feelings of unrest. It also gives rise to elements of chauvinism in the public religion of the land.

So we turn for a last look at *The Land* of Walter Brueggemann and his Bible, to the chapter on "Jeremiah and the Terror of Land-Loss." Jeremiah is "the poet of the land par excellence." Therefore, "Jeremiah more than anyone else is the embodiment of terror." And "his message to Israel, which thought it was ultimately secure and at home, is the coming ultimate homelessness." Brueggemann says he uses "homelessness" here "not simply [to mean] being away from Palestine but in the more radical sense of *anomie.*" We are taught to observe that "Jeremiah articulates to Israel his own pathos, the pathos of Yahweh which is pathos over land-loss," and "land-loss means the end of history." No wonder that historic American sermons decrying failures to keep the covenant and threatening colonial or national destruction were called jeremiads.

Jeremiah also announces a new history: "The Lord of history gives history to the landless who should have no promise," and thus a way beyond the exile of *anomie.* He

> takes the barren as the mother of promise. He takes the slaves as the bearers of freedom. He takes the desperately hungry as heirs of the new land. And now he takes hopeless exiles as his new people. [In Jeremiah 29] what had seemed homelessness is *for now* a legitimate home. . . . What had seemed alienation is for now a place of binding interaction. (Italics added)

B. The Case of American Terrors and Dreams

It would be absurd to picture the American majority being radically theocentric as Jeremiah was. It may be absurd to believe that his contemporaries were or that even much of a remnant among them was. But in diffuse yet sustaining ways, there has been a sense that the

Creator of the natural world set the right things in motion for America, and that the Lord of history rules there. Doctrines of Providence or Progress, stories associated with Paradise past or Millennium promised, may come and go; they may be held only by subcommunities. But they are part of the larger sense that the bounded nation called the United States and its antecedent colonies are and were a place where "the terror of land loss," experienced by most immigrants, or the *anomie* of unsettlement and noninstallation (which we will see were Jacques Maritain's terms), made a contribution to collective and personal meaning alike.

The theme of this volume is congenial to me because so much of my historical work has been a reflection of the theme of "home" and "land" and "homeland" in America. The literature and the actions of Americans through the centuries suggest that most of the people successfully conflated home with land as natural environment and land as national experience: homeland.

Many actions of citizens demonstrated "terror of land loss," particularly in wartime or other occasions of crisis, or when they dealt negatively with conspiracies, putative subversions from without or within, or threats to public order and survival. Similarly, they displayed it positively in calls for loyalty and patriotism, when they were asked to sacrifice lest they lose credentials to hold the land. Their terror of land loss was a reaction less to lands most of them never knew in their parents' places—Africa, Asia, Europe, or elsewhere—than to the American homeland. They both possessed this land and they longed for it.

Most of the more than 50 million immigrants America absorbed came not for religious or political but for economic reasons. They were ordinarily not themselves landed, so they had no land to lose or reasons for evincing terror in respect to such loss. In the Europe that sent so many immigrants, industrialization and urbanization did not allow for land-based economic security. Most Africans came as slaves and thus were landless. They were forced to dream more of a land "across the Jordan" than of land once owned back in an Edenic Africa. The case was similar with Asians, especially the Chinese, since immigrants from there had almost never been landed before they came to America. They all may have known terrors and dreamed dreams, but a particular terror of land loss and a dream of replacement developed in America. The case is similar to that of Jeremiah, who prophesied about such loss to people of Israel who were not looking back to Egyptian exile but forward to a return to the land from exile in Babylon.

II. THE AMERICAN LAND AS SOMEHOW REVELATORY AND REDEMPTIVE

Pilgrims in Their Own Land is the title of the only effort I made, should have made, or will make, to try to tell, in miniature, the "whole" story of *500 Years of Religion in America*.[2] The first page of Chapter One began, as such whole stories must, longer than five hundred years ago. Called "The First Migrants," it spoke of the "tens of thousands of years ago" when "geological motion turned America into a stage for human drama." This occurred at the Bering Strait, where "the first crossing" of humans, from what today we call Siberia, is presumed to have occurred. "We can only imagine the first crossing" of some "one of the band, nameless to us, [who] had first crossed an unmarked boundary. He had discovered America" and was the first of those who remind us

> that all Americans are peregrine people. That is, they all came from foreign shores and were, at first, alien. They had to make sense of their new surroundings and neighbors, to find meaning for their lives, to discover America on their own—and themselves, while doing so.

One can only speculate, after viewing archaeological remains, how they did make sense of things. But the oldest traces, with their suggestions of ceremonial burial, lead to hunches that these early settlers were being religious, as scholars in our half-millennium might have called it. So I speculated about a continuity:

> In all . . . respects, not least of all religiously, they set a precedent that restless Americans have lived with ever after. Never have there been so many systems of spiritual striving existing so close together as in America. The neighbor or newcomer of a different faith or way has always represented a threat or an opportunity to those already here. The great difference between the modern pilgrims and their native American ancestors involves the pace of change. More kinds of strangers keep coming,

and they disrupt established ways. Meanwhile, modern media of communication make citizens more aware than before of alternatives to their own beliefs and customs.

What, I had to ask, was the most important thing one could say "religiously" *in respect to their American situation* about the largest possible number of men and women who have lived on the land that became the United States of America? It had to be a theme that connected Native Americans, who were aliens and immigrants from Asia, and the later aliens and immigrants, from Europe, Africa, latter-day Asia, and elsewhere. Such a theme had to relate to the colonial period, from 1492 or at least 1565 (the date of the first permanent settlement in Florida) to 1776 or 1787, as well as it related to the period of nationhood, 1787 to 1997 and beyond. The guiding theme had to be as grounded in the story of women as of men, that of the outsider as of the insider, the urbanite as of the farmer, the religiously affiliated and the unaffiliated seeker alike. In the seasons of musing, I came to deal more and more with a paradox:

On one hand, Americans seemed, and still seem to me, to be a set of peoples who regard *the land they call their home as being somehow revelatory and redemptive*—a high-risk notion, if there ever was one, from the viewpoint of prophetic faith.

On the other hand, since the framework of paradox demands two kinds of approach, these same Americans reflected their alien or immigrant status. They were aware of their having been uprooted. Those schooled in otherworldly religion, a majority concept, could have repeated and often did repeat hymns like the one asserting "I'm but a stranger here, Heaven is my home." They therefore dared not be fanatically attached either to the land under their houses or to the dwellings and other artifacts they or others had placed on it. They were settlers but not settled, at home but still dreaming of a lost innocence in a remote past, *in illo tempore*, or of a millennium, paradise, or utopia still to come. My designation of Americans as unsettled and uninstalled is taken from an observation by Jacques Maritain, the French Catholic philosopher who at mid-century was commuting across the Atlantic and who left behind a book of *Reflections on America*. He wrote:

> Americans seem to be in their own land as pilgrims, prodded by a dream. They are always on the move—available for new tasks, prepared for the possible loss of what they have. They are not *settled, installed. . . .*

This sense of becoming, this sense of the flux of time and the dominion of time over everything here below, can be interpreted, of course, in merely pragmatic terms. It can turn into a worship of becoming and change. It can develop a cast of mind which, in the intellectual field, would mean a horror of any tradition, the denial of any lasting and supra-temporal value. But such a cast of mind is but a degeneration of the inner mood of which I am speaking. In its genuine significance this American mood seems to me to be close to Christian detachment, to the Christian sense of the impermanence of earthly things. Those now with us must fade away if better ones are to appear.[3]

I was not and am not ready to carry Brueggemann's word about Israel into an American analogy and say that his "land is . . . *the central theme* of biblical faith" translates into "land is . . . *the central theme* of American faith." But I am ready to say that it is *a* central theme. The reference now, however, is to *land* as in nature + history = homeland, the dreamed-of place.

III. SETTLEMENT AS SACRALIZATION OF LAND AND PLACE

Centuries after the first Europeans and Africans came to America, their descendants or the later comers still lived with this sense of "settlement" and unsettlement alike. They realized more than most had dreamed of in the old country, but they also still dreamed. Along the way, most of them, even those who suffered because of their forced presence in America, evidently sanctified it. Mircea Eliade liked to say that when you stop being a visitor or explorer and settle a place, you are rendering it sacral. But even those whose very existence as reservated Indians or as forcibly uprooted and then enslaved people—which meant that their destiny in respect to place became a market item in the eyes of someone else, a possessor—engaged in this sanctifying of "God's Country." Evidences that Native Americans did and do this are so extensive that it would be idle to quote them. The African-American, already in slave days, spoke similarly. Examples that are both classical and typical abound from the nineteenth-century experience. Thus when an American Colonization Society, made up chiefly of benevolent Northerners, whites, thought they could serve freed slaves and white America well by sending blacks back to colonize Africa, they were greeted by what must have been to them astounding claims. Thus Bishop Richard Allen, patriarch founder of the African Methodist Episcopal church in 1827 wrote in *Freedom's Journal:* "This land, which we have watered with our tears and our blood, is now our mother country, and we are well satisfied to stay where wisdom abounds and the gospel is free." Another opponent of colonization, the equally eloquent David Walker, drew a line of challenge: "America is our country more than it is the white's—we have enriched it with our *blood and tears.*" Blacks had enriched the soil "which their blood and sweat manured."[4]

In the African-American antagonism to African colonization there was a terror of land loss, the American land, South and North. Later, whites experienced this, in the westward movement on paths like the Oregon Trail, where they were beckoned with the promise of land and society in the Northwest. In the Depression of the 1930s, "Okies," the Oklahoma poor white victims of the Dust Bowl, had to move to California, where they went ahead to sacralize "the tractored [already occupied] land" and wherein they had to make their home in the subsequent half century. In John Steinbeck's *The Grapes of Wrath,* "Pa" sits on the truck, not able to leave the dry land because, as it was then said, "Pa is the land." Pa, landless, is dead a few days later before the family comes to "the tractored land."[5]

Extending Brueggemann's motif of "the terror of land loss" to this nation, over 97 percent of whose citizens do not claim to be blood descendants of Israel, might demand a bit of explanation, especially to visitors or newcomers from, for example, Asia or anywhere else that the Hebrew scriptural motifs did not dominate. I am arguing that the sacralizing motifs on which the American majorities drew through most of their centuries derived from biblical themes, either by explicit reference or as the result of the osmotic picking up of cultural elements in their environs.

The "terror of land loss" for most of them could not mean only the loss of a particular piece of land in the Old Country or the New. Maritain was right about their sense of being migrants, temporaries in particular places, the uninstalled and unsettled. To this day, a time when, as it is observed in folklore based on fact, a state like Minnesota loses three farms a day, the victims of this land loss may shed tears when they auction off farm implements. One corner of their mind may always have them cherishing the farm, though we must note from the record and experience of state universities that just as many have been eager to get away from the farm. Other corners of their mind help them cherish the new place, as long as it is in the land called America. They may sputter about the loss of freedom and innocence and talk about moving to Australia as a land of putatively more freedom and innocence. But few do; the continent of Australia has fewer people than does the one state of California to which so many of the uninstalled and unsettled but still lovers of the American land did and do migrate.

The terror of land loss, we have been arguing, refers not just to nature but also to history. It connects less with particular soil connected to the "blood" or the "Volk" or folk, but to the politically boundaried place called the United States.

The American place became a holy land to so many, not because it was a scene of hierophanies, some sightings of God or divine agents, and thus a place for shrines that marked where heaven met earth. Most religions and lands revere such places. The number of guidebooks to sacred sites increases also in America. Here and there is a map to a place like Hill Cumorah, where young Joseph Smith saw the next-worldly figures, heard their voices, and had a revelation.

Walter Ong, S.J., once observed that any place could serve the American pilgrim as long as it was an American place. It could be the home. Ong also observed that instead of pointing to shrine locations as so much of the rest of the Catholic world did, American Catholics wore St. Christopher medals—Christopher being the patron of travelers. Or theirs was the Holy Family, in imagery that had Joseph, Mary, Jesus, and the donkey on the move to any place. In the American Catholic case, the "any place" could not have been an Egypt, an alien country for exile. Instead it was some other site where members of an unsettled people could settle, where an uninstalled citizenry could be temporarily reinstalled.[6]

That the one-fourth of America that is Catholic could draw on the Holy Family figures or that the American majority of Protestants could draw on other biblical imagery is taken for granted, almost unnoticed. Yet it belongs only to the accidents of history that this should be the case. The Native Americans, lacking bullets and Bibles and being the despised "other" who could be and had to be dis-placed, were ruled out by whites. Without moral inhibitions and usually with positive theological justifications, Americans of European descent ruled the Indians out, except when they served as negative figures. Only in recent decades has there been a kind of romantic attempt by other Americans to draw on Native American lore to interpret the environment.

Similarly, the Africans who manured this land with their blood stood little chance of preserving memories of the old land sufficiently to sustain them in the new. Debates about the transmission and survival of Africanisms and Africanity have gone on for decades in African-American and larger communities alike; we cannot begin to settle these, or even address them extensively. For most black Americans, Africa may be "mother" land but it is also "other" land. Forcible removal through slavery centuries ago and, ordinarily, the absence of written scripts, led them to devise their own new plot. They gained the freedom to stay connected with each other after Emancipation. The choice of most to do so meant that sacred Africa had to be dealt with in general, not specific, terms. Ceremonial occasions like Kwanzaa were invented long after profound breaches with African memory had occurred. In any case, the nonblack majority was no more ready than blacks, from 1619 until the recent past, to want to see themselves in the African plot.

Asia? Obviously the Siberia of the Beringian experience tens of thousands of years ago was unavailable for "homeland" reference. Modern Asians, the laborers unwelcomed by organized labor but useful to management, tended to have local influence. On the West Coast, usually in enclaves only, they remained "other" to everyone else. In fact, as late as 1942 the United States government, acting with virtual impunity and little effective stigmatization, could forcibly remove citizens of Japanese descent from their homes, lands, and places, and imprison them behind barbed wire in detention camps. Such Asians, often single men who wore tradition lightly, were not likely to be able to provide the myth, the story, the plot, the script, of "home" for others.

The Arab and Muslim worlds? They in their faith through the centuries displayed considerable sense of both place and migration, of *hajj* and sacred hierophanic sites to one of which all devout Muslims aspired to make pilgrimage. In *Pilgrims in Their Own Land* I briefly traced the fortunes of Muslims in Spain up to the fateful year of 1492 when Catholic Spain forced Jews into exile and defeated the Moors, concluding: "Had there been a different military outcome in the Iberian outpost of Christendom in the 1490s, it is possible that mosques would dot the New World landscape where Christian churches now stand."[7] But the mosques do not stand except at a few hundred locations. The Qur'an did not rule or provide the pre-script for non-Muslim America. But again, only in the recent decades of vivid "multicultural" awareness and curiosity, and in the face of a large Muslim presence, has there been occasion to explore the meanings of home and land and place among peoples who elsewhere around the globe make up one-fifth of the human race.

That left Israel, which provided the pre-script for the Christian script that guided the hegemonous Christian establishment parties at least until the eighteenth century. That is when a Jeffersonian covenant, Enlightenment-style, brought new influences in the understandings of home, land, nature, and history, and came to dominate in the American myths. The Jeffersonians and many other decisive national founders spoke not of the God of Abraham, Isaac, and Jacob or of Jesus of Nazareth, but of the God of Reason, the God of Nature. Most later citizens, however, deftly, subtly, and reflexively fused the two partly contradictory plots. For the majority, the story of home and land, exodus and exile, promise and settlement, as they knew it in "God's Country," had been prefigured in Israel.

IV. THE ISSUE OF AMERICAN EXCEPTIONALISM IN LAND LOSS AND THE DREAM OF HOME

That people in isolated but intense small colonies like Massachusetts Bay, Plymouth, Oglethorpe's Georgia, or experiments in Pennsylvania spoke of their experience of land loss and the terrors it brought, and developed dreams of finding home(s), is not by itself remarkable. It became worthy of remark when they came out of isolation and lost some of their particularized intensity as they formed a nation. They communicated across colony boundaries. Then they became a single "union," God's Country. They found new ways to translate the originating myths and developing stories and somehow fuse them. That is noteworthy. They combined nature and history, environmental land with political land.

In 1848 an English Methodist cleric, James Dixon, upon visiting Pittsburgh and turning in a report to readers back in England, wrote in language that still could overstress Christian-and-American fusions in an exuberant way. He typically reinforced this theme through some observations. For Dixon as for so many, the American dream of home represented innocence, purity, simplicity:

> It can be no matter of surprise that the American people, being favored with opportunity, the soil being clear, and no old institutions standing in the way, should be disposed to adopt a new principle, and, discarding all authoritative church-organization, try the effect of Christianity itself, in its own native grandeur and divine simplicity. This they have done.

Then, after arguing a bit too vehemently that Christianity was the American adoption, he went on:

> All the interests of society converge to this point; religion is its life, its power, its beauty. It is like the *substrata* of the world, on which all the soils whence the vegetable productions spring repose in security.

Dixon is interesting here for the interplay of realities and metaphors with his references to "soil" and "substrata," environmental land and biblically storied foundations. Immigrants found and founded a land. They did not have to be Protestant biblicists to do so. German poet Ludwig Kempert said of and for Jews: "It is to America that our longing goes forth. . . . In your adopted fatherland . . . a man is worth what he is, and he is what he does. Before all else, be free—and go to America." Like Jews with one eye on Zion, blacks, in W. E. B. Du Bois's terms, had to live with "doubleness," which meant with "two souls in one dark body." But there was no doubt that for almost all of them that body belonged in America.

As for Catholics, usually unwelcome in Protestant America, novelist Evelyn Waugh as late as 1949, in terms more exceptional than one might need to make the positive point, could locate them:

> Catholicism is part of the American spirit. . . . Americanism is the complex of what all Americans consider the good life and . . . in this complex Christianity, and pre-eminently Catholicism, is the redeeming part. . . . The lay American Catholic insists more emphatically on his "Americanism" than do Protestants or atheists of, perhaps, longer American ancestry. There is a purely American "way of life" led by every good American Christian that is

point-for-point opposed to the publicized and largely fictitious "way of life" dreaded in Europe and Asia.

The Catholics, as readily as others, had left behind the terror of land loss in famined Ireland or on the European continent, where in the industrial era there were not resources or opportunities for all. In America, they may have lived in urban ghettos and some adopted a fabled "ghetto mentality," but for the most part they were super-Americans, claiming the land and its promise as their own, even as they dreamed of more.[8]

V. SACRED LAND AS A BOUNDARIED POLITICAL ENTITY

Americans did their interpreting of land and place independently of what went on in the rest of the Americas. Especially if one begins with physical geography, geology, landscape, and land, the boundaries on the map appear to be quite artificial.

Joel Garreau some years ago experimented at book length with the notion of *The Nine Nations of North America*.[9] They exist on both sides of Mexican-U.S. or Canadian-U.S. lines. One of them obviously crosses the Rio Grande; he calls it *Mexamerica*. He points out that Los Angeles is the second-largest Mexican city in the world, and that Hispanic growth north of the Rio Grande is bringing about a new reality or realization of what people in the southwestern United States and northern Mexico have in common. There is no doubt that Mexamerica will grow in numbers, power, and influence, but it is more likely to merge its myth into a preexisting story than it is simply and completely to transform the rest of the United States. The nation will capably and reflexively integrate Mexamerica into its own founding and evolving myths while contributing to the alteration of perspective and substance in the other myths.

A second of the nine nations spills over northern borders; Garreau calls it *Ecotopia*, which extends from Alaska to just north of Los Angeles in a thin strip. Citizens there are oriented to the Orient; the Pacific is their lake. Ecotopia, he says, is definitely an "Anglo place," though there are significant pockets of Asians in several urban areas. Physically, Vancouver has much in common with Seattle; environmentalists and advocates of Native Americanness share a poetry that includes the British Columbian coast with the coasts of Washington and Oregon. Yet the Washington-British Columbia border is a high barrier in the United States citizen consciousness. It is not, of course, simply "our" land; when the *Exxon Valdez* spills oil in Alaska, it is an environmental problem for two nations. But for the most part, the two nations do not share a common story.

This aspect is equally true for the largest of the nine nations of North America, the *Empty Quarter* that includes the Arctic regions down through the mountains and deserts all the way to Mexamerica. Within it is the Mormon kingdom, ever expanding in size and numbers and prosperity, spreading its private myth involving the terror of land loss and the dream of finding home. But it is unequaled in its particularity by the others in this "Empty Quarter," to say nothing of the rest of the nation. Here as so often, it is the Latter-Day Saints who contribute to and adapt to the larger story. They provide super-Americanism in politics and ethos, and set examples designed to ward off *anomie*. But the story of what is north of the Canadian border is not "ours" in the rest of that Quarter.

The *Breadbasket*, similarly, overlaps the political boundary. Certainly there is a common literary imagination in that crossing, as chronicled in Robert Thacker's *The Great Prairie Fact and Literary Imagination*. Thacker prints as an epigraph a paragraph by Indian novelist N. Scott Momaday, one that certainly reveres the land in a way that ought to move it above history and politics, and merits quotation in the present context:

> Once in his life a man ought to concentrate his mind upon the remembered earth, I believe. He ought to give himself up to a particular landscape in his experience, to look at it from as many angles as he can, to wonder about it, to dwell upon it. He ought to imagine that he touches it with his hands at every season and listens to the sounds that are made upon it. He ought to imagine the creatures there and all the faintest motions of the wind. He ought to recollect the glare of noon and all the colors of the dawn and dusk.[10]

Yet "he" will define and refine this by identifying the land with homeland, the country with "God's country," in one's national interpretation. One could turn to Willa Cather; Thacker describes her accurately as "the most subtle artist yet to record the landscape," and quotes her in a line that became her chapter title: "the great fact was the land itself." Cather remarkably transgressed boundaries in her fictional corpus, with *Shadows on the Rock* set in Quebec and *Death Comes for the Archbishop* in Mexamerica, before New Mexico was part of the United States. She is appreciated by French critics and is read around the world.

Cather showed little interest, in her fiction at least, in nationalism and political boundaries. Her chosen faith tended to be an Episcopal Catholic transcendent ritual affirmation. But to Americans far from the prairie she remains "our novelist," too, in a way that even the most talented Saskatchewan, Manitoban, or Albertan, who shares the Breadbasket physically, cannot be. They write of the "other," and Cather is, as one of her novels calls its subject, about *One of Our Own*.

Space does not permit a visit in detail to the others of the binational "nine nations" in Garreau's atlas. *Quebec* spills over into northern New York and New England, but is a separate Separatist place even in Canada. Thus it represents another other, a different difference, twice removed in plot. *New England* is marked as one New England in the United States. But there is another one, not physically contiguous (thanks to Quebec), which includes Newfoundland, Prince Edward Island, and Nova Scotia. Landscapes in the two New Englands may be similar, but the physical geography and the story are not one. Nor is that of the *Foundry*, which spills from the United States into industrial Ontario. Toronto, ethnically and religiously pluralist and richly multicultural, may be more like United States cities are dreamed to be than many of them are, but it is not part of that generalized landscape or environment seen as being somehow revelatory and redemptive to citizens of the United States.

In sum, politics, events like the American Revolution and the Civil War, "our own" heroes and heroines and story, lead United States citizens to express their terror of land loss and the search for home in respect to what is contained with some rather arbitrary, "unnatural" northern and southern borders. They see that contained land as somehow the arena for revelation and redemption, if not an agent of revelation and redemption itself.

VI. THE ENDURING BUT COMPLEX DREAM OF "GOD'S COUNTRY" AS THE AMERICAN LAND

If I have spoken in terms that might evoke romantic national-ism when dealing with the myths, stories, or other evocations of the American dream of finding home in its landscape and historical ex-perience, that was not the intention. I am ready to argue that the vast majority of Americans, no matter what their physical circumstances in respect to actual land and home, thought of it as "God's Country," and did not want to be divorced from it. But between the idolization of land as soil or land as nation on one hand and the ironic distancing called for in the texts of the scriptural "substratum," there is, of course, a very large range of options for American people and peoples.

Also, far from suggesting that the terror immediately ends for immigrants who have come from elsewhere and made the United States their home, I have to note the stories of first-generation immi-grants as revealed in the literature and behavior of many Americans. The terrors around them do not disappear and can be internalized. Harold P. Simonson has illustrated that with an instance that we can use as a typical case study. He explores the work and life of Norwe-gian-American novelist Ole Rolvaag, author of *Giants in the Earth*. Simonson called his book *Prairies Within: The Tragic Trilogy of Ole Rolvaag*.[11] The desolation—indeed the terror—of loneliness and up-rootedness represented by the "prairie without," was also a "prairie within" in the case of Rolvaag and the kind of people about whom he and so many others had written. Like his characters, says Simonson, Rolvaag

> felt himself still standing on the promontory, still gazing at the world left behind and also at the engulfing darkness lying ahead. Rolvaag was still the immigrant—to the end of his days a spiri-tual denizen of "Nordland"—but one who now was intent upon transforming his painful internalization into psychological and artistic truth. He had found his governing metaphor in the wanderer alone in space, another Ishmael. The measure of his success would come in the fictional character of Beret who, locking her past inside a trunk, stood a stranger in the American wilderness, a place of crisis where light and dark held tryst and where the terror beyond the promontory filled the earth and sky.

Simonson relates this to the sacralization theme:

> This fundamental truth that Rolvaag paid dearly for is one Mircea Eliade describes as the consequence of living without roots, of stepping into unconsecrated space and inhabiting a world in which nothing connects with the *axis mundi*. Something primal is at issue. Primitive consciousness—the *homo religiosus* in all of us—requires ontological orientation. Everyone shares a thirst for being, the essence of which is relationship or connection. We require a place (house, temple, village) that serves as a symbolic extension of the world's axis, a paradigmatic cosmos in which we are at home because we exist in a place made sacred by its connection to the axis. Thus, as Eliade explains, settling somewhere represents a serious decision because one's very existence is involved. Likewise, changing habitation is serious business because such a move means the abandonment of one's world and the threat of cosmic alienation and nonbeing.

The thread or the axis for this nation of immigrants, of strangers, is story—the story of ancient Israel. Then it is the story of Enlightened founders; of those who participated in political events such as the fighting of wars of independence and civil wars, the abolition of slavery, and the gaining of civil rights by women or racial minorities. It is the narrative of those dying in the space shuttle Challenger, where a multiracial, multireligious crew and cast came to an end together. The story grows in length, richness, complexity, and multicultural experience.

VI. PROBLEMS ASSOCIATED WITH THE STORY OF LAND AND LAND LOSS

If story plays such a large part in warding off the terror of land loss and nurturing the dream of finding a home, there are three main problems that demand mention but cannot receive development here. The first of these relates to forgetting, failing to tell the engendering stories—the Grand Narrative, if such is accessible—or failing to tell the small narratives that make up a whole.

Much of the tradition in the United States "possesses" people more than they possess it. That is, amnesia, indifference, neglect, carelessness, and even repudiation become problems in postmodern

America. The custodians of the story are haunted by the fear that precisely at a time when the story can be enriched by the inclusion of more kinds of characters, it will instead be forgotten by citizens all across the population pool. The haunting is in the mood of a Rolvaag character, a senior figure, Pastor Kaldahl, who blurts in Norwegian to the embarrassment of the younger generations:

> You have been entrusted with a rich inheritance, an inheritance built up through the ages. How much of it, what portion, are you trying to get? Isn't it your irrevocable duty to see how much of it you can preserve and hand down to those coming after you? *A people that has lost its traditions is doomed!*

To which protagonist Peder responds, "We're Americans here!" Then the pastor protests in language that from Euro-American lips anticipates multicultural complication today:

> If this process of leveling down, of making everybody alike by blotting out all racial traits, is allowed to continue, America is doomed to become the most impoverished land spiritually on the face of the earth; out of the highly praised melting-pot will come . . . a dull, smug complacency, barren of all creative thought and effort. Soon we will have reached the perfect democracy of barrenness.

That exchange introduces the second theme that complicates an address to the terror of land loss and the dream of finding home; it goes by the code word we have already mentioned, multiculturalism. As Muslims come to outnumber Jews; as Mormons expand; as Eastern Christians become expressive; as a "pentagon of hyphenated peoples" (Euro-, Afro-, Native-, Hispanic-, and Asian-Americans) share the same land, as do similarly expressive advocates of women alongside men, homosexuals alongside heterosexuals, each with their at least partly separate traditions and stories—can the terror be addressed, the home still sought? Will there not be land loss in the United States because the pre-script is forgotten or given conflicting interpretations until Babel results? Since the separate stories are usually stories of trauma and victimage which need, and include, an inducer of trauma, a victimizer, in the plots, can they become part of a common lore of narratives and myths?

Answers to those questions belong to another day, or a life's work. At this point I can only mention my own observation and tentative conclusion. I answer that the terror without and within, the dream of home, can be addressed but, of course, not satisfied within history. The pre-script does not have to be rejected or to disappear; the separate stories need not be part of the plot of exclusion but they can be in the drama of enrichment. One need not reduce the multicultural stories cynically to say that they are all predictable variations on a common theme that must homogenize the custodians of the larger culture, presumed to be hegemonic.

The third problem is enduring but has contemporary rings. I refer to the idolization of land—not land as place but land as nation. Those tempted to this idolatry wear different political guises in different periods. The John Deweyite left verged on it in its celebration of the democratic process, fifty years ago. Abraham Lincoln, as described by Edmund Wilson in an essay on "The Union as Religious Mysticism," came close to idolatry of the land as nature and nation, but was rescued by his own sense of irony and the mysterious and transcendent character of the God who stood above the nation. The Manichaean absolutizers of our side over against the "evil empire" near the end of the Cold War, and their antecedents throughout it, always invoked the Communist as the demonic agent who threatened America with the terror of land loss.

Today many in the New Christian Right have done a complete about-face from their earlier premillennial postures. These had led them to be seen as transcending earthly political concerns and worldly love of the material scene, including land. That land and all that was in it was to have passed away, soon, with the apocalypse and the second coming of Christ. The lure of the American environment, landed and storied, is so overpowering, however, that it helped lead many of these Christians to attribute the terror of land loss to Antichrist, liberals, secularists, humanists, socialists, pornographers, and different subverting Others.

Far from wanting to forget the traditions, the new millennialists, longing for a home in the future, have tried to take over America as home. They want to claim The Tradition as their monopoly, to invent a Christian America (sometimes coded as Judeo-Christian America). From being least political they have become most political, even as they have all along been most nationalist, most militarist among the religious forces.

In their hour of access to local and national political power, the temptation will grow for the Right to suggest that through their reading of the pre-script and obedience to it, in their interpretation, their multimillion-member remnant can, through earthly politics, finally come to or produce, or at least find, "home," leaving behind the terror. If so, they will have joined a procession where liberals once marched. And, if one is given to ironic interpretations, it will be interesting to see whether a Jeremiah or preachers of jeremiads will reach them with the message that the terror remains; that their Lord still threatens an end to the history of this people. Or will a Psalmist have to remind those who bring forth a strategy for adducing absolutes a message that will effectively keep the terror at bay and the triumphant at home: "He that sits in the heavens shall laugh"? That laughing, too, is part of a story. It makes a contribution to the possibility of seeing the revelatory and redemptive in the traditions of land and history.

NOTES

1. Walter Brueggemann, *The Land: Place as Gift, Promise, and Challenge in Biblical Faith* (Philadelphia: Fortress Press, 1977), especially chap. 7, pp. 107–29; specific references in the paragraphs that follow are from pp. 1–5, 107–11, 125.

2. Martin E. Marty, *Pilgrims in Their Own Land: 500 Years of Religion in America* (Boston: Little, Brown & Co., 1984); in the paragraphs that follow I shall cite pp. 3–5, xiii.

3. Jacques Maritain, *Reflections on America* (New York: Charles Scribner's Sons, 1958), pp. 93–94.

4. Allen, DuBois, and Walker are quoted in Marty, *Pilgrims in Their Own Land*, p. 241.

5. For seeing Steinbeck's *The Grapes of Wrath* in context, see Robert Thacker, *The Great Prairie Fact and Literary Imagination* (Albuquerque, N.Mex.: University of New Mexico Press, 1989), pp. 188–89.

6. Walter J. Ong, S.J., *Frontiers in American Catholicism* (New York: Macmillan, 1957), p. 117 on the Holy Family; St. Christopher came up as a parallel in conversation.

7. Marty, *Pilgrims in Their Own Land*, p. 17.

8. For the references to Dixon, Kempert, DuBois, and Waugh along with contextual comment see Martin E. Marty, *Religion and Republic* (Boston: Beacon Press, 1987), pp. 172–73, 174–75, 183.

9. Joel Garreau, *The Nine Nations of North America* (Boston: Houghton Mifflin, 1981), passim.

10. Thacker, *The Great Prairie*, p. vii.

11. Harold P. Simonson, *Prairies Within: The Tragic Trilogy of Ole Rolvaag* (Seattle: University of Washington Press, 1987), pp. 15, 78.

Author Index

Agamben, Georgio, 160–162
Allen, Bishop Richard, 252
Aquinas, Thomas (see Thomas Aquinas)
Arendt, Hannah, 1
Augustine, Saint, 43, 81

Bachelard, Gaston, 112, 115
Baum, Frank L., 128
Bloch, Ernst, 8, 177
Bowne, Borden Parker, 34
Brague, Rémi, 5, 6, 12, 95–111
Brueggemann, Walter, 12, 245–46, 247
Buber, Martin, 149
Buechner, Frederick, 4, 13, 63–78
Bunyan, John, 43

Campbell, Joseph, 154
Camus, Albert, 18, 37, 38, 44, 45
Carter, Angela, 134
Cather, Willa, 259
Cohen, Herman, 159
Conrad, Joseph, 101

Deleuze, Gilles, 188, 195, 196, 198, 201
Descartes, René, 35, 43
Dewey, John, 82, 85
Dixon, James, 255–56
Doniger, Wendy, 6, 7, 128–47
Donne, John, 74
Doré, Gustave, 37
Douglas, Mary, 113
Duncan, James, 113

Edwards, Phil, 194
Eliade, Mircea, 251

Foucault, Michel, 197
Freire, Paulo, 10

Frost, Robert, 33

Gandhi, Mohandas, 1
Garber, Marjorie, 143
Garreau, Joel, 257
Giacometti, Alberto, 162–63
Guattari, Felix, 188, 195, 196, 198, 201
Gundersheimer, Werner, 3, 9, 47–62

Halevi, Yehudah, 152
Hall, Edward and Mildred, 6, 114
Hamilton, Cynthia, 224
Haughton, Rosemary L., 9, 10, 11, 204–16
Hegel, Georg Wilhelm Friedrich, 31, 40, 41, 46
Heidegger, Martin, 6, 33, 35, 42, 105–7, 173, 191
Hobbes, Thomas, 31
Hocking, William Ernest, 4, 88
Husserl, Edmund, 34

James, William, 84
Jammer, Max, 181
Joyce, James, 97

Kafka, Franz, 18
Kant, Immanuel, 6, 104–5
Kierkegaard, Søren, 92, 101
Kohák, Erazim, 2, 3, 4, 9, 11, 13, 30–46
Komenský, Jan Amos (Comenius), 43–45, 46
Korosec-Serfaty, Perla, 112

Langland, William, 32
Leavy, Barbara Fass, 134, 138–39
Levinas, Emmanuel, 193

Maimonides, 152
Malamoud, Charles, 133

Maritain, Jacques, 12, 250–51
Marty, Martin E., 12, 245–65
Marx, Karl, 41, 102
McMurtry, Larry, 195–96
Miller, Arthur, 89
Moltmann, Jürgen, 8, 9, 170–84
Momaday, N. Scott, 258
Montaigne, Michel de, 107
Murthi of Banaras, T. R. V., 82
Myerhoff, Barbara, 116–18

Nahman, Rabbi, 24, 27
Naipaul, V. S., 237
Nietzsche, Friedrich Wilhelm, 23, 41

Oliver, Mary, 86–87
Ong, Walter, 253
Orwell, George, 102–3

Parekh, Bhikhu, 11, 12, 230–42
Pascal, Blaise, 107–8
Patočka, 34
Percy, Walker, 99
Plato, 81, 82, 98, 99, 100–101
Platt, Katherine, 6, 9, 112–27
Plotinus, 6, 103–4
Popper, Karl, 172

Rais, Karel, 32
Rank, Otto, 132
Reid, Robert Leonard, 5, 91, 92, 93
Ricoeur, Paul, 88
Rosenzweig, Franz, 8, 158, 177, 179
Rouner, Leroy S., 1–13, 81–94, 117
Rousseau, Jean-Jacques, 35
Royce, Josiah, 89, 188
Rushdie, Salman, 128

Saarinen, Esa, 200

Said, Edward, 123–24
Sayigh, Rosemary, 123, 124
Scholem, Gershom, 149
Shakespeare, William, 141–42
Shamir, Simon, 122, 124–25
Showalter, Elaine, 143
Shulman, David, 141
Simonson, Harold P., 260–61
Solzhenitsyn, Alexander, 106
Steinbeck, John, 170, 252
Sue, Eugene, 37

Tauber, Alfred I., 7, 8, 9, 148–69
Taylor, Mark C., 200
Tepl, Johannes von, 32
Teresa, Saint, 198–99
Thacker, Robert, 258, 259
Thomas Aquinas, 97
Thompson, Stith, 138, 140
Tuan, Yi-Fu, 114

Virgil, 35

Walker, David, 252
Walter, Victor, 6, 112
Warren, Karen J., 10, 11, 217–29
Waugh, Evelyn, 256–57
Wiesel, Elie, 2, 3, 9, 17–29
Wilde, Oscar, 143
Williams, Charles, 89
Wittgenstein, Ludwig, 161–62, 164
Wolfe, Thomas, 18
Wordsworth, William 86
Wright, Susan, 120
Wyschogrod, Edith, 9, 187–203

Yeats, William Butler, 144

Subject Index

Age of the Refugee, 1, 6, 9, 19, 187–201
Americans, 12, 47–49, 153, 171, 188–89,
    195–96, 206, 245–64
anti-Semitism, 37
Arabs, 6, 213, 231, 254

beauty, 4, 6, 66, 103, 109–10, 208
bioregions, 217–18, 221, 223, 224, 228
body, 6, 34, 40, 41, 96–97, 172, 190, 194,
    199, 218–19, 228
boundaries, 6, 112, 115, 120–22, 171–72,
    188, 192, 193, 212, 255, 257–59
Buddhism, 83, 137, 230–31

Catholicism, 12, 84, 253, 256–57
Christ, 75–78, 173, 178–83, 263
Christianity, 3, 4, 5, 8, 37, 39, 42–43, 47, 49,
    52–54, 70, 74–78, 81, 82–83, 84, 96, 100,
    132, 139, 154–56, 177, 178–83, 251,
    255–56, 263
Christmas, 50, 52, 53, 68, 75
community, 172, 191, 195, 196, 200, 208–11,
    217–18, 235

death, 22, 23, 26–27, 34, 38, 44, 92–93,
    135–37, 183, 187, 210
diaspora, 8, 11, 28, 149, 151, 230–41
Displaced Persons, 19
domination, 220
dualism, 83, 88, 204–7, 210, 213, 214–15,
    220
dwelling, 2–3, 10, 30–46, 151, 171, 174–83,
    192

earth, 2–3, 9, 11, 32–33, 96, 98, 102, 103,
    104, 171, 187, 193, 205–6, 218, 225–28,
    258

ecofeminism, 10, 217–28
ecosystems, 205, 217, 218
empiricism, 82
Enlightenment, 9–10, 157, 204–5
Epicureanism, 5, 6, 39, 100, 102
exile, 1, 2, 3, 9, 18–24, 44–46, 70–71, 73,
    101, 151–52, 153, 155, 170, 174–78, 197,
    249
existentialism, 88–89
experience, 81–93, 112–26

family, 3, 4, 17–18, 20, 21, 27, 55, 59, 72–73,
    109, 118–22, 123–25, 134, 136–37, 153,
    173, 205, 213, 214, 232–33, 253
fantasy, 6
feminism, 143–44, 220
freedom, 3, 18, 42, 173, 188, 196, 199, 216,
    253

gender, 142–44
German language, 171, 172
Germans, 170
Gnosticism, 5, 7, 100–102, 103
God, 7–9, 12, 17, 20–21, 24, 26, 28–29, 39,
    47, 78, 83, 84, 96, 102, 150–52, 154–59,
    170–83, 199, 208, 225, 245, 248, 251,
    253, 258, 260, 263, 264

Hasidic Jews, 21–22, 24, 164
Hinduism, 81, 83, 85, 231, 236, 240
Holocaust, 2, 116
homelessness, 4, 9–11, 20, 44, 71, 95, 126,
    187, 201, 213–14, 245, 247
hospitality, 9–10, 110, 204–16
human beings, 2–3, 7, 17, 19, 32–33, 36, 39,
    41–43, 87–88, 93, 95–96, 97–99, 102,
    107, 129–39, 161–62, 171–72, 177–78,

(human beings cont.)
   205, 207, 213, 241, 249
humanness, 81, 83

immigrants, 116–19, 213, 232–41, 248–50,
   260–61
incarnation, 3, 34–35, 39, 41–42, 45–46
India, 7, 11, 128–34, 135, 139, 213,
   230–41
individualism, 88, 129, 205
Indonesia, 135, 231
Iran, 6, 115, 119
Islam, 231, 233, 234, 235, 254–56, 262
Israel, 12, 19, 21–23, 24, 28, 174, 177, 178,
   182, 245, 249, 251, 252, 255

Jerusalem, 2, 23, 27–28, 151–52, 155, 164,
   174, 176, 181–82, 212, 213
Jews, 1, 2, 3–4, 6, 7–8, 11, 17–19, 21–28,
   37–38, 48–49, 50, 52, 53, 115–19,
   148–64, 170–71, 183, 209–10, 212, 213,
   230, 256, 262
Judaism, 5, 39, 54, 60, 61, 81, 96, 100, 117,
   148–64, 170–71, 174–78, 179–80, 181,
   183

loneliness, 88–89
love, 34, 41, 55, 66, 82, 89, 91–92, 188, 191

marriage, 18, 20, 129, 136–42
memory, 8, 25, 112, 148–64, 240
men, 17–18, 120–22, 142–44, 170, 205, 223,
   232, 262
metaphors, 2–3, 30–46, 149–50, 154, 160,
   162, 164, 256
morality, 1, 6, 9, 98, 100, 103–4, 109-10, 113,
   158–59, 209–12, 215
mysticism, 24, 93, 161–62, 177, 263
mythology, 7, 129–42, 154, 163, 255, 262

nature, 5, 33, 35, 41, 84–86, 89–93, 105, 190,
   196, 218, 220–23, 225-28, 246, 255, 263
nomads, 9, 188–201, 213
nostalgia, 1–2, 25, 71, 81, 236

Palestine, 115, 122, 124-25
Palestinians, 122-25
patriarchy, 11, 120–22, 219–22, 224–27
permanence, 65, 70
pilgrims, 3–4, 9, 11, 12, 13, 43–46
place, 6, 30, 36, 63, 95, 97, 112-26, 171–72,
   190, 198, 245–48, 253–54, 261, 263
Platonism, 5
prison, 18–19
Protestantism, 47–48, 57, 81, 253, 256

Quakerism, 48, 52

racism, 220, 223–24, 225, 239
rationalism, 82
refugees, 19, 48, 122–26, 213

selves, 5, 84, 87–88, 97, 99, 144–45, 160,
   164, 200, 225
Shekinah, 8, 23, 24, 151, 154–55, 170–83
socialism, 10, 172, 215, 238
solipsism, 82
Stoicism, 5, 39, 190

Talmud, 17–18, 139, 151, 156
technology, 5, 7, 35, 102
Telugu, 7, 139–41
transcendence, 4–5, 13, 81–93
Trinidad, 237–38

Wandering Jew, 37, 154–55, 197
wayfaring, 3, 30–46
women, 6, 17–18, 113, 119–22, 142–44, 170,
   189–90, 205, 220–25, 232, 261, 262